Advanced Criminology
or
Crime Control and Reduction

ISBN-13: 978-93-88937-80-1

First Published 2021

Published and Printed by

Concept Since 1974

Concept Publishing Company Pvt. Ltd.
A/15-16, Commercial Block, Mohan Garden,
New Delhi-110059 (INDIA)
T : 91 11 25351460, 91 11 25351794
E : publishing@conceptpub.com; *W* : www.conceptpub.com

Cataloging in Publication Data--Courtesy: D.K. Agencies (P) Ltd. <docinfo@dkagencies.com>

Vadackumchery, James, author.
Advanced criminology or crime control and reduction / Dr. James Vadackumchery.
pages cm
Includes bibliographical references and index.
ISBN 978-93-88937-80-1

1. Criminology—India. 2. Crime prevention—India. I. Title.

LCC HV7092.V33 2021 | DDC 364.954 23

To

Mary

Preface

Crimes are offences if and when a person violates the criminal laws of the State. All crimes are not offences under the State made penal laws; at the same time, all offences are always crimes. Crimes can be looked at from two angles—namely, (i) the act-centered, (ii) the person-centered. If we see the crimes, from the point of view of 'act-centered', then it is a violation of any law, *viz.*, social, cultural, moral, ethical, State-enacted, institutional etc. No doubt, the violation of law is bad and to that extent, the crimes must be prevented. If the law is bad, then the law must be changed so that crimes against that law do not come for consideration. Of course, there are written and unwritten laws. Sometimes, the unwritten laws are more powerful than the written laws. Accordingly, the **crimes committed against the unwritten laws too must be prevented**. The question is: **'Can the crimes in society be prevented?** The immediate answer to the question is that crimes cannot be prevented in toto eternally. If there exist no crimes, there is no need for any laws against such acts. A law has relevance and meaning only if there are crimes in society. 'No law-No crime'; 'No crime-No law': that is the law.

When a crime is evaluated from the point of view of 'act-centered', then there will be such crimes, even if there exist no laws against such acts. In the absence of a law or in spite of a law, the act is seen. Therefore, such an act cannot be prevented permanently. One may make a law and see to it that acts against such laws are controlled by means and methods which are effective. The control will be weakened when the means and methods become ineffective.

If crimes are assessed from the point of view of 'person-centered', then the crimes committed by that person can be prevented permanently if he is punished by capital punishment or imprisoned till his death. Imprisonment for a period of time will prevent his further commission of crimes so long as he lives in the prison. However, there is no guarantee that such people will not commit crimes during his incarceration. A few people in prison does not mean that all people living outside will not commit crimes. The criminal laws of the State look at the offences from the point of view of 'person-centered' act and therefore the offender is punished. Of course, the punishment to an offender does not mean that crimes in society is thereby prevented. There was a time when offenders were punished following *'Lex Taliones'*—i.e., the law of retaliation. Accordingly, the eyes of the offenders were plucked off and the country became a nation of blind people. The hands and legs were cut off and the country became a nation of crippled and physically handicapped people. The sex organ was removed and the country become a nation with men having no reproductive organs. Women then raised voice and it led to chaos in society. The law of retaliation could never prevent crimes, rather it created more and more issues. It was proved that a person centered approach is not a fool-proof solution for the total eradication and prevention of crimes in society. Let us therefore accept in fairness that crimes can never be prevented permanently, rather they can only be controlled and thus reduced. This book is about the control and reduction of crimes by the effective application of **push-pull-ego** factor theory of crime causation.

I say that 'my crimes are my unique choices and nobody else's and therefore I say further that' 'I alone can reduce my crimes in society by controlling myself and no one else can do it for me'. Crimes—'act centered'—cannot be controlled, reduced or prevented; nevertheless, crimes—'person centered'—can be controlled and thus reduced if and only if the 'person' decides so. In my opinion, crime is purely an individualistic act which has social impact. Corporate crimes, *Mafia*, Organized Crimes, Crime Syndicates, Nexus Crimes, Bureaucratic Crimes, JEL Crimes, Political Crimes or any crimes of any description are individualistic. The law enforcement agencies can cause deterrence in some and it does not mean that the deterrence will work always with all sorts of criminals with the same intensity. With all efforts to prevent crimes, statistics show that the crimes are on the increase incredibly. Why? Does it mean that the strategems are ineffective? There was a time—even now—one of the prime duties of police has been prevention of crime. They believe that prevention is better than cure. However, experience shows that no crime can never-ever be prevented in toto and researches confirm that every crime can be temporarily controlled by strong police action. Crime is an expression of a man's energy and it is now admitted that the criminal energy can never be destroyed. It can at best be converted into another energy. Police action can and will convert the crime energy to another energy which will generally be criminal in nature. This is the reason why criminologists always speak about the 'Quota Theory' of crime. In other words, the quota of crimes in a given society—in a given situation will be almost constant. By strict police action, one kind of crime will be converted to another type of crime. Crime control strategies should be more personnel oriented—value oriented and situation oriented. This book discusses how can we make use of the **push-pull-ego** factor theory of crime causation for the control of crime via personnel oriented—personnel centered approaches. In my opinion, crime must be placed more in one's **ego** rather than in his wrong deeds or criminal acts. A change in the **ego** means a change in his personality. Accordingly, I may say emphatically that a crime is an inner attitude and disposition of the crime-doer, making himself a criminal. He commits crimes of 'commission' as well as crimes of 'omission'. A 'no' to the existing penal laws of the State is an 'offence' under the law and to other laws (social, cultural, moral etc.) is a 'crime' or 'criminal behaviour', then there will be 'nos' if the individuals are not prepared to abide by the laws, rules or regulations. Hence, if we want a reduction in offences or crimes or criminal behaviour, we must try to strengthen the **ego** factor in man by *Morality/Ethics, Spirituality and Intelligence.* How can we do it? It is discussed elaborately in this book. Man is linked closely with the social life and he causes harm to his fellow men through his offences/crimes/criminal behaviour. Every offence/crime/criminal behaviour injures the person who commits it as well as others who are affected by it. Inculcation of the moral principles into the **ego** of an individual, I believe, will help him realize his responsibility to withdraw from such unacceptable acts. Efforts should be made to inculcate moral values and infiltrate spiritual principles in an intelligent way to the crime-doers and it may be a good option to control and reduce crimes in society. Police, other law enforcement officials, judiciary, legislators, moralists and civic minded citizenry, NGOs, spiritual men, teachers, parents, religious preachers, educationalists, teachers, lawyers, social workers, prayer-men, concerned citizens—all should come forward to take up this noble venture for the benefit of humanity and society. To exist for a man means to co-exist with other fellow men. To be in the world is nothing but to be with other fellow beings. In such a situation, a crime doer must realize that he exists for him and for others on earth. He must co-exist and the commission of crime is not the means for it. Acceptance of this value will make him to understand his role in society and social life. How to make him understand his role in society is a matter of great concern for criminologists and penologists. Punishments alone will not solve the issue.

There are any number of criminals in police department and criminalization in police is a widely discussed problem. Criminals are seen in judiciary—in Bench and Bar—and the crimes crimitted by them are numerous. What is happening among the legislators and in the Legislatures? Violation of laws does take place and the JEL crimes are notorious in these days. There are monasteries and one takes note of monastic crimes. Many crimes committed in convents and *ashramas* do not come to public visibility although reports about such crimes do appear in the media at times. Human gods are punished, and the 'holy crimes' committed by these 'holy men' become recurring realities. I saw a film in Niagra Falls, U.S.A. and I saw the aborigines involved in the commission of crimes about 10,000 years ago. Look at the Code of Hammurabi, the Babylonian King [18th century B.C or earlier] which dealt with criminal matters. In my view, the history of man is a history of crimes and law violations too. Politics is full of crimes and the politicians have their justification and rationalization for everything they do. Crimes are seen in the Legislature, among the Executives and in the Judiciary in a democracy. The media which may be called the IVth Estate in a democracy commit various types of crimes. This book contains a litany of crimes seen in the society today and they are in addition to various crimes I had enumerated in my book **Contemporary Indian Criminology** [ISBN: 13:978-93-5125-100-2].

This book speaks of the importance of morality/ethics to control crimes and reduce criminality in society. The values should be inculcated to the unborn while he is in the uterus of its mother. The mission should be continued from its birth, during infancy and childhood... etc. and the family is the best place to initiate strategies for control and reduction of crimes in society. A family means a **home**—a dwelling place where emotions, esp. love and sharing, become very prominent. It is a communion in intimate love and affection. The ancient love poems from Egypt, Mesopotamia and Sumeria are examples to show the rich traditions of love in ancient families. The Greek culture and the Roman tradition and the Indian scriptures and mystical writings emphasized the holiness of family life and the importance of value inculcation to the new generations. Since the parents are responsible for the birth of a child, they are obliged to educate and train their children uprightly in the right direction. Nothing can compensate the failure of parents if they fail in their obligation. Hence, start thc work from home if one wants to control and reduce crimes in society. Parents cannot and should not delegate their responsibility to others or they should not allow others to usurp their obligations. *Delegatus non delegare.*

The personal growth and personality development start from the family. Children are taught how to control their animal instincts and emotions like bursting anger, unsettling anxiety, sickening irritability, uncontrollable greed etc., etc. so that they can live in society in peace. By meaningful education and training during the early infancy, a child will surely gain self confidence, a feeling of security of life and dignity of human person, an ability to face life problems and internal freedom—all of them are necessary to control crimes and reduce criminality in society. Sigmund Freud said the same thing in his theory of psychoanalysis and Eric Berne repeated the same in his theory of Transactional Analysis (TA). **Push-Pull-Ego Factor** approach of crime causation too accepts their approaches when it discusses the control and reduction in crimes and criminal behaviour. Teachers have a responsibility and obligation to train and educate children. A good family coupled with good schools produce responsible children who will become responsible citizens and parents later in their life. It has been found that the gruesome crimes which are seen large in society today have their roots either in the family or in the schools. Sometimes, both family and schools are seen to be responsible. Family is the starting point and the schools are the next points developing everything initiated in the family. In the family and schools, various generations come together and help one another to grow wiser by detaching from criminal behaviour. All said and done, today's families are found to be disorganized and the schools are seen to be contaminated with all sorts of organized defiance to authority. Strikes, boycotting of classes, *gheraoing* of teachers, fights, affraies etc. and the question is how to control and reduce crimes in such an atmosphere. **Push-Pull-Ego Factor** approach of crime causation makes an attempt to find out a solution to such aching problems in families and schools. Here, I may emphatically advise the police not to interfere with the family and school life of children unless it is that essential and inevitable. Of course, there is a juvenile wing in many police departments and their role is very limited and only to the extent to offer help to problem families and schools in a child friendly manner. **Push-Pull-Ego-Factor theory** of crime causation urges the family and schools to plant moral and ethical values in developing children with the help of the Juvenile Police Unit if and only if their services are found to be that necessary. Of course, religious agencies, NGOs and counsellors who do things for the best interest of children may offer their valuable services to control and reduce crimes in society.

Spirituality is as important as morality and intelligence in controlling and reducing crimes. There is a school of thought which argues that **Man** minus **Spirituality** is an animal. Conversely, **Animal** plus **Spirituality** is **Man.** Of course, spirituality does not mean religion or theism. Atheists, agnostics, rationalists, empiricists, idealists and so on can have spirituality in them. Spirituality is based on faith or belief or both. Faith in an invisible being—a spiritual God/gods will surely and without doubt make many to desist from involving themselves in crimes. Belief in certain values or principles which is as powerful as faith in God/gods helps some to keep away from committing crimes. The **Push-Pull-Ego Facto**. approach extensively discussess this aspect in this book. Man has physical and spiritual strengths in him. Every human behaviour is psycho-somatic. So long as one's behaviour is controlled by the psychological energy, the spiritual strength has a power to control and reduce crime. Even a superstitious belief will control man's behaviour, especially, his criminal behaviour.

What about the role of man's intelligence in the control and reduction of crimes in society? Goddard said long ago that man committed crimes because of low intelligence. His theory was rejected as found to be unscientific and against factual evidence. Today, the theory is that intelligent people commit crimes intelligently and those who have less intelligence commit crimes in an unintelligent way—both being motivated by instincts and impulses. Cessare Lombroso (Italy, 1835-1909) spoke of atavism as the cause of crime and his atavistic explanations too were thrown off by later researchers. Intelligence controls human behaviour including criminal behaviour. If intelligence has the power to control criminal behaviour, it has the needed power and strength to reduce crimes and criminal behaviour. People having high I.Q. commit crimes and their intelligent crimes can be controlled only by intelligence and nothing else. Of course, morality and spirituality can come to aid the intelligence to arrive at the correct decisions to desist from the commission of crimes. **Push-Pull-Ego Factor** theory of crime causation explains how effectively can intelligence control and reduce crimes.

Animality, Morality/Ethics, Spirituality and Intelligence which form the Push Factors interact with the Pull Factors (They are in thousands) and thereby an **ego** is formed. This **ego** Factor formed during early infancy and developed during the childhood commits crimes. How does it commit crimes has been discussed at length in many of my research articles and books, namely (i) **Contemporary Indian Criminology** and (2) **Advanced Criminology or the WHY of crimes.** This book titled **Advanced Criminology or Crime Control and Reduction** brings out the means and methods by which the **Push-Pull-Ego** Factor Theory of crime causation is effectively applied to control and reduce crimes in society. Once again, I repeat that crime is a human act and very much a social fact. It cannot be prevented in toto, rather can be controlled and thus reduced in a limited way. The police argument that crimes can be prevented in toto and permanently is at best a pious hope and a wishful thinking.

I thank my wife, Mary and my daughters Neethu and Neethie for their lavish help in very many ways to write this book. Again, I thank the publishers for bringing out this book beautifully well.

Thiruvananthapuram
17.03.2020

Dr. James Vadackumchery,
Criminologist & Advocate

Contents

Preface vii

List of Figures xvii

1. Aquinas, Bentham, Beccaria, Freud, Berne and Crime Reduction, Control and Prevention 1

2. Push-Pull-Ego Factor Theory of Crime Causation: Animality 23

3. Morality/Ethics: The Law of the Conscience to Control and Reduce Crimes 56

4. Push-Pull-Ego Factor Theory of Crime Causation: Spirituality 114

5. Push-Pull-Ego Factor Theory of Crime Causation: Intelligence 134

6. Push-Pull-Ego Factor Theory and Control: Reduction of Crime and Criminality 171

Appendix: Crimes and Criminality: Seen and Unseen 203

Bibliography 207

Index 211

List of Figures

1.1:	St. Thomas Ego	
1.2:	Sigmund Freud	3
1.3:	Ego of Bentham and Beccaria	5
1.4:	Showing three parts of the multiple nature of man	6
1.5:	Satan, id, pleasure, child are the animal instincts	6
1.6:	Controlling and Restricting Energy	8
2.1:	Animal Behaviour	34
2.2:	Human Behaviour	34
2.3:	Animal Behaviour	35
2.4:	Human Behaviour	35
4.1:	Spirituality Dominated Ego	130
5.1:	The Ideal Squares in an Individual	163
5.2:	The Contaminated Squares in an Individual	163
5.3:	Contamination of morality/ethics with intelligence	163
5.4:	Blocked Morality/Ethics	165
5.5:	Blocked Spirituality	165
5.6:	A Person with the Blocked-out Intelligence	166
5.7:	Conflicts Between Spirituality and Morality/Ethics	167
6.1:	Areas in the EGO	189
6.2:	Pull Factors of Powerful Forces on Ego (KNEAD)	192
6.3:	Individual Mind (Pull Factors Around) [Pull and Push Factors shaping the Ego and the Ego factor of an Individual	193
6.4:	Animality, Morality/Ethics, Spirituality and Intelligence represented as [A], [M/E], [S], [I] for Further Discussion	196

6.5: Intelligence Analysing a Situation by [S], [M/E], [A] values 196
6.6: Introspection-1 198
6.7: Introspection-2 198
6.8: Self Analysis by a Group 199
6.9: Transaction resulting no crime 201
6.10: Third Party Analysis and Intervention resulting in no crime 201

1

Aquinas, Bentham, Beccaria, Freud, Berne and Crime Reduction, Control and Prevention

Throughout the history of man, the human nature has been consistent and the man has a multitude of animals in him. I am a lion—a leopard—a lamb—a snake—a bull/cow—a camel—and an ass—a tiger—an elephant—a cat—a giraffe—a pig—a hyena—a hippopotamus—a monkey....For, I show their behavioural patterns and nature. Man's animal nature is expressed differently in different books of anthropology, sociology, psychology, criminology, law, justice and religion etc. Sometimes, I look into myself—my behaviour—my character, then I recognize that I am showing the behaviour of several animals and that the particular animal in me at the moment has the upper hand and it will invariably give place to another, if that is necessary. The animal behaviour in me is necessary, natural and inevitable for my existence and survival. Any animal behaviour up to a limit is permitted in society. Beyond a limit it is not tolerated by the society and further is resisted by the society and then finally punished. It is necessary for human existence and survival to punish those who exhibit animal behaviour beyond the permitted limit and the control is exerted by the intelligence/morality—ethics/spirituality either alone or along with another or all of them together. The *Push Pull-Ego Factor* theory of crime causation is all about the behaviour—especially the criminal behaviour—of man.

Animals behave because they have the instincts. Man behaves because he has the drives. The drive for me is nothing but the instincts plus intelligence, morality/ethics or spirituality either alone or along with another or with all of them together. This is what St. Paul has said: "The fact is, I know of nothing good living in me—living, that is, in my spiritual self—for though the will to do what is good is in me, the performance is not, with the result that instead of doing the good things I want to do I carry out the sinful things I do not want. When I act against my will, then, it is not my true self doing it, but sin which lives in me" [St. Paul, Romans, 7:19-21, New Testament]. What are these sinful things I do not want to do?

When Sigmund Freud (1856-1939), the Austrian neurologist and founder of psychoanalysis] appeared on the scene in the early twentieth century, the enigma was subjected to a new probe. Until then, the demons were believed to be mostly responsible for the causation of sins as St. Paul conceived of. Satan, the chief evil spirit, the great adversary of man—i.e., Lucifer, the proud rebellious archangel (identified with Satan) expelled from heaven and his army were at constant and continuous work to instigate the humans to commit sins (crimes). This is what St. Paul categorically said: "When I act against my will, it is not my true self doing it but sins which lives in me". After this demonological theory came the classical, neo-classical, crackpot approaches, positive, neo-positive, ecological, sociological, psychological, victimological theories of crime and all of them made attempts to explain the etiology of crime and criminal behaviour. According to Freud, the human mind had three layers—namely, *Conscious, Sub-conscious* and *Unconscious* with *Ego, Super-ego* and *Id* as its contents. His theory was that the warring functions existed in the *unconscious*. The *Super-ego* was said to be the restrictive and controlling force over the *Id* (i.e., the instinctual drives), with the *Ego* as a referee operating out of the enlightened self interest.

In philosophical psychology of St. Thomas Aquinas [1225 ?-'74], the Italian scholastic philosopher and the major theologian of the Roman Catholic Church, the warring functions existed in the human mind which had two functions—viz., **will** and **consent**. The human mind with the **will** and **consent** had an **Ego** and it was this **Ego** which operated in man. The Satan (Devil) instigated the man to commit sins and thereby to violate the commands of God. In fact, it was the devil [the instinctual drives] which made the man to go against the dictates of God. According to the scholastic thought, man had an innate weakness to become a victim to devil's temptations. If man wants to overcome the devil's temptations, he needs to pray to God for his blessings. Only with the blessings of God, man can live without committing sins (crimes). Therefore, God's dictates are the **superego** and it alone has the restrictive and controlling force over the **Ego.** They are pictorially drawn as under:

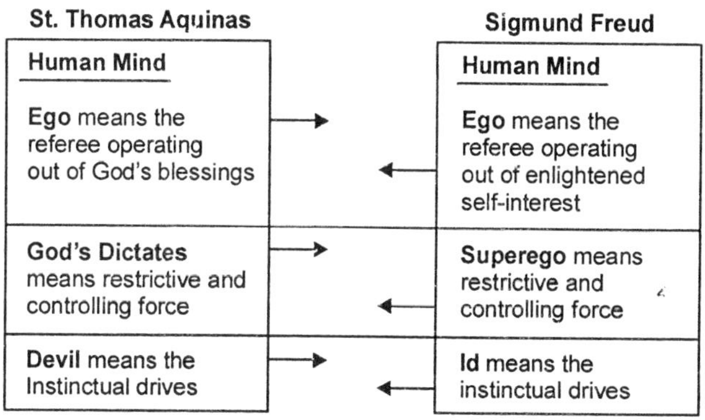

Fig. 1.1: St. Thomas Ego **Fig. 1.2:** Sigmund Freud Ego

Thomist view was that the human mind had **will** and **consent** as its main functions and Freudian view was that the human mind had **Conscious, Sub-conscious** and **Unconscious** Layers for its various functions.

Of course, Sigmund Freud stands on the shoulders of St. Thomas Aquinas to explain human behaviour. Thomist approach was to explain the etiology of sin (crime) and the remedy for the sin. The concepts of mortal sins and venial sins of the Catholic Church as well as the concepts of heaven, purgatory and hell necessitated St. Thomas Aquinas to bring devils, God and prayers etc. to explain the causative and controlling forces behind sins (crimes). Of course, he was not talking about crimes (offences) although his thoughts influenced the Italian Cesare Beccaria [1735-1795] and the English Jeremy Benthem [1748-1832] to formulate the concepts of **Felony** and **Misdemeanor** and Lord Macaulay to define **cognizable** and **non-cognizable** crimes in India.

Sigmund Freud succeeded to a great extent to establish the theoretical foundation upon St. Thomas Aquinas for the purpose of treating patients by his psychoanalysis. The sinners needed mental relief and Thomist approach was through God's intervention via ardent prayers. However, there were exorcists who sought to expel an evil spirit, Devil by adjuration or religious or solemn ceremonies. The Thomist approach was rejected by criminologists as they found it to be unscientific. The demonological approach of crime found to be a pre-scientific explanation of the causation of crime. Although contemporary criminology rejects Thomist approach, the classical school of Jeremy Benthem and Cessare Beccaria accepted it to a certain extent. Instead of the devil and its instigation, they spoke of *hedonism*—i.e., the doctrine that pleasure or happiness is the highest good. On the other side of pleasure or happiness, there is pain and they made an attempt to explain the cause of crime on the basis of this pleasure-pain approach. People committed crimes because they got pleasure when they did so. They avoided the commission of crime because it gave them pain. They brought the concept of hedonistic calculus which was intended to decide the extent/intensity of pain by way a punishment. Accordingly, they prescribed more severe punishments for those who committed more heinous crimes. As St. Thomas Aquinas classified sins into two categories (motal sin and venial sin), they classified the crimes into Felony and Misdemeanor. It was so because those who committed misdemeanor were convicted for short term imprisonment or fine or both whereas those who did felony were awarded death or transportation or life imprisonment. St. Thomas Aquinas had purgatory—i.e., a condition or place in which according to Roman Catholics and others, the souls of those dying penitent were purified from venial sins or undergo the remaining temporal punishment for mortal sin forgiven on earth. The purpose of imprisonment was then deterrent, incapacitation for them to do anything freely, corrective and reformative etc. The Thomist's God for Bentham and Beccaria was the laws, rules and regulations and thus the roots of classical school and to some extent the foundation of the present criminal justice system is found to be in Thomist explanation of the causation of crime.

Going back to Sigmund Freud (1856-1939), we may notice that the Devil of St. Thomas and the pleasure of Bentham and Beccaria are seen in the **Id** of Sigmund Freud. The **Id** of Freud was in the *unconscious* of man. The 'Id' was the part of the psyche that is the source of instinctive energy. It's impulses are modified by the **ego** and the **superego,** the source of the **libido.** As the **id** complexes are the instincts, it activated the man to behave and it was controlled by the **Superego** which was nothing but the God of St. Thomas and the laws/rules etc. of Bentham and Beccaria. Freud was not a criminologist. He was a therapist and his theories were for psychoanalytic treatment. Nevertheless, he explained the causation of crimes in the following way:

(i) Crime is committed because of the inadequate formation of the **superego.**
(ii) Crime is committed owing to the excessiveness of **id** complexes

Bentham & Beccaria

Human Mind
Ego (crime-doer) means the referee operating out of pleasure
Laws, rules and regulations mean restrictive and controlling forces
Hedonistic energy means instinctual drives

Fig. 1.3: Ego of Bentham and Beccaria

(Fig. 1.3) may be compared with (Fig. 1.1) and (Fig. 1.2) of Aquinas and Freud respectively. Aquinas was a theologian and Bentham & Beccarica were jurists and Freud was a neurologist (psychotherapist). Though they were not criminologists, yet, their theories could reduce, control or prevent crimes to a certain extent.

Here appeared Eric Berne (1910-1970) who proposed a theory, i.e., P-A-C., or Transactional Analysis. He was not a criminologist, yet his theory of Transactional Analysis can be used to explain criminal transactions to a limited extent. According to him: "The unit of social intercourse is called a transaction. If two or more people encounter each other... sooner or later, one of them will speak, or give some other indication of acknowledging the presence of the others. This is called the transactional stimulus. Another person will then say or do something which is in some way related to the stimulus and that is called the transactional response" [Eric Berne, *Games People Play,* New York: Gorve Press, 1964]. For Berne, human mind has three natures and they are P-A-C [i.e., Parent-Adult-Child] which are the three parts of this multiple nature of man.

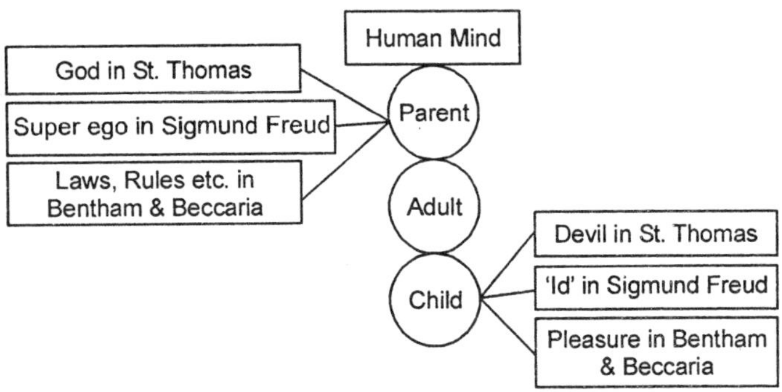

Fig. 1.4: Showing three parts of the **multiple nature** of man

Putting St. Thomas Aquinas, Bentham and Beccaria, Sigmund Freud and Eric Berne together, it may be diagrammatically represented as under—

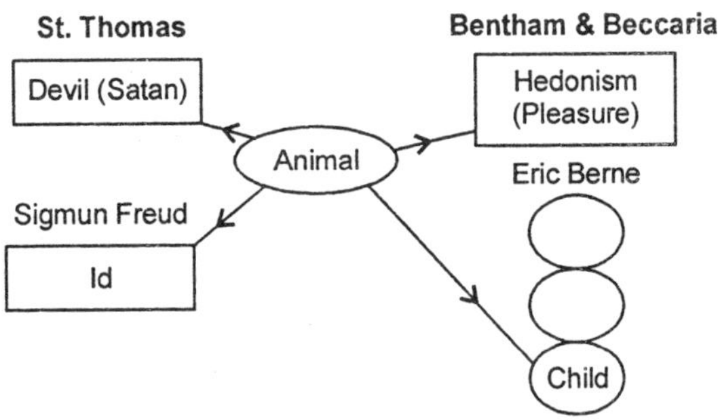

Fig. 1.5: Satan, **id**, pleasure, child are the animal instincts

To repeat, animals have instincts to activate them and they behave accordingly to satisfy their instinctual energy. The 'Devil' in St. Thomas was nothing but the animal instincts (Animality) in the pre-scientific era when no body knew anything much about animal instincts. The 'Id' of Sigmund Freud was nothing but the animal instincts which were found in the 'unconscious' of man. The 'pleasure' (Hedonism) of Bentham and Beccaria was also the animal instincts. Hence, I may say that all of them were talking the same thing using different terminologies or words. If the postulate of Charles Darwin (1809-82) is accepted, man is an evolution (the process of formation or growth of man from apes) from **apes,** then he cannot but behave to some extent like the animals do. Nevertheless, man is not just or merely an animal. He is animals plus 'something else' and what is called that 'something else?'. That 'something else' is his **intelligence** and therefore, he cannot behave just like animals do. He is controlled and restricted in his behaviour.

How is the man restricted or controlled? St. Thomas Aquinas had only supernatural beings like the God and the Satan. Hence, he brought God and God's punishments to restrict and control man. He wanted the Satan to be made inactive, ineffective or inoperative. He wanted the man to overcome the influence, instigation or temptation of the devil by God's intervention. He wanted man to pray to God in an ardent way and thus the animal behaviour of man is restricted and controlled by deep, continuous, ardent and persistent prayers offered to God in many ways. Thus, we see in all prayers to God—

(i) Praising and glorifying God.
(ii) Exposing and confessing one's sins and exposing his inability/helplessness/need to get out of them.
(iii) Praying ardently and craving for divine intervention and God's blessings to escape from Satan's temptations. For this, prayer is the only panacea for him.

What do Bentham and Beccaria speak about restricting and controlling animal behaviour in man? For them, pleasure should be restricted. For it, they said about the laws, rules and regulations and the punishments to the violators of the laws, rules and regulations by applying the hedonistic calculus—i.e., the more heinous is the violation, the more harsh and severe should be the punishment. Thus we see capital punishment, transportation, life imprisonment, imprisonment with hard labour, imprisonment without labour (simple imprisonment), short term incarceration, fine, forfeiture of property etc. as punishments. There was a time when corporal punishments were in vogue in some countries and the cruel ways an offender was punished were unimaginable or so severe that only human imagination could conceive of. The punishments were not only deterrent but were retributive too. Corporal punishments are seen in a few countries even today.

According to Sigmund Freud, the animal (instinctual) behaviour—i.e., **'Id'** was controlled and regulated by **Super-ego** which was nothing but the laws, rules, regulations, traditions, customs etc. According to him, the **Superego** was the **human conscience.** According to him, the formation of human conscience in an upright way in the right direction was an effective method to control and regulate the **'id'** in man. However, as repeatedly said above, he was not a criminologist, rather he was a psychotherapist with his **conscious, subconscious** and **unconscious** layers of human mind.

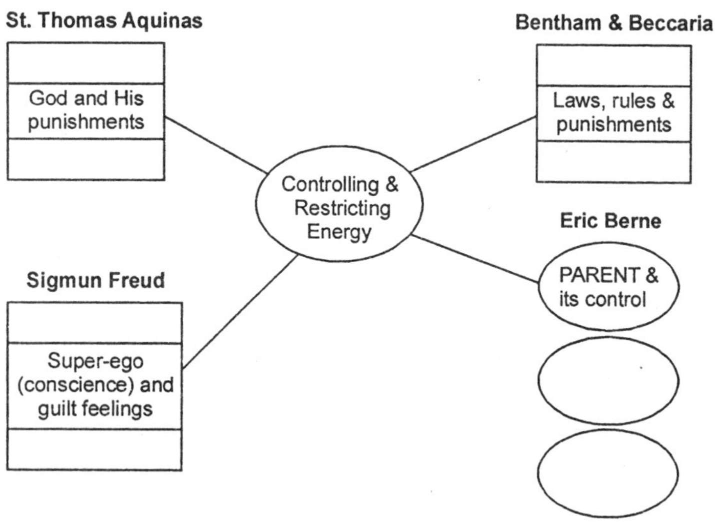

Fig. 1.6: Controlling and Restricting Energy

The **Parent** in Eric Berne contained all the laws, rules, regulations, customs and traditions. Nothing more and nothing less. God and God's punishments were deterrent for people not to commit sins. For, the sinner is punished to hell for mortal sins and to purgatory for venial sins. History proves that St. Thomas Aquinas succeeded in controlling and restricting the animal behaviour of man to a great extent down the centuries and even now among the faithful in Christian (Catholics) Churches. The priests, god-men and the religious promoted and propagated Thomist approaches and it was found more amidst the Roman Catholics. Christians other than Roman Catholics too promoted and propagated God's punishments in their own way. All religions promoted and propagated the punishments either on the earthly life, or in the life after death. Certainly, animal instincts instigated human behaviour and is controlled and restricted by God, religions and divine punishments among the faithful. St. Thomas Aquinas, though a theologian, was a penologist as well to a limited extent. Sin is the violation of God's laws and religious rules. Offence is a violation of State's laws. Crime is a violation of the society's written and unwritten laws, customs, traditions including the institutional laws. Thus, we may say that the Thomist's theological explanation of sins had an impact to control the violations of laws enacted by the State or seen in the society by way of traditions, customs, etc. St. Thomas, Aquinas is a 'criminologist' or a 'penologist' in that sense only in a limited way.

Italian Beccaria (St. Thomas Aquinas too was from Italy) and the English Bentham took away God and God's punishments from Thomist's explanation. They put, as said above, the State in the place of God and State's laws and punishments as the restricting and controlling forces of animal instincts—i.e., pleasure giving energy. If St. Thomas spoke about God's punishment after the death of man, Bentham & Beccaria said about the punishments on this terrestrial life. They punished the human body and the mind while St. Thomas punished the human soul after death. Thus, a shift in approaches from the Thomist's supernatural world to the terrestrial world is seen in Bentham & Beccaira. Of course, the Bentham & Beccaria approach to punish the violators of laws was certainly a deterrent weapon to control, reduce and prevent temporarily crimes to a certain extent.

What about Sigmund Freud? He talked about Superego—i.e., the *human conscience*. Human conscience is pregnant with **moral laws** and every law—whether it is God made or man made—has a moral content. If the moral law is violated, then there will be guilt feelings. A person who does not have such normal guilt feelings is treated as a psychopath. Freud, I repeat, was the founder of psychoanalysis-school—i.e., a systematic structure of theories concerning the relation of *conscious* and *unconscious* psychological processes. The psychoanalysts subscribe to the following doctrines:

(i) The principle that human behaviour is determined largely by the unconscious psychological forces or drives;
(ii) The corollary principle that the functional behavioural disorders arise primarily because of conflicts related to the *unconscious* drives (to their repressions or inadequate socialization) which interfere with the normal or required activities of the individual.
(iii) The therapeutic principle that the most appropriate treatment to those disorders is to help the patient to gain insights into his *unconscious* drives. They believe that psychoanalytical techniques will be able to cure the patients.

Dr. Gregory Peechat, formerly a school psychologist in New York was practising psychoanalysis in Thiruvananthapuram and he did his Ph.D. in Kerala University on a topic: 'Guilt Feeling and Psychoneuroses' and I had an opportunity to closely associate with his studies and practice in psychoanalysis. He established, from his studies, that guilt feeling was a powerful cause for all kinds of psychoneurotic disorders. My research observations of convicted prisoners in the jails in Kerala State proved beyond doubt that many incarcerated had guilt feelings. Whatever that be, Sigmund Freud, his associates and followers were not concerned with the legality or the criminal liability of their patients. According to them, *'Id'* is the lowest and the most fundamental content of human personality. It is the collection of primary and instinctive urges or is a deep reservoir of instinctual drives—or animal instincts. When a child is born, its behaviour is motivated/activated by *'Id'* and as it grows older and older, it learns the laws, rules, traditions, customs and regulations etc. They control him and all those which control him are combined together in the term **Super ego**. Thus the **Super ego** represents the norms, values and ideals of the society which a person internalizes as his own. In short, according to Freud, the 'Superego' functions to police the individual by laying down the *dos* and *dont's* in society. According to the school of psychoanalysis, the **Super ego** sometimes may become dominant with the result that guilt feeling about repressed instinctual drives may be created. Thus one sees (Fig.1.6) the—

i. God and His punishments of St. Thomas Aquinas.
ii. The State and its laws and punishments of Bentham & Beccaria.
iii. The Super ego and its dictates in Freud play the same role as far as the control, the reduction and the temporary prevention of crimes to a certain extent is concerned. Thus, it may be specially noted that the controlling, restricting and regulating forces are—
   a. **Spiritual** in St. Thomas Aquinas.
   b. **Legal** in Bentham and Beccaria.
   c. **Moral** in Sigmund Freud. All of them, no doubt, are very powerful energies.

Eric Berne, again was concerned with the transactions in human beings. Here, I may consult Edmond Locard (1877-1966) who is eulogised for his **principle of Exchange** in crime investigation. The **principle** is: *Whenever two entities come in contact, there is an exchange of traces mutually.* It means that—

(i) when two things come into contact, there is always an exchange of materials.
(ii) The more the contact, the better will be the exchange.

Edmond Locard was a contemporary of Eric Berne (1910-1970) and therefore, I think that the Locard's Principle of Exchange in crime investigation can be meaningfully applied to human transactions as well. I do not have any material to show that Eric Berne was influenced by Locard's Principle of Exchange, nevertheless, I may apply the same principle in human transactions in the following way. Human transaction may be a criminal transaction as well.

Let me put the principle as under:

(1) When two persons come into contact behaviourally, there is always an exchange of human transactions. A transaction, as stated earlier, is a unit of social intercourse.
(2) The more the behavioural contact, the more will be the exchange.

(3) The exchange of transactions can become criminal, if not properly or well controlled, restricted or regulated.

Who is the **parent** in Berne's P-A-C.? He says that the "parent is a huge brain of unquestioned or imposed external events perceived by a person in his early years, a period which we have designated roughly as the first five years of life". According to him, "in the parent are recorded all the admonitions and rules and laws that the child heard from his parents and saw in their living. In this set of recordings are the thousands of 'no's directed at the toddler, the repeated don'ts that bombarded him, the looks of pain and horror in mother's face when his clumsiness brought shame on the family in the form of Aunt Ethel's broken antique vase"....

To continue what Berne said: "The significant point is that whether these rules are good or bad in the light of a reasonable ethic, they are recorded as truth from the source of all security... It is a permanent recording. A person cannot erase it. It is available for replay throughout life". [Thomas A. Harris, *I'm ok—You're ok,* London & Sydney, Pan Books 1977].

In criminology, I want to emphasize the fact that a transaction can or may become criminal if the exchange is between two Child Ego States. Whenever, the exchange is found to be not proper, then the **parent** has to interfere to settle it right. If the **parent** does not interfere at the right-appropriate time, the exchange will land in criminality. More about it will be discussed in the chapters which follow. In short, the **parent** of Eric Berne is the **God** of St. Thomas, the **State** of Bentham and Beccaria and the **Super ego** of Sigmund Freud.

Reduction, Control, Prevention of Crime and Criminal Behaviour

How can we make use of St. Thomas, Bentham and Beccaria, Sigmund Freud and Eric Berne to reduce, control and temporarily prevent crimes and criminal behaviour? It may be stated at the outset that no crime can be prevented *in toto*. It can only be reduced or controlled—and that too for a period of time only.

Let us go to St. Thomas Aquinas, the Catholic Theologian once again. He has God, God's punishments and Satan to explain sins—

i.e., violation of God's laws or religious laws. It is found that most of the people in the world believe in some God/gods as they have faith in God/gods. Faith in God/gods means faith in the supernatural beings in a spiritual world. Look at the temples, churches, gurudwaras, mosques, prayer halls including the abodes of tribal gods and the number of people who visit/or gather at such places. It means that many people want a God/gods for their existence, mental pleasure and survival. They want to get out of the clutches of evil spirits (?) and escape from their temptations, instigations and influences. People pray ardently for divine blessings and precisely therefore, **prayer** is said to be an effective weapon to control, reduce and temporarily prevent crimes. A genuinely religious man—believer in God/gods—desists from the commission of crimes. If he commits a crime, his mind is normally disturbed and there will be unsettling of his mind. His mental peace is lost.

There are people who are not believers in God/gods. In other words, apart from theists, we take note of atheists, agnostics, rationalists, empiricists and so on. They do not have faith in God/ gods or other divinities. Nevertheless, they have **belief** in certain absolute principles, universal truths or such other eternal realities. Belief is not faith as belief means 'to have confidence in the truth or the reliability of something without absolute proof'. One needs 'Belief' if he wants to go forward. Therefore inculcating a belief that the crime-doer will be caught one day and certainly he will be punished will control, reduce or temporally prevent crimes. In criminology, we say that certainly of punishment is more effective than severity of punishment. 'Effective' means to reduce, control and prevent crimes. This principle should be promoted and propagated if one wants to reduce or control crimes. The theory of *Karma*—i.e., the vicious will surely be punished makes some people to desist from committing crimes. Effective law enforcement and the belief among the people that the vicious will be punished will certainly control, reduce and prevent crimes. In fact, criminologists put both (i) **faith** and (ii) **belief** under a common nomenclature—i.e. **spirituality**. Anything done towards promoting and propagating the finer aspects of **faith** or **belief** will reduce, control and prevent crimes. In other words, crimes can be controlled, reduced or prevented via **spirituality**.

Let us again go to Bentham and Beccaria who made the State and its laws/punishments to control, reduce or prevent crimes.

How? The methods are—

1. Enact effective laws and enforce them strictly.
2. Appoint effective, impartial and efficient enforcement machinery to ensure strict and stringent action against law violators.
3. Punish the guilty and protect the innocent. The purpose of punishment shall be the development of human personality in an upright way in the right direction. Abolish death penalty.
4. Stop corruption and all types of malpractices in and during law enforcement. Respect human rights and the dignity of man.
5. Create an awareness among the people about the laws, punishments and the need to abide by the laws.
6. Make the justice delivery system free from abuse of power and misuse of authority or exercise of pseudo-authority or abstaining from the use of power and authority.
7. Concurrently with the strict enactment and enforcement of State-made laws with punishments for law violators, create an atmosphere/environment [pull factors] for inculcating the social, cultural, ethical, moral, institutional, traditional, custom-made laws, rules, practices and regulations for all from their childhood. Crime can be controlled, reduced or partly prevented only in a conducive environment for the same.

Coming again to Sigmund Freud, the reduction, control and temporary prevention of crime can be effected if and only if—

(i) The **Superego** is adequately formed. How? There are many ways and methods by which values can be inculcated in a neonate and later during the development of his/her personality.
(ii) The **Superego** is also known as the *conscience* of the mind and the moral/ethical laws are otherwise called the **laws of conscience**. Moral laws are absolute moral principles of the society and ethical laws are the principles which an individual has in himself about the right and wrong—i.e., individualistic or subjective.

(iii) Human **conscience** is to be uprightly formed in the right direction. Family, parents, schools, teachers, religion and catechism classes, religious platforms, moral exhortations and enlightenment, cultural programmes having moral/ethical values, songs, dramas, films, media etc. can be meaningfully and fruitfully utilized for the purpose of creating a moral ***conscience*** among the people. The individual, group, society, national and international morality must be respected and honoured to control, reduce or prevent crimes.

(iv) The animal instincts should be controlled. If there is an excessiveness of certain instincts in an abnormal way, it must be treated. Counselling, psychoanalysis, psychiatry etc. can be used meaningfully for the purpose. There must be mental health promotion and projects for the purpose. Though crime is not the impact of mental disorders in all cases, the importance of mental disorders cannot be ignored. There should be proper treatment centres.

Like the **spirituality** in man, we may notice **morality/ethics** in him working very powerfully. As there exists a spiritual atmosphere, there is also a moral atmosphere in every society. Immorality is not tolerated as man is basically a moral being. Thus, man has **spirituality** and **morality/ethics** as two important contents in his personality.

Looking at Eric Berne, we notice the **Parent Ego** controlling and regulating the **Child Ego**. According to Eric Berne, the **child** in human mind is:

A child sees, hears, feels and understands many things from its birth. The little child has no vocabulary during its early infancy and precisely therefore most of his reactions are expressed via *feelings*. Berne says: "He is small, he is dependent, he is inept, he is clumsy, he has no words with which to construct meanings" [Thomas A. Harris, *ibid*.]. It being the case, the child expresses its feelings. Feelings are expressed by emotions and the emotions are connected to instincts. Every instinct is accompanied by emotions. For example, the **Fear** is an accompanying emotion of the instinct **Escape**; **Disgust** is an accompanying emotion of **Repulsion**; **Anger** is an accompanying emotion of **Pugnacity**; **Lust** is an accompanying emotion of **Sex** etc. Thus, one sees animal instincts working very strongly in a neonate, little infant, child and so on.

If an instinct interacts with another instinct, naturally and necessarily an instinctual behaviour is resulted. As Edmond Locard said, we may admit the fact that there will be an exchange and may add to that the exchange can be an exchange of instinctual forces. It is just like animals behaving—dog against dog, cat against cat—etc. Here, I may add—

When an instinct comes in contact with another instinct, the result will be an instinct. The more the interaction, the more will be the instinctual exchange.

Example: A gets angry, B in return gets angry and the transactions go on until one of them makes his emotion to become inoperative or inactive. If it is not done at the correct time, there may be aggressive attacks which may end/even in the murder of one of them. How do one's God/s, Super-ego, Parent State and State's law control and reduce crimes?

God/s, Super-ego, Parent State, State's laws cause stresses in an individual. A stress is a threat—i.e., physical, psychological or imaginary—which puts a person in any form of jeopardy by pain, unkind words, mental disturbance, unsettling human mind or unexpected confrontations of various forms. No one wants to have stresses in life and precisely therefore, everyone usually keeps away from committing crimes or violating laws.

Examples

(1) Sodomy is an unnatural, especially anal copulation; copulation of a human with an animal (bestiality). In Genesis (19:24) in the Old Testament, one reads the story of God destroying Sodom and Gomorrah because of its wickedness. "As the sun rose over the land and Lot entered zoar, Yahweh rained on Sodom and Gomorrah brimstone and fire from Yahweh. He overthrew these towns and the whole plain, with all the inhabitants of the towns, and everything that grew there. But the wife of Lot looked back, and was turned into a pillar of salt" (Gen: 19: 23-26). What does it mean? It means that the sinners (i.e., crime-doers or those who commit evil things) are punished by God in a very cruel way. In all religions, one notices the divine intervention to punish the guilty/sinners or the. These stories are conveyed to generations

and certainly they cause fear in the growing children. God is a punisher of the sinner is/guilty and he punishes very cruelly. This sort of frightening approach creates fear (Fear is the emotion accompanying **escape**—an animal instinct) in the developing children. Resultingly, the God's punishment deters many not to commit sins (crimes). Thus, God and religion have a deterrent effect on people and it prevents people from committing crimes.

Coming again from Thomist school of thought to classical school of criminology, one sees hedonism as a single cause of crime. Classical criminologists (Bentham & Beccaria) brought the concept of hedonistic calculus to prescribe punishment to the crime-doers. In other words, the more the pleasure derived from the commission of crime, the more severe would be the punishment awarded to him. Laws were enacted by States prescribing punishments according to the headonistic calculus. Nevertheless, the punishments, it has been noticed, did not have any perceptible impact upon a total and permanent prevention or eradication of crimes although they could control and reduce crimes to a limited extent.

The retributive theory of punishment has a long history. *Lex Talionis*—i.e., the law of retaliation has been in existence during the period of the Hammurabi. An eye for an eye and a tooth for a tooth principle was followed during the period of Moses, the Hebrew Patriarch who led the Istalites out of Egypt and was their leader and law giver during their years of wandering in the wilderness. History proved that his approach of retaliation did not have much effect or impact on the Israelites. They committed several crimes which ultimately paved the way for Ten Commandments. People adored the golden calf and the Decalogue of the 'Ten Words' inscribed on the tablets at Sinai laid down the fundamental law—which was at once moral and religious (The Jerusalem Bible). Researches conducted in the west regarding retributive punishments show that they resorted to all sorts of cruel, brutal, barbarian and inhuman corporal punishments. Burning at the stakes, drawing and quartering, boiling, pulling the body apart, mutilation, Ducking stool, stock and pillory, Scold's bridle, flogging or whipping (using cat-o-nine lashes), confinement in irons, chaining criminals together at work or in a cage at night etc. were a few among them. Corporal punishments were given in the east as well. Multilation of half of the feet was awarded for stealing a female slave. Cutting of the little finger and thumb was the penalty for first offenders. Cutting off hand and foot was awarded as punishment for second offenders. Death was for the third offenders. Amputations of limb was the punishment for robbery. People committed crimes and the retributive approach created a multitude of physically handicapped people. Why? So long as man has got animal instincts, he continues to commit crimes in spite of severe and very severe punishments—corporal or otherwise. Self control is the best control if one wants to control and reduce crimes in society. The approach of the classical school of criminology based on 'pleasure-pain' theory did not yield results as expected. Cruel punishments have an inevitable tendency to produce cruelty in people. Certainly it did more harm than good to the society and social welfare.

What about the **Superego** of Sigmund Freud in preventing crimes? The Freudian *'Id'* was a powerful energy in every human being and an over-effect of the *'id'* energy could be controlled only by a psychoanalytic treatment. His theory was primarily for the treatment of patients who had psychological problems by psychoanalysis and how far or how much can it be used for preventing crimes is at best doubtful. **Superego** will control a person who suffers from an excessive *'id'* energy. As said earlier, Freud was not a criminologist or penologist and precisely therefore his theory cannot be fruitfully applied for the reduction, control and prevention of crimes. Freud was not talking about crime and criminal behaviour and therefore his theory has little or no much importance either to the explanation of the causation of crime or to the control, reduction and prevention of crimes.

Eric Berne was not at all concerned with crime and criminal behaviour. His **parent** consisted of huge collection of recordings in one's brain and they are the **dos** and **don'ts** which his parents [Father, mother, grandfather, grand mother, teachers and so on] have inscribed. Thousands of simple rules about 'how to do' a thing are recorded in one's brain from his/her birth onwards. It is a rich treasury containing the right and wrong—and tells a man "Never do it', "No, never". For example, a person may have recordings in his brain: "Don't cheat others"; "Don't forge a document"; "Look after the old parents properly"; "Tell the truth always". Thus, a child develops his personality with values and principles in an upright way in the right direction. If he violates the values and principles thus recorded in his brain from childhood, he feels guilty. On the other hand, a child may develop his personality in the wrong way with perverted values and principles of questionable nature. The reason for it is the **pull factors** or the environment in which he is born and brought up. I had visited prisons and had discussions with the prisoners there. I published a book titled 'Kolayalikalude Pinnampuram' in Malayalam (*Behind the Murderers*) after interviewing 306 convicts who were punished for life imprisonment. I found almost all of them were having severe guilt feelings for the murder they committed. I studied their past and could learn that most of them were brought up by parents who had right values and principles. A few who had no guilt feelings were from problem families which did not inscribe right values and principles in them. When I asked "would you commit another murder after leaving the prison?" most of them said: "No, never". I am sure that the strong decision which each one took while they were in the prison would certainly work with them and thus the crimes could be controlled. I say that a 'Crime is one's choice and if that one takes a decision not to commit a crime later, certainly he will not commit the crime thereafter'. My interviews with the pick pockets, burglars and so on convinced me that most of them had no guilt feelings for the crimes they committed. They told me that they would commit the crimes again when they were freed from the jails. I interviewed a person who came to the prison (18 times) as a jail bird and he said that he would commit burglary again if he got chances. He was a recidivist who never felt bad or guilty in his criminal acts. When his childhood was studied, I could learn that he was an orphan who never had good environments [**pull factors**] to develop his personality in an upright way. He never had any guilt feelings and he never had any difficulty to come and stay in the prison. Every official in the prison knew him well and the officials used to ask him: "When is your next visit?" when he left the jail after his 'comfortable' stay as a convict for a short term. According to TA theory, he had always a psychological position: "I am OK and you are not OK". In my opinion, people often commit crimes because of this psychological position they hold in life. If they examine the **parent** data in them, they will understand that the *parent data* in them is far away from being moral and to that extent, not satisfactory. Moral values which control crime and criminal behaviour must come from the parent. As the adequate formation of **superego** is a powerful energy oı force to control crimes, a strong **parent** with strong moral values will be a powerful energy or force to control crimes and criminal behaviour. Develop a moral **parent** or form an adequate **superego** may be one of the ways to control and reduce crimes in society.

What about the **child** in TA and ***id*** in psychoanalysis to control and reduce crimes? The **parent** is external just like the **Superego** is. They are the **dos** and **don'ts** coming from outside. Simultaneously, there is another recording being made internally and concurrently with the external events being recorded in the T.A. It is the **child**. The responses of the little person to what he sees or hears. The **child** has instincts and emotions to respond to the situations, events and individuals. He sees, hears, feels understands and responds instinctively and emotionally. The **child** is dependent, enept, clumsy and he does not have words or vocabulary to express his feelings to give meanings to his internal experiences.

People face situations where they are put into frustrations and conflicts. They may feel rejected, abandoned, frustrated, depressed, dejected etc. and in such circumstances, their reason flies way and passion comes to play. Sometimes, anger dominates their reason and they may react instinctively. T.A. says that the **child** in them command in such situations and they commit crimes. The only option to control the **child** is to call the **parent**. The same strategy is found in Freud's ***id*** which contains the instincts and impulses. ***id*** impulses which cause crimes can be controlled by **superego** (The **Parent** in TA) formed in an upright way in the right direction. Freud says that an excess of the ***id*** energy would causes crimes and it could be treated by psychoanalysis.

Yes, I said earlier that my 'Crime is my Choice' and that was what Bentham and Beccaria of the classical school said during 18th century and St. Thomas Aquinas during the 13th century. In TA, the **child** and the **parent** never allowed a man to choose his responses to a situation or to manipulate his surroundings. The **parent** dictates and the man obeys. The **child** behaves instinctively and he behaves accordingly. Between the **Thought Concepts** (*parent*) and the **Felt Concepts** of the **child** of life, the man should have **Thought Concepts** of life to behave to situations. Yes, my crime is my choice—and to say so, man must have **Thought Concepts** of life. This is what the **adult** in T.A. says and the **adult** asks several questions to himself and he finds answers to them. The **adult** is a data processing computer. It grinds out directions after computing the information and knowledge from three sources, namely, (i) from the **parent**, (ii) from the **child** and the data which the **adult** in him has collected. The important functions of the **adult** are:

(i) to examine the data in the **parent** and to see whether or not they are acceptable or applicable to the present situations. He may accept it or reject it as he decides.
(ii) to examine the **child** and to see whether or not, the felt feelings are appropriate, acceptable and commendable to the present situation. It also examines whether or not the feelings are archaic and in response to archaic **parent** data.

The purpose here is not at all to do away with the **parent** and the **child**, but to be free to examine these bodies of data. What happens when a man commits crimes? The answer is simple—an unrealistic, irrational, immoral, unacceptable, illegal **adult** response will cause crimes. If the **adult** examination of the data is praiseworthy, then no crime will be committed. Training people to make an **adult** examination in a way acceptable to the laws, rules, regulations etc. will create a crime free society. But it is not possible as there are venomous people living around us. In Freudian approach, one does not see an **adult**, rather he explains every behaviour on the concepts like '*Conscious, Sub-conscious, Unconscious, Ego, Super-ego* and *ID* and therefore there is no need for any further discussion on the subject for controlling and reducing crime.

A word about the four Life Positions in TA needs a brief discussion before we proceed to the next chapter on **Push-Pull Ego Factor** approach on crime causation, control and reduction, The four Life Positions are:

(i) I'm not OK—You're OK
(ii) I'm not OK—you're not OK
(iii) I'm OK—You're not OK
(iv) I'm OK—You're OK

(1) Taking each life position one by one, I may say that a person who takes the first position—i.e., I'm not OK—

You're OK—cannot and does not commit a crime. If he commits the crimes he is to suffer the consequence. This is a fine position.

(2) 'I'm not O.K—You're not OK' position means a position in which an individual may or may not commit crimes. Evil should not be won over by Evil. If one decides to do so, it means that he has a defective personality development. This sort of criminal behaviour is seen in politics, police crimes against criminals, communal bigotry and organized defiance to authority etc. The life position is harmful to control and reduce crimes.

(3) 'I'm OK—You're not OK' position becomes fine if one goes to initiate legal action against the one who has a 'not OK' life position. On the other hand, if he takes law in his hand and attacks him physically or otherwise, he is liable for legal action against him. This life position is good if no crime is committed and is acceptable to control and reduce crimes.

(4) 'I'm OK—you're OK' position is the best and no crime is committed. There is harmony and peace in society and as such, the life position is encouraging.

The life positions said above are for individuals. It can be applied to groups, communities and the society at large. A society which ensures welfare and happiness will take the life position (4) if it wants to control and reduce group crimes. The authorities and the law enforcement officials can adopt the best life positions as per the demands of the situation prevailing in the society. There should be the OK-ness in every transactions. Remember always that the first three positions are based on feelings and the fourth—i.e., 'I'm OK—You're OK'—is based on thought, morality, spirituality, intelligence etc. One can not decide on the fourth position without having a great deal of information about many things including the Pull Factors or environment/circumstances. More about the control and reduction of crimes and criminal behaviour is discussed in the chapters that follow.

2

Push-Pull-Ego Factor Theory of Crime Causation

Animality

Why do people commit crimes? Why does the neonate bite the nipple of its mother when it experiences difficulties to get breast milk? What activates the little infant to behave the way it does? The infant is totally dependent on its mother; it cannot walk; cannot talk; cannot even recognize its mother who breast-feeds. The infant expresses its difficulty in an aggressive way by biting the nipple—i.e., negatively. The helpless child bites its breast-feeder instinctively. The simple explanation is the instinct called *pugnacity* (combat) which works strongly in it and resultingly the emotion called *anger* follows. The infant does not choose it. It comes automatically. If this is what happens during the oral stage of personality development (Sigmund Freud) of a neonate, the behaviour during its anal stage is not different from what it shows during its biting stage (oral stage is divided into *sucking stage* and *biting stage*. 0-6 months come under *sucking stage* and 6-18 months come under *biting stage*). Whenever the child has biological need for emptying its bowels, it does it anywhere—everywhere even on the lap of the caring mother. The mother, 'at times', punishes the child by disallowing it from enjoying the breast-feed when it bites the nipple. Some mothers used to gently throw the child from the breast and it cries further with anger. In rare cases, the mothers used to give a soft beating at the thigh of the little infant with love, care and concern. Similarly, whenever the infant empties its bowel, the mother takes the child to wash in the beginning. Gradually, the mother gives instruction to go to the toilet. Sometimes, the child fails or refuses to obey the mother's instruction, then the mother too gets angry. She may even beat the infant gently with love and care. Toilet training is given to the child and thus the child is getting socialized. Socialization is a process by which a new born child is given training to become a socialized human being. If it is not done, the infant becomes like Kamala and Amala, two girl children found in the Indian forest. They were behaving just like how the animals did.

Control the emotions and instinctual behaviour—is the best advice we can give or we must give to growing children. Education, training and instructions become necessary for an infant to grow as a human being with desirable personality traits. Man is an evolution from monkeys and therefore the behaviour of animals will be shown by humans too unless they are trained to behave like a man. There is a common saying that 'the child is the father of man'. Though the saying is in a different context, it can be very well applied even in the commission of crimes. ***Transaction Analysis*** (T.A.) of Eric Berne admits that there is a child in every man. Yes, there is. Otherwise, why should a 70 year old man cry when he faces frustration or conflicts. Crying is a pattern of behaviour of children to resolve their frustrations and conflicts. It is called *regression* in psychology. A child often responds or reacts instinctively and expresses its emotions without any control.

Push-Pul-Ego Factor theory of crime—causation (it is not a theory of causality) speaks of *animality* in man as he is an evolution from monkeys. He has an animal ancestry and precisely therefore he has animal instincts and they activate him. After Charles Robert Darwin's (1809-1882) theory of evolution, came the De Vries' (1848-1935) theory of mutation. Mutation in biology is the (1) Sudden departure from the parent type, as and when an individual differs from its parents in one or more heritable characteristics caused by a change in a gene or a chromosome; (2) It is an individual species or the like resulting from such a departure. Accordingly, De Vries held the view that mutations are responsible for evolution. I am not in any way concerned with the theory of mutation. Nevertheless, I infer that man did emerge through a process of evolution just like any other organisms.

It is noted that some animals like lemurs, monkeys and apes have many features which are very much similar to the same in human beings. (1) The comparatively large brain case with large brain, (2) the forward looking eyes, (3) the position of thumb being or becoming opposite to other digits, (4) presence of flat nails on the fingers etc., are examples in point. No doubt, a man is an animal—said philosophers of the past. Aristotle said that man is a *rational animal* and I differ from his view as I find that a man is not just a rational animal, but many animals. Tiger, lion, cheetah, horse, camel, ass, giraffe, gila monster and thus we may see many hundreds of animals in him. I do not agree with the great Aristotle. I describe man not as a rational animal, but as a moral, spiritual, intelligent animal. I have my reasoned arguments to say so and I have brought them out in my **Push-Pull-Ego Factor** theory of crime causation discussed in my earlier articles and books.

Scientists who postulate evolutionary theory argue that man is rightly included in a group along with these animals like lemurs, monkeys and apes. They call the group **Primates**—i.e., any mammal of the order *Primates,* including man, the apes, monkeys and lemurs. According to the evolution postulate, there is good and convincing reason to believe that today's man and other **Primates** must have emerged from a lower **Primate** stock.

Look at the studies of fossils. They reveal that the earliest creature that seemed to be on the evolutionary line leading to the emergence of man was **Ramapithecus**. The studies show that the **Ramapithecus** appeared on the earth about 12 million years (or more) ago. Studies further show that the next group of modern man's ancestors were collectively called **Australopithecines** which were believed to have lived on earth two millions (or more) years ago. They were called **Bipes**—i.e., two-footed animals and they had teeth, limbs and pelvis almost similar to those of the man today. One of the species of this ancestor of today's man was known as **Homo Transvaalensis**. It is believed that they existed about 1.7 million (or more) years ago. They had the ability to make tools and make use of them. It has been further brought out by the scientists that the **Homo Transvaalensis** was replaced by another species called **Homo Erectus** about eight lakhs years ago. The **Homo Erectus** resembled man in cranial capacity. As far as crimes and criminal behaviour are concerned, **Homo Erectus** occupy an important place. For, organized social life and improved technical know-how for better way of life were found to be some other attributes to the group called **Homo Erectus**. This species has a number of traits—all possessing features resembling those of today's man.

Criminologists are concerned more with the organized social life of people and their technical know-how for honouring social laws for people's co-existence. A social law without morality/ethics is not and cannot be a social law. Every social law presumes morality/ethics. For example, 'Do good and avoid evils' is a moral law. The social law accepts it and incorporates it in the social fabric of life. 'Avoid evil' is a moral law. The social law accepts it and incorporates it in the social fabric of life. 'Avoid evil' means 'don't commit a crime'. A moral 'wreck' cannot and does not live a good social life.

'Improved Technical know-how for the better way of life' means a lot. It shows the intelligence of man. Earlier it has been stated that the **Homo Transvaalensis** (existed 1.7 million years ago) had the ability to make tools and use them. What does it mean? The **Intelligence** which the modern man has its root in the **Homo Transvaalensis** and the **Intelligence** thus in its earlier nature got developed further. **Homo Erectus** which replaced the **Homo Transvaalensis** had improved 'technical know-how' for better living. **Intuitiveness** is a function of intelligence along with (i) memory, (ii) comprehension, (iii) expansion and (iv) analysis.

Push-Pull-Ego Factor theory of crime causation is built on modern man's **Morality/Ethics, Intelligence** and **Spirituality**. Spirituality is nothing but a belief or faith in the invisible. It may be the God/gods or a principle, superstition, invisible reality or anything of like nature—real or unreal. Man has a hope and he looks ahead with that hope to the better. We have no valid information whether or not the **Homo Transvaalensis** and the **Homo Erectus** had spirituality. However, the **Homo Erectus** had hopes for a better way of life as revealed from his improved 'technical know-how'. The ***intuitiveness*** (invention capability) is a proof for the same. In my considered view, the **Spirituality** of the modern man has its roots in the *intuitiveness* (inventiveness) of the **Homo Erectus**. He had hopes for a better life.

Evolution-researches prove that the fossil record of the man today—viz., **Homo Sapiens**, dates back only about three hundred thousand years. **Homo Sapiens** (the modern man, the single surviving species of the genus *Homo* and of the primitive family *Hominidae*, to which it belongs), as the scientists say, belong to the common genius *Homo* (means the primate genius that includes modern man). According to them, a few other species closely related to **Homo Sapiens** also existed. One such was **Homo Neanderthalensis.** It is popularly called **Neanderthalman.** This race was short necked and massive in built. Criminology is not concerned in such matters although Kretschner identified body mind types with all kinds of criminal behaviour. Of course, William H. Sheldon too spoke of constitution of man as a cause of crime. Nevertheless, we have no evidence to show that **Neanderthalman** involved in the violation of law which existed from the time of **Homo Erectus** or earlier. Anyway, **Neanderthalman** disappeared from the earth and that race was replaced by a tall race called the **Cro Magnon Man.** It is now established that the **Cro Magnon Man** was similar to the modern man in appearance and in intelligence. There exists no information about the violation of laws by the **Cro Magnon Man. Cro Magnon Man**—that race is not considered as a modern man although there was some similarity in appearance.

The modern man—i.e., **Homo Sapiens** is believed to have co-existed with **Neanderthalman**. It is postulated that the **Homo Sapiens** became dominant since the extinction of the **Neanderthalman.** It is further believed that the **Homo Sapiens** ultimately might have absorbed the **Cro Magnons Man** through interbreeding and they flourished throughout the surface of the earth. The difficulty which the criminologists face today is that they cannot study the criminal behaviour of the **Homo Sapiens** now. They had, I believe social laws and morality, spirituality, and intelligence to control their behaviour. Cesare Lombroso (Italy 1836-1909) made attempts to relate man's criminal behaviour with his morphological features with atavism. Atavism postulates a revision to the primitive or sub-human type of man. Atavists are characterized typically by a variety of inferior morphological features reminiscent of apes and lower primates. According to Cesare Lombroso (the father of Modern Criminology), the atavists were similar to the primitive man psychologically too. He said that the criminal's behaviour would be contrary to the rules, laws and expectations of the modern man because of the atavist's physiological and psychological '*throw backness*' to an earlier stage of evolution. I do not know how he came to such conclusions on the psychology and behaviour of the atavists. He could be right(?). He brought the concept of '*degeneration*' which meant and included a kind of pathological component in the individual which he inherited from his ancestors. He concluded that the criminals would show rudimentary physical and psychological attitude of the primitive man. So far, so good.

The modern man has, no doubt, dominated the other creatures. He could achieve this, according to me, because of his morality/ethics, spirituality and intelligence. Because of the morality/ethics he could ensure rapid progress in his social life. Because of his spirituality, he could act with a hope and confidence to achieve his goal. Because of his intelligence he could ensure scientific, technological, cultural and legal progress. His bipedal and erect posture, free movement of hand and legs to do a variety of works, his opposable thumbs, ability to communicate via verbal and non-verbal language (tongue and other parts of his body) helped him to be unique in body and functions. His ancestors were not blessed with such organs and capabilities. His (1) Eye-hand coordination helped him to perform a variety of psychomotor activities. (2) Highly developed brain enabled him to memorize, comprehend, expand, analyse, assess, critically evaluate, logically think, associate, integrate, interpret, invent and make decisions. (3) Unique locating of eyes, colour sensitive retinal cones, special antigravity postural muscles, language ability and other communication skills—all helped him to have advancement in social, moral, intellectual, spiritual, ethical and cultural spheres.

Everything is admitted and criminologists do not question the postulates of evolution. They wanted to know how did the modern man's ancestors behave? What activated them to behave the way they did?

Psychologists generally admit that the animal behaviour is instinctive. An instinct in psychology is an inborn pattern of activity or tendency in action common to a given biological species. It is a natural or innate impulse—i.e., a natural intuitive power. There are many instincts. Man is an evolution from the animals and just like the animals have, man too has two eyes, two ears, one nose, one mouth, one tongue, one neck and thus the internal and external body organs are alike. In my studies and observations, I find that the same energy which activates the animals activates the man too. Animals in the forests or animals which are not trained are the real animals. The dogs, elephants, horses, camels etc. are trained. There are domestic animals tamed or trained. They live with human beings and therefore their behaviour cannot be normally considered as animal behaviour. Likewise, people who are not trained or socialized behave just like real and naked animals. Earlier I have brought the case of Kamala and Amala, who were found out from Indian forests. Their behaviour was almost like or exactly like animal behaviour—instinctive in nature. My studies show that behaviour—whether that of animals or human beings—is instinctive to begin with. As far as human beings are considered their instinctive behaviour to a certain extent is tolerated in society. Beyond that level, the behaviour becomes slightly abnormal (border-line) and then if it goes further and further it becomes abnormal proper. In such situations, his behaviour must be controlled by morality/ethics, spirituality and intelligence. Thus, I have seen that the instinctive behaviour (to begin with) of the human beings are controlled by laws which are innumerable in numbers. Yes, "I am born free, but chained everywhere"—said so by the French Philosopher Jean Jacques Rousseau [1712-78] long ago. Animals which behave instinctively are not chained unless they come into contact with human beings. If animals go beyond the permitted level by human beings, they are punished in many ways—even are killed.

I find that instincts are natural, necessary and inevitable for animals and human beings. They activate them and as a result they behave. In the case of human beings, the activating instinctual energy beyond a level is found to be harmful for human co-existence in a society. Hence, they are controlled by laws of many kinds. Some violate the laws, and they are dealt with in different ways to reduce the violations. Even in the animal world, the instinctual behaviour of animals are controlled by animals themselves in a lesser way. If the animals tolerate them and I have seen such tolerance in the animal world telecasted in the TV. There exists a sort of justice administration even in the animal-kingdoms!—at least in the case of certain categories of animals. It may be clarified that the observations are purely individualistic and as such subjective in every sense. My personal and subjective observations need more research findings to come to conclusions which are objective.

The instincts I have noted among human beings and animals (dogs, oxen, pigs, goats, elephants, asses etc.) in a visible way are given below:

	Instincts	*Animals*	*Humans*
		...Seen...	
1.	Escape	√ √ √ √	√ √ √ √
2.	Repulsion	√√√√	√ √ √ √
3.	Curiosity	√	√ √ √ √
4.	Pugnacity (Combat)	√√√√	√ √ √ √
5.	Parental	√√√√	√ √ √ √
6.	Appeal	√√	√ √ √ √
7.	Submission	√	√ √
8.	Self-assertion	√√	√ √
9.	Gregariousness	√√	√ √ √
10.	Food seeking	√√√√	√ √ √ √
11.	Acquisitiveness	√ √ √	√ √ √ √
12.	Constructiveness	√	√ √ √
13.	Laughter	√√	√ √ √
14.	Sex	√√√√	√ √ √ √

√ √ √ √ √ – seen Very High
√ √ √ √ – seen Moderately High
√ √ – seen High
√ – seen

Instincts like (i) Escape, (ii) Repulsion, (iii) Pugnacity (Combat), (iv) Parental, (v) Food seeking, sex etc. were observed to be very high in both animals and human beings. Nevertheless, instinct like Acquisitiveness was observed to be moderately high in animals. The instincts called Submission, Appeal, Self-assertion, Laughter etc. were observed to be high (not very high or moderately high) in animals and instincts like (i) Submission (ii) Self assertion were high in human beings. As stated above, I could judge the intensity of the working of instincts in human beings and animals by evaluating them subjectively—by keenly observing the emotions which accompanied each instinct. They expressed (i) fear to escape, (ii) disgust to repulsion, (iii) anger to pugnacity (combat), (iv) lust to sex (v) tender emotions to parental, (vi) appetite to food seeking etc. It was further observed that they showed (i) distress to appeal, (ii) humility to submission, (iii) feeling of superiority to self assertion, (iv) feeling of loneliness to gregariousness, (v) feeling of ownership to acquisitiveness, (vi) amusement to laughter etc. I presume that the same may be seen in reptiles, amphibians, birds, insects etc.

Some psychologists during the earlier years of the development of psychology as a science made attempts to explain human behaviour resulting from instincts. They said that every human behaviour is instinctive like animal behaviour. Naturally, that approach led to the development of more researches in the area of instinct and human behaviour. Resultingly, a few psychologists found out that human behaviour was not purely instinctive. They said that human behaviour which was thought to be instinctive actually varied widely from culture to culture and individual to individual. Hence, they stated that instincts had nothing much to do with human behaviour although they have importance in studying animal behaviour.

Criminologists in general do not fully subscribe to the views of the psychologists who endorsed the above view. According to them, human beings are animals basically and everything working in animals does work in human beings as well. This is the reason why criminology holds the view that man is not an animal, but many animals. Earlier philosophers said emphatically that man was a rational animal. Today, that view of the earlier philosophers is almost rejected as found to be only partly true or untrue. Man is an 'intelligent' animal. Rationality is only one function of intelligence as intelligence has many more functions like, 'memory, comprehension, expansion, analysis and intuitiveness, etc. Criminologists say further that man is not only an intelligent animal but also he is a moral and spiritual animal. Thus, **Intelligence, Morality/Ethics** and **Spirituality** make the human beings different from animals, reptiles, amphibians, birds, insects etc.

Just see the investments man makes in the area of **Spirituality**. The churches, temples, mosques, gurudvaras, shrines, chapels etc. are found everywhere and many men cannot live without them. Go to a tribal settlement. There too one observes spiritual activities and prayer centres. The tribal gods have great importance in their life. Though there may be some who are not theists or are not having any faith in God/gods, all of them have strong beliefs in invisible things. Faith or belief or both play an important role in the life of human beings. It is observed that a vast majority of people have faith in the God/gods although a small minority may have belief only as they are rationalists or atheists or humanist as the case may be. A considerably vast majority of people have **Faith** and **Belief.**

Just see the investments made in the area of **Intelligence.** The schools, colleges, other educational institutions, training centres, institutions for higher learning, universities and centres for researches etc. are no less than spiritual institutions seen in the world. People are plenty in both. It means that human beings are spiritual as well as intelligent.

Coming to morality, we take note of the fact that man is basically moral. He dislikes immorality. He constructs institutions for the disabled, mentally retarded, the aged and the infirm, the mental patients, the destitutes etc. People are concerned with the humanitarian issues of others and they spend their time, money and energy for the development of human beings. Everybody has concern over the **Essence** and **Existence** of human beings. Everybody has equal rights for everything and man's morality or moral sense works for it. Any immoral news appearing in the media is resisted against; any immoral act is reacted against. People organize protests against immorality in very many ways. Human beings are, as said above, basically moral.

Look at the investment man makes in the area of instincts. Theatres, entertainment halls, hotels, restaurants, museums, zoos, maternity centres and thus many things on earth are just for instinctual satisfaction of man. This is the reason why criminologists emphatically say that—

Animal + (plus) Spirituality, Morality/Ethics, Intelligence = Man

or

Man—(minus) Spirituality, Morality/Ethics, Intelligence = Animal

Human beings have **Humanity** and humanity means **Animality + Morality/Ethics + Spirituality + Intelligence** combined or mixed together and this mixture **[KNEAD]** is **Man.** It being so, the criminologists say that culture alone will not make a man. Culture is only a logical consequence of humanity in man. Animality, morality/ethics, spirituality and intelligence are the **Push Factors** in man.

Why do People Commit Crimes?

No doubt, man has morality/ethics, spirituality and intelligence. Still, why does he commit crimes of cruelty, of greed and against sexual morality. Why does he murder other fellow men? Why does he speak foul words and call epithets? Why does he commit sexual crimes? Why does he rob others? Why does he persecute people? Even people who claim to be 'religious' persecute people. According to Ludwing, during the period between 325 AD to 1912, one sees 2,43,21,000 human beings were butchered by non-Christians and 1,73,90,000 by Christians. How many people were killed during the two World Wars? Encyclopedia Britannica says that the Allies lost more than 5,00,000 lives and the Central European Powers lost nearly 34,00,000 lives during World War I. The total number of people who lost their lives in World War II are put between 3,50,00,000 and 6,00,00,000. Why? Even today religious fundamentalists and political terrorists murder people in large numbers. What is a genocide? Why? Man preaches self-denial, self sacrifice, selflessness, love, concern, consideration etc. and the same man commits crimes after crimes. Why? I have no doubt to say loudly that man commits crimes after crimes as he is activated by instincts which are not controlled by (i) Morality/ Ethics, (ii) Spirituality and (iii) Intelligence. He becomes emotional and not rational, moral, ethical, spiritual or reasonable. People lack emotional self awareness. Emotions expressed beyond a level lead to criminality and that is what Sigmund Freud said when he spoke about the excessiveness of '*id*' impulse as a cause of crime. Emotions (passion—i.e., any powerful or compelling emotion) which accompany instincts will appear as panic, rage, hilarity, sexual passion, greed, feeling of superiority etc. Destroy everything that causes fear—and people are slaughted thus. This is visible in politics, religion, race, caste, finance etc. Fear is a distressing emotion aroused by an impeding pain, danger etc. and people are afraid of it or that causes fright. Animals do it and it is seen that the deers fly away from the lion which is running after it. Ultimately, the lion kills it. Rage means fury or violent anger. What do the terrorists, fanatics and insurgents do? What do we see in communal fights or religious bigotry?—arson, looting, destruction of public property and mass murder? Why do the mother-in-law burn her daughter in law? What is rage or violent anger? There is something called the traffic rage. Why? Policemen who are duty bound and expected to protect the life and property of the people pelt stones at a mob! What laws do they observe in such situations? Laws are on one side and violations are concurrently on the other side.

What are the **Pull Factors?** Pull Factors mean the environment. Animals too have environments. Every animal reacts to its environment instinctively. But, unlike the animals, the man is controlled by *Morality/Ethics, Spirituality* and *Intelligence*. The formula is—

$$S \rightarrow O \rightarrow R$$

Where, S means Stimulus
O means Organism
R means Response

Both animals and men respond to a stimulus. Animals respond to the stimulus instinctively whereas the man is expected to be controlled by *Morality/Ethics, Spirituality* and *Intelligence*. If he is not thus controlled, he reacts instinctively and thus commits violations of law.

The instinctual behaviour of animals and men is shown in Fig. 2.1 and Fig. 2.2.

Fig. 2.1: Animal Behaviour

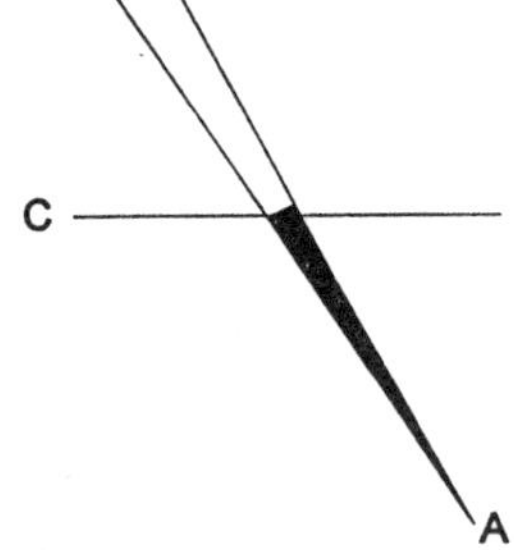

Fig. 2.2: Human Behaviour

In Fig. 2.1, animals behave instinctively and there is no control over their behaviour. In Fig. 2.2, man behaves instinctively, then he is not allowed to go beyond a limit or level (in Fig 2.2). The limit or level is fixed at C beyond which he is controlled by *Morality/ Ethics*, *Spirituality* and *Intelligence*. If his instinct overpowers the controlling forces, then he violates the law and thus commits a crime. The instinct is the root of every crime. No crime is committed without an instinct or more than one instinct.

Some psychologists speak of drives in man as the activating energy. But many criminologists do not accept it. An instinct becomes a **drive** only if it is controlled by *Morality/Ethics, Spirituality* and *Intelligence*. **Drive** in psychology means an 'inner urge that stimulates a response'. Random House College Dictionary says that drives are the basic or instinctive needs. Criminologists like me also say that a **drive** is an instinctive need.

Animal behaviour		**Human Behaviour**	
AB = S/I		HB = S/I	
Where AB-	Animal behaviour	Where HB-	Human behaviour
S-	Situation	S-	Situations
I-	Instinct not controlled by Morality/ Ethics, Spirituality and Intelligence	I-	Instinct controlled by Mortality/ Ethics, Spirituality and Intelligence

Fig. 2.3: Animal Behaviour

Fig. 2.4: Human Behaviour

In both cases, Fig. 2.3 and Fig. 2.4, instincts play a role. In the case of animals, instincts play the role without any control and in the case of human beings, instincts play the role with controls— i.e., controlled by *Morality/Ethics, Spirituality* and *Intelligence*. If the instincts are not controlled, crimes will be the outcome.

Frustrations and Conflicts in Animals and Human Beings

As far as an animal is concerned, the frustration is the difficulty encountered by the animal when its instinctual satisfaction is thwarted by some obstacle which blocks or impedes the progress towards the instinctual satisfaction. For example, a dog which feeds the puppies becomes violent when someone disturbs it. It will bite those who disturb it. Why? The maternal instinct is so strong in it. As far as a man is concerned, the frustration is the experience which a person has when his motives are thwarted either by some obstacle that blocks or impedes his progress towards a desired goal or by the absence of an appropriate goal (James C. Coleman). For example, a person who creates difficulties for a man to reach his goal may be beaten or killed. How many such instances are seen every day?

What is working behind a mob behaviour? Instincts and emotions play an important role in mob behaviour as well as in riots. For examples: (1) a communal riot, (ii) a political agitation. Instincts are seen in hostile or aggressive crowds. People become a lawless throng to be led by instincts—to be led into lawlessness. Again in an escape crowd, people are led by instincts. They are terror stricken—survival instincts which are very forceful and in an acquisitive mob (e.g., food riots), one may see very powerful instincts. People in an expressive crowd give expression of their emotions. Joy is the emotion of great delight or happiness accompanying the instinct called laughter.

Animals and human beings face conflicts of various types. How will the animals in hunger behave? Criminologists may attest the view that they behave exactly like the human beings who are not controlled by *Morality/Ethics, Spirituality* and *Intelligence*. A conflict is a stress for animals and men. No one can predict how hunger/thirst will make people and animals to behave. They may get wild. There is a village saying: 'Don't teach Bible before a wild animal which is hungry'. Again, many people believe that anything is justified for a hungry man. They say further that it is the right of the hungry man to misbehave—to behave in an undesirable way-in a criminal way.

In custodial torture and in custodial death, policemen behave instinctively. They are to enforce law in society. Corruption and bribery are rampant among the Government employees. Researches show that acquisitiveness (greed) is the instinct powerfully seen in such people. Officials of the income tax, of the sales tax, excise and customs, health services, education, local administration become corrupt even though they know the laws, rules, regulations and moral principles etc. 'Religious' men and godmen become corrupt although they preach divine scriptures. What is seen in crimes of affluence? Greed and nothing more. Intelligent people give justification for their instinctual crimes. 'So called' moral/ethical men give convincing explanations for their instinctual crime. In many situations, people commit the crimes first and later, they give rationalization, justification and moral explanations. People commit crimes because their activating forces—i.e., instincts—are not controlled morally/ethically, spiritually and/or intelligently.

Instincts and Emotions in Animality

People generally and commonly think that they are moral/ethical, spiritual, reasonable and rational. My researches in criminology give me enough proof and evidence to prove that relatively a small part of a man's behaviour results from rational thinking and reasonableness. We live in a culture which is said to give high value for mortality/ethics and on reasoning and thinking. Therefore, people are inclined to think of themselves as basically moral/ethical and primarily rational and reasonable. Precisely therefore they overlook non-rational, immoral factors in their behaviour. There are instinctual factors and accompanying emotional processes behind every human act. The forces which one calls 'instincts' and accompanying 'emotions' may lead to many human activities or inhibit the activities.

The migrating and nest-building habits of birds are often quoted as the common examples of instinctive behaviour in birds. The speciality of man is that he has *Morality/Ethics, Spirituality* and *Intelligence* so much so that he can modify his instinctual behaviour. For example, a scientist has *constructiveness* as his instinct and the accompanying emotion is a *feeling of creativeness*. His endeavour reaches to many inventions. There too, instincts and emotions are the activating forces on him. Again, laughter is an instinct and *amusement* is the accompanying emotion. With his intelligence, morality/ethics and spirituality, he can raise to the level of a renouned artist or a performer. The only thing to be cared is that the instinctual and emotional energy and force should not cross the limit or level permitted by the society and its culture. If they cross the limit or level, they violate the laws which impose restrictions on their behaviour.

If a man does not have an instinct and accompanying emotion, he cannot act as a man. For example: (1) A man devoid of the instinct **sex**, then he will not have the accompanying emotion called **lust**. Is he a man if he does not have sex and lust? If a man does not have the instinct called **escape** and the accompanying emotion known as **fear**, he cannot be called a man. The fact that animals behave in a particular way because they have instincts, it goes without saying that a man who is an animal behaves instinctively at the beginning and then he modifies his behaviour by *Morality/ Ethics, Spirituality* and *Intelligence.*

I.Q., E.Q., A.Q., M/E.Q., S.Q. in MAN

A **quotient** means in Mathematics the result of division; the number of times one quantity is contained in another. Thus, I.Q.—i.e., **Intelligence Quotient** is calculated as:

$$\boxed{IQ = \frac{MA}{CA} \times 100}$$

Where, I.Q. — Intelligence Quotient
M.A.— Mental Age
C.A. — Chronological Age

Scientists today speak of E.Q.—i.e., **Emotion Quotient,** HR.Q—i.e., Human Relations Quotient. E.Q. consists of five important dimensions, namely: (1) knowing one's own emotions, (2) controlling one's own emotions, (3) recognizing emotions in others, (4) controlling emotions in others, (5) improvement in emotional control etc. More about E.Q. will be discussed later in this chapter. As the scientists today speak about HR.Q., criminologists are thinking about A.Q. (Animality Quotient), M/ E.Q. (Morality/Ethics Quotient), S.Q. (Spirituality Quotient) etc. to explain criminal behaviour. In a nut shell, we may say—

$$C.B. = \frac{M/E.Q.}{A.Q.}$$

$$C.B. = \frac{S.Q.}{A.Q.}$$

$$C.B. = \frac{I.Q.}{A.Q.}$$

$$C.B. = \frac{S.Q.+M/E.Q. + I.Q.}{A.Q.}$$

Where C.B – **Criminal Behaviour**
M/E.Q. – **Morality/Ethics Quotient**
S.Q. – **Spirituality Quotient**
I.Q. – **Intelligence Quotient**
A.Q. – **Animality Quotient**

A.Q. or the **Animality Quotient** should not go beyond the instinctual level or extent permitted by the culture and society—i.e., the **Morality/Ethics, Spirituality** and **Intelligence** (See Fig. 2.2). How to decide the extent or level will be discussed later in this chapter.

The algebraic formula reads that—if the **A.Q.** (i.e., Animality Quotient—i.e., instincts and emotions) is more than the **S.Q.**; **M/E.Q.**; **I.Q.**, or all of them put together then criminal behaviour is the outcome. The formula emphasizes the fact that the **A.Q.** should always be lower than the other Quotients or all quotients put together 4 permitted?

How to Decide the Instinctual Level or Extent

There are scales to decide the instinctual level/extent permitted and they are: (i) **Individualistic Scale,** (ii) **Normative Scale,** (iii) **Majority Scale,** (iv) **Socio-cultural Scale,** (v) **Diagnostic Scale.** They are discussed below.

(1) In **Individualistic Scale,** the individual decides the instinctive level/extent. The Naxalites, the terrorist, the *Mafia* criminal, the corrupt man, the human god, the political leader and so on will decide the level/extent. It is purely subjective and crime will be the outcome if the person has a defective personality, philosophy or outlook. The root cause of genocide may be the defect of the individualistic scale. The **A.Q.** is very high.
(2) In **Normative Scale,** the instinctive level/extent will be decided by forces which are outside the individual. Adherents of Maoism or insurgency will have a level which is decided by those who promote the '*...isms* and *...ologies* or*...sophies*'. Victory or success through the barrels of a gun; the end justifies the means; poor man has a right to violate the laws etc. are examples in point. If the normative scale is acceptable to the dominant culture/

society, then there is no issue or crime or criminal behaviour.

(3) **Majority scale** decides the instinctive level/extent on the basis of how majority of the people think about it. Majority of the people in a given society/culture say that adultery is bad, then the sexual instinct leading to adultery is to be controlled. In all cases, the majority judgments may not be acceptable. Nevertheless, in most of the situations in a democracy, majority decisions can fix the level/extent of instinctual forces which can be functional.

(4) **In socio-cultural scale**, it is well defined the extent or level up to which the instinct can be operative. The society and culture play their role to fix the extent/level of instinctual expression. Every instinct is natural, necessary and inevitable, but beyond a level it becomes crude or unrefined, indecent or obscene, vulgar and unacceptable. The society and the culture make laws and rules for controlling the instincts. The morality and ethics have their laws and rules. The religion and institutions will have their own. The State does enact laws and makes the violations/offences under the State laws.

(5) **Diagnostic Scale** is also called the Clinical Scale. The instinct one expresses should give individual pleasure and social welfare. A rapist may get individual pleasure by the rape, but no social welfare. His act is a crime. Democracy is for social welfare and in such a system the political leaders or party men enter into nexus crimes or exploit the people for their selfish achievements. The instinct beyond the level must be stopped and anything done should be punished for making people in a society happy and to ensure the welfare of the society.

Crime Control and Reduction

No doubt, crimes can be controlled and crimes can be reduced only by controlling instincts and the accompanying emotions—only by reducing the intensity of the instincts and the accompanying emotions. But how?

1. Accept the truth that man is basically an animal or better, many animals and he has all the animal instincts in him. They do work in everyone. However, the instincts in man work or ought to work under the control of **Morality/ Ethics, Spirituality** and **Intelligence**. Emotions accompanying instincts are a very powerful energy which sometimes overpower the **intelligence, morality/ethics** and **spirituality**. Make the children aware about this fact from their birth so that they develop their personality in an upright way in the right direction. If that is done, the animality can be controlled and crimes can be reduced.
2. Although emotions are accompanying animal instincts in man, researchers show that changes from one emotional state to another can and do take place rapidly. A mild, sensitive and concerned person may become suddenly violent resulting in the commission of crimes. Emotional self control becomes necessary in such situations. This can certainly be achieved by practice and training. One's emotional behaviour must be more stable and children should learn it from their infancy. When do children start learning to control their emotions? According to criminologists, the children learn the rules, regulations, customs, traditions etc. to control their animal instincts (impulses) from their birth onwards. It is through the interaction of their internal needs and external restrictions that the children (little infants) learn them. The mother, father, family members, schools, neighbourhood, community have to play special and specific roles to educate little infants and children to internalize the means, methods, rules, regulations etc. so that their animality is put under control or is not allowed to cross the permitted limit or level.

Immediately after the birth, the baby sucks the breast of its mother for feeding. It is nothing but an expression of the baby-infant's animal instinct called **food-seeking** followed by the emotion named **appetite** (i.e., a desire for food or drink). Animals too do the same thing and I have observed it in many domestic animals like cows, goats, pigs etc. A baby-human infant is no different from the puppies, kittens, calves etc. What is shown by the baby-infant without control at its birth will be continued if it is not properly trained or educated. Mother is the principal and the only socializing agent at the birth of a child and she does it in very many ways. The manner in which the child is fed by its mother (mother substitute too) is of great importance. Socialization means, as said earlier, the process by which a new born child is socialized—i.e., is made a social person obeying the various rules, regulations, rules of morality/ethics, spirituality, customs, traditions etc. Why do we socialize the infant? The reason is that we do not want to 'animalize' the child. 'Animalize' means to excite the animal passions of; brutalize etc. 'Animalism' again means *'preoccupation with or motivation by physical appetites rather than moral, spiritual or intellectual forces'*. The meaning of 'animalism' given in Webster's Dictionary is to be taken seriously as it implies that *moral, spiritual* and *intellectual* forces alone can make an infant to abide by law—not to become a law violator—by controlling animal instincts in him. **Push-Pull-Ego Factor** theory of crime causation too teaches the same emphatically (if one wants to control and reduce crimes in society). What about the bowel control of the baby-infant? No control at all at birth. Breast feed and bowel emptying are the two needs of the baby-infant. It needs the cleaning of its body. All these are well looked after by those who are near and close to it. But, they cannot and will not continue for a long time. The sucking stage (i.e., up to 8 months after birth) ends when the baby infant becomes 8 months old. Sigmund Freud says that the infant naturally passes to a stage named 'biting stage' in the **oral stage** of socialization, humanization and personality development. How does the baby-infant behave during the biting stage? I have observed that the baby infants bite the nipple of their mothers causing pain to them. The incisors (Four anterior teeth in each jaw used for cutting) appear by that time and the little infants mercilessly bite the nipple of their feeding-mothers whenever they have difficulties to get the breast milk freely. How can they do so? Their bites cause, sometimes, injuries to the nipples of their mothers and they need, sometimes, medical attention. The biting of the nipple by the infants is nothing but an act of aggression. In other words, it is the expression of the animal instinct named **pugnacity** (combat) and the accompanying emotion of **anger**. 'Pugnacity' means excessively inclined to quarrel or fight and the little infant fights with its mother by biting. No, that should be controlled and should not be encouraged. The mother then assumes the role of policing the infant and she punishes the little baby forcibly removing it from her lap. Sometimes, she gently throws it denying not only the breast feed but also the pleasure which the infant has in its touching the body of its mother. The tactual pleasure is a real pleasure which little infants enjoy during that period. Thus, the loving mother imposes two types of punishments—i.e., (i) denying the breast feed, (ii) disallowing the tactual pleasure derived by the infant by touching the body of its mother. Punishment is a mild method of humanizing the infant. It gently teaches how to control its aggressive instincts and thus to become a socialized or law abiding child.

The Anal Stage starts at when the infant is 18 months old and lasts up to 4 years. The bowel-functions are very important and the child needs toilet training. The child should have control over the bowel and it cannot urinate at any place as it likes. It cannot answer the nature's call everywhere without any control. Parents and other family members teach them the rules, regulations etc. with an aim to inculcate in them the values of 'how orderly, neat and planned should one be in later life to live as a socialized human person'. By the end of the biting stage, one develops the feeling of self and others in society—i.e., 'I am a self different from other selves in society'. This awareness [**I-Thou**] is necessary as it will help him to develop morality/ethics in him.

During the **anal stage**, there will come a variety of situations in which conflicts may arise between the socializing-humanizing agents and the little children. The pull factors in **Push-Pull-Ego Factor Theory** of Crime causation include such agents as well. The children then realize or internalize more about others selves around them. No doubt, the internalization to children means 'adjustment' with other selves. It also means the control of animal instincts and emotions. There are many situations—**Pull Factors**—in which the children rebel against their parents. Children may become aggressive or stubborn then.

Controlling the animal instincts and emotions is found more when the children go to nursery schools at the age of 4—a little earlier or later. Children are entrusted to baby care centres by the working parents in these days and it is seen even earlier or before the children are sent to nursery schools. In both cases, the humanizing functions are shared by the family and the baby care centres/nursery schools. Parents, other family members, schoolmates, teachers, baby care takers, the environment (**Pull Factors**) etc. are important here. Cases are reported that babies and nursery school kids are abused sexually even during this period. Necessarily, such sexual misuse or abuse of children may result in **repulsion** (animal instinct) accompanied by **disgust** (emotion). Such misbehaviour may be responsible for the development of a defective personality—eventually to crimes and criminal behaviour.

There is a period called '*Phallic*' stage (4-6 years of age)—says Sigmund Freud. Oedipus Complex—i.e., the unresolved desire of a child for sexual gratification through the parent of the opposite sex, especially the desire of a son for his mother. This involves first, identification with and, later, hatred for the parent of the same sex, who is considered by the child as a rival (Webster's) and Electra Complex—i.e., the unwanted desire of a daughter for sexual gratification from her father (Webster's) are supposed to come into being. Freudian view is opposed by many later psychologists. Criminologists have no evidence to show that Freudian view is right or wrong. Nevertheless, they have ample evidence that some parents misuse their little children of tender ages even sexually. Investigation of such cases reported to police reveal that the children are victimized by their parents having pervert personality, unethical sex values or psychic problems. Investigating officers generally do not go to probe into the role played by children in such situations. Children are presumed to be innocent victims of sexual attack by their parents and the Protection of Children from Sexual Offences Act [POCSO Act] in India registers criminal cases against such parents. The children during the *Phallic* stage are sexually, sometimes, misused by their teachers as well and there are many reasons for such acts against children.

Anyway, the animal instinct—i.e., sex and accompanying emotion, lust,—is seen in children during the *phallic* stage as well. Any honest attempt on the part of their socializing and humanizing agents will help them to develop mental power to control their animal instinct during that stage of personality development. Children do develop sexual feelings towards members of their complimentary sex. This certainly makes them to love others and share their sorrows and pleasures. Never inculcate wrong values. Some agents wrongly say 'members of the opposite sex'. This is wrong. There is only complimentary sex and no opposite sex. We need both sexes and such values will be helpful to control their lust and bring it to the permissible level/extent. Teach the children moral values which are laudable at home, in schools etc.

There is a period known as ***Latency Stage*** (Sigmund Freud) during which the children supposedly lose interest in sexual matters. The sex energy during the ***Latency Stage*** is still very powerful. Nevertheless, it is repressed. Resultingly, the energy is not that patent. During the ***Latency Stage,*** only the sex instinct is suppressed. Others are in full swing. Look at the pre-delinquency behaviour of juveniles. Comparing to the adults, no doubt, the juveniles face greater difficulties to adjust with situations which frustrate them. Owing to the parental control, the watchful eyes of the teachers, poverty at home, unemployment in the family, quarrels between the parents etc., the children may experience frustration or mental conflicts. These **Pull Factors** may compel them to engage in doing things which are violations of law. To escape from these frustrating or conflicting situations, they may (i) steal money, (ii) fight with others, (iii) engage in the sale of lottery tickets, drugs etc. or engage in gambling or begging. Some may run away from home. My studies prove that more than 90 per cent of children who were caught by the police had frustrations, mental conflicts, stresses at home, schools or both.

Truancy and vagrancy are said to be pre-delinquency stages. My observations of truant or vagrant children give enough evidence to say emphatically that most of them are uncontrollable children who in the absence of proper guidance, supervision and parental control become delinquents. Children develop their **ego** from infancy and if adequate **Pull Factors** (Environments) are not provided for the development of their **ego** (Personality) properly, the possibility of their becoming delinquents will be very high.

'Escape' is an animal instinct and they must be provided with **Pull Factors** (environments) which teach them the right and the moral ways by which they can exercise their instinct (escape) in an upright way in the right direction. Committing suicide just on the eve of the examination (that is seen in Kerala in an incredible way) is not the right way. Killing a fellow student is not the correct way to become a student (political) leader. Of course **self assertion** is an animal instinct accompanied by **feeling of superiority**. Murdering a student or boycotting classes or destroying public property may not be the acceptable method. Yes, **repulsion** is an animal instinct followed by disgust as the accompanying emotion. Neglecting the old and the infirm at home is not the way to express **repulsion** and **disgust**. Parents are morally bound to teach them to control their **repulsion** and **disgust**. There is a spiritual canon which says that the elderly at home should be nursed and cared. This spiritual rule should be inculcated. Parental instincts—especially the maternal—are found to be the strongest instinct among the animal instincts. The accompanying emotion is **tender feelings**. In the ten commandments believed to be given by God to Moses at Senai Mount, one sees such a canon and it must be inculcated into little children to develop their **ego** uprightly in the right direction. Thus one sees that the children are taught the moral, ethical, spiritual laws and values, in an intelligent way from their infancy so that their instincts are controlled well—are not allowed to go beyond the limit, extent or level permitted.

Just before puberty, children have a short period—may be one year, a little less or more, which (Sigmund Freud) is called **Homosexual Stage**. According to Sigmund Freud, it is universal, but many well-meaning and pious spiritual men do not openly accept it. My criminological investigation shows that everyone faces or passes through this stage. I have asked many children about it and most of them told me 'Yes'. Some refused to answer my question. There were a few who said 'No' to me. I had a bio-feedback gadget (Audio) with me. It measures the level of perspiration [GSR] on the finger when the questions are asked. The sound produced by the gadget varies according to the strength of the perspiration. Those who said 'No' to my question openly produced 'high sound' when the gadget was fixed on their index finger. My questions regarding homosexuality disturbed them very much producing more perspiration. The sound produced by the gadget when questions unrelated to homosexuality at that specific stage was quite normal and it did not reveal deception or mental conflicts.

After the homosexual stage, one sees the **heterosexual stage** (Sigmund Freud) getting developed. My observations as a criminologist are—

(1) Interaction between parents and children matters a lot in the development of **ego** (personality). I observe that the basic values, moral convictions, spiritual principles and

attitudes in the life of every person are formed and strengthened by the time he/she reaches the puberty. The foundation of the values are put before one reaches puberty. The superstructure is constructed on this infrastructure.

(2) The environments (**pull factors**) play a very important role in shaping the **ego** (personality) and there are hundreds of such pull factors—known and unknown—operating in a man. Bad neighbourhood, slum life, deterioration of the moral standards of the people around, delinquent sub-culture, generation perverted values, defective mass media, films and cultural programmes, decline in values seen in social media, filthy literature, cartoons, internet etc. exert a lot of influence in the formation of the ego.

(3) Children identify with values of their parents, teachers and so on. They identify with film stars they like. False adventurism, untrue criminal heroism, delinquent attitudes, crime movies, sex-stimulating scenes do attract them. They imitate their parents and teachers. Sometimes, religious preachers and spiritual men—real or fake—exert influence on children. They have suggestive effects. The **pull-factors** give very fantastic—i.e., conceived or appearing as if conceived by an unrestrained imagination—ideas of making easy money by smuggling, looting, pocket-picking, gang activities, *Mafia*, robbery etc. and they become criminals in later life. 'Tell me who is your father, I shall tell you who you are'—this is a village saying which is partly true in real life. No doubt, the social, cultural, economic, educational, financial, political etc. background of everyone has a decisive say in controlling and regulating one's animal instincts.

What to do and how to Control Animal Instincts to Reduce Crimes and Delinquency?

The answer to the question: 'How to control **animal instincts** to reduce crimes and delinquency?' lies in **managing oneself.** How? One can and he should manage himself by emotional self control. Emotional self control can be effected through controlling the animal instincts in each one. The instincts should not cross the limit. This can be done by: **(1) Morality/Ethics, (2) Spirituality, (3) Intelligence.**

Morality means conformity to the rules of right conduct. In other words, behaviour with a moral/ethical values acceptable to the society—the dominant culture. Everyone should consciously develop emotional self control, techniques inculcating universal values to their personality.

Spirituality means supernatural-incorporeal-metaphysical. Depending upon the **pull factors** from the early infancy, everyone becomes a theist, an atheist, a rationalist or an agnostic etc. Nobody can live on this earth without having a belief (not faith) in certain cosmic truths—nature's truths—which he cannot physically see or experience.

Intelligence means the capacity of reasoning, understanding and for similar forms of mental activity such as memory, comprehension, intuitiveness etc. More about morality/ethics, spirituality and intelligence will be discussed in the chapters that follow.

The methods and means for instinctual and emotional control—**Managing Oneself**—are:

1. Education

Education does not mean 'the act or process of imparting or acquiring general knowledge and of developing the process of reasoning and judgment'. It means formation of character with values. Character is the aggregate of features and traits that form the individual nature of some person or thing—i.e., moral or ethical quality; qualities of honesty and integrity. Certainly, the formation of character will refine people and help them to control their animal instincts.

2. Training

It is nothing but the education, instruction or discipline of a person or thing that is being trained. The training is meaningfully given from infancy by parents and others to control their instincts and emotions so that they may live observing laws and norms and respecting positive values.

3. Intellectual Infiltration

It is the process or act of infiltrating—i.e., to permiate. The purpose of infiltration is to penetrate into the mind values—moral and ethical—in order to control negative emotions. The purpose is to control the animal instincts not to go beyond the permitted limit. By many methods, the values can be put into a person's mind. Terrorists, fundamentalists, fanatics and so on do it so that they make people to become very aggressive in their thoughts and actions.

4. Exposure

It is a disclosure, as of something which is considered to be valuable in the formation of character. For the formation of character, there is the need of information. The information is obtained by exposure to situations. For example, repeated exposure to cruel situations (**Pull Factors**) will normally make a man to become cruel. Just like the butcher's son who is repeatedly exposed to the sight of butchering becoming cruel (?) to animals, a child exposed to 'instinct controlling situations' repeatedly will become soft and sober in his behaviour. The more the exposure, the better it is to control one's animal instincts.

5. Reinforcement

Reinforce means to strengthen with some added piece, support or material. It is nothing but strengthening the moral and ethical values in a person so that he can control his animal instincts. This is needed and that is the precise reason why children and adults are exposed to religious sermons and preachings which contain moral and ethical values.

6. Model

It is a standard or example for imitation or comparison. Parents are, no doubt, models for their children. Teachers become models for their students. Saints, *sadhus*, *sannyasees*, human gods, politicians, film stars, literary writers, religious men, extremists and so on can be the models. The biographies of saints and greatmen are taught to children or told in sermons/speeches. The intention is to inculcate the good aspects of their lives to developing children. The models teach and the people learn the good and bad aspects of their lives. There will be many situations in which the models have resorted to controlling their instincts and emotions—ultimately become successful to reduce crimes in society.

7. Examples

Every human person is an example to someone—i.e., a pattern or model, as of something to be imitated or avoided. Company with good friends in schools or later in life will help a lot to learn how to control one's negative emotions and to learn more about positive emotions. The role of the associates is important in character formation. Research studies to date indicate quite conclusively that association with antisocial people make us to have recourse to antisocial activities. It is because people in such situations do not learn how to control their animal instincts. Bad neighbourhood, slum life, decline of the moral standards of the associates, physical deterioration of areas, urban slum, delinquent sub-culture, gangs etc. are really bad, as they do not help to control one's animal instincts and negative emotions.

8. Prayer

Prayer is a devout petition to, or any form of spiritual communication with God or an object of worship—the purpose here is to get divine blessings to control one's animal instincts. It is a spiritual communication for getting God's grace to live without committing sins (crimes). There is a village thinking—i.e., a family which prays together lives together. The meaning is that they acquire necessary spiritual strength and psychological capability to live together by effectively controlling animal instincts and negative emotions. Many people do believe that prayer is a very powerful weapon or energy against crimes and delinquency.

9. Penance

Penance is a punishment undergone in token of penitence for sin (sin is violation of God's law—i.e., religious law). Penance is different from penalty which is a punishment imposed on a crime-doer. Penance is self-inflicted penalty or a punishment willingly taken. Realization of one's defects and behavioural aberrations is a positive step taken for controlling the animal instincts. Many people go to pilgrim centers after taking a variety of self-inflicted sacrifices and they control their animal instincts during such periods. Penance and prayer go together.

10. Mortification

Mortification has many meanings. In criminology, we mean the practice of asceticism by penitential discipline to overcome desire for sin and to strengthen the will. No doubt, it is a self-inflicted humiliation. Mortification will, certainly, subjugate (the body, passions etc.) by disciplinary austerities. It is found to be very effective to control one's animal instincts and negative emotions. In Christian religion, Lent is an annual season of fasting and penitence. In Islam too, there is such season before Ramzan. All religions have it and it is intended to encourage the people to mortification.

11. Disciplining

Disciplining has many meanings and they are (1) training to act in accordance with rules; (2) instruction and exercise designed to train to proper conduct or action; (3) punishment inflicted by way of correction and training; (4) a whip or scourge, used in the practice of mortification or as an instrument of chastisement in certain religious communities etc. All these methods are primarily intended to control one's animal instincts and thereby coexist with others in society without violating the laws, rules and regulations. Even animals are disciplined with an intention to make them control their instincts. Certainly, it is an effective method for human beings as well.

12. Persuasion

To persuade means to prevail on (a person) to do something. The synonyms to persuade are (i) urge, (ii) influence, (iii) entice, (iv) impel etc. In many prisons, the principal role of the correctional staff is to persuade the inmates to control their animal instincts. Even in such controlled institution like a prison, the inmates exhibit their animal instincts in sexuality, aggression (leading to prison riots, protests etc.) etc. Persuasion is an often resorted stratagem in prisons.

13. Advice

It is a recommendation offered as a guide to action/omission. Advice and admonition go together and the purpose is to reprove or warn a person from acting instinctively (beyond the permitted limit/level). Children with problem are sent for professional counselling and they are advised to behave like human beings. Moral advice is given in very many ways during infancy and childhood. There are grandma-stories which have good morals—the moral teachings or practical lessons contained in the stories. Advice in the form of instructions is seen everywhere—from nursery school onwards—and the purpose is to enable people to control their instincts.

14. Gentle Punishment

Punishment means causing pain—physically, psychologically, morally, spiritually or more than one stated above—to a wrong doer. Parents give gentle punishments to children when they do wrong things; a court convicts a person to fine, imprisonment and even to capital punishment. While the former corrects the child or reforms him, the latter sometimes annihilates the wrong-doer. Punishment, no doubt is a very powerful weapon to put down the animal instincts. Certainty, the certainty of punishment works stronger than severity of punishment to compress down the excessiveness of animal instincts in a person.

15. Treatment

This is the systematic effort to cure illness and relieve symptoms, as with medicines, surgery etc. It can be psychotherapy, moral therapy, faith therapy or any of such methods of curing diseases. Even exorcism has been employed to get away from the excessive instinctual disturbances. Demonology explained criminal behaviour as the work of evil spirits and people said so because they were not aware of the animal instincts in man. They attributed every evil behaviour caused by the animal instincts as instigated by demons. Hence, they made attempts to get away from the clutches of demons to get out of the criminal bahaviour. They did not know that excessive animal instincts were the demons in man. There is always a fight going on between good spirit (God) and bad spirits (Demons) in every human beings. If the bad spirit wins in the fight, a crime is committed. On the contrary, if the good spirit wins in the fight, no crime is committed.

16. Meditation

'Mediation' means to think contemplatively or reflect. It is an introspection about one's good and bad ways of thinking and acting. It is a sort of self-reflection and the resolutions taken by a person will help to refrain from evil things. In seminaries, convents monasteries and other ascetic places, meditation is a usual method adopted to control animal instincts.

17. Surveillance

Surveillance simply means a watch kept over a person, group etc. especially over a suspect, prisoner or the like. In the case of children, certainly they are not suspects or prisoners. Nevertheless, parents, teachers, elders and close associates can and will smell or sense their inclination or proneness to undesirable activities (**Pull Factors**) which may result in the development of perverted personality formation. In such cases, they must be put under surveillance for proper parental control/teachers' watch so that they do not deviate from the moral/ethical values.

My studies prove that the parents who neglect to watch the activities of their children cry loudly when they find their children involved in criminal activities without any guilt feeling. In one case, a child said to his parents: "One does not become a father just by reproducing children. He should be a responsible father". Responsible parenting is essential for the development of enviable values in children. Surveillance and counselling with responsible parenting attitude will ensure good dividends.

18. Shadowing

'Shadowing' in criminology means to follow a developing child (a person too) secretly in order to keep a watch over his movements. No doubt shadowing is generally used in police work, but in criminology it means to keep a secret watch over children who are likely to develop a criminal personality through wrong association with people who are criminal minded. This is a time of internet communication and certainly there must be a healthy shadowing of children's interest in internet. There is internet addiction and it can cause perversions. I have noted children who are 3 years of age using smart mobile phones having internet access. Social media produces havoc and promote animal instincts to grow in the wrong direction with questionable values. Shadowing of mobile phones, internet chatting, SMS communications becomes essential now and never keep away from the rooms of children and don't permit them to misuse their phones and internet connectivity.

19. Association with Peers

A 'peer' means a person who is one's equal in rank and children's association with the peers is important in the development of proper personality. A number of studies conducted in the West have proved the influence of peers in the commission of crimes. Today, one may notice social media peers and they become close. Police records show that they do not show any remorse for the wrongs they commit. The drug addicts, alcoholics, rebels, fundamentalists, extremists, terrorists and so on come under this category.

20. Cultural Injections

The songs, films, mimicry, dance etc. have their impact. Knowingly or unknowingly, many ideas are injected to the growing children. The pornography which comes via internet may be enjoyed by immature minds and the children may experiment it for deriving erotic pleasure-sex instinct. Films show many things and every cinema has a formula which contains murder, aggression, sex, bed room scenes, vulgar language, filthy conversation, suicide, smuggling, crimes, etc. and they inject false notions and instinctual values to developing children. I had the bad experience of meeting such children in my researches and in criminology, the foul values injected by the cultural media do a lot of damage/havoc to growing children.

The chapters which follow discuss more about the working of the good spirit-morality/ethics, spirituality, and intelligence—in every human being so that he controls his animal instincts and thus reduces crimes in society.

Note

1. 'id' in psychoanalysis means the part of the psyche that is the source of instinctive energy. Its impulses are modified by the ego and superego: the source of libido (Webster's).

3

Morality/Ethics

The Law of the Conscience to Control and Reduce Crimes

Clara Calero took me to a restaurant at Rochester in New York State. We ordered for meals and waited for the food to be served. Before paying the bill, she asked for a container to carry the food items which we ordered, but could not eat. I asked her: "What are you doing?". She smiled and said: "The money for purchasing the food is ours; but the resources belong to the society". I did not fully understand her and therefore, I asked her to explain her statement further and more. She said: "The food items which we do not eat become waste and no one will eat it. It is not morally right to waste food when millions of people do not have much or anything to eat". Yes, there is a point in what she said to me. 'Wasting food is a crime'—that is what she thought and her moral conviction did not allow her to commit such a crime. Moral values do have an impact on the reduction of crimes in society.

Clara tells me that there are countries which punish people if they waste food items. In India, we observe many people ordering a lot of items in hotels and they leave the hotel without eating the food fully. If we go to a marriage party, we see people eating food and wasting food. Once I saw a beggar eating food-waste from a barrel in which people deposited the waste-food. Morality—moral values—moral principles will certainly control crimes and reduce them.

In India, we have any number of orphanages, charity schemes, old age homes, destitute houses etc. and all of them are run with the money collected from the people who feel that they have a moral responsibility to look after the poor and the needy. The Cancer Care Center near to my house provides palliative service and the director told me once that money was never a problem for them. There are many patrons and sponsors for the various services they render to cancer patients. People contribute liberally to charity and the money flowing to areas affected by natural calamities in Kerala recently is incredible. Some N.G.Os involved in human service have an annual budget more than some States in India. People do not tolerate crimes in society. They hate murder, kidnapping, rape etc. and are against terrorism, fanaticism, fundamentalism, insurgency etc. They spend a lot of money to control and reduce all sorts of crimes such as adulteration, drug traffic, human traffic, prostitution and sex trade etc. The moral conscience in man—in society—questions all sorts of injustice, wounded justice, less justice, miscarriage of justice etc. There are 'Charity Mafia' flourishing in society.

'Man is a rational animal'—the specific difference [s.d.] between man and animal was found to be 'Rationality' by ancient philosophers. Animals are not rational—hence they are not moral too. Therefore, the specific difference between animals and men is, like rationality, morality as well. The earlier philosophers had little or no knowledge about intelligence which has memory, comprehension, expansion, analysis and intuitiveness as its functions or characteristics. 'Rationality' means 'endowed with the faculty of reason'. Reasoning is just one of the functions of intelligence and it comes under analysis of it. Morality is not a pure function of intelligence alone and therefore it is necessary to say that 'man is a moral animal'.

Because of the morality in man, he fights against all sorts of injustice. For example—

(1) Human Rights Justice

People in authority or power misuse their authority or power. They abuse their power or misuse their authority. They exercise pseudo-authority. They refuse to exercise their power and/or authority. Resultingly, they commit moral wrongs—injustice. The history of man is a history of human rights violations and a history of fighting against such crimes. Communalism, racism, apartheid, slavery and slave-trade, genocide etc. speak a lot about human rights violations and such crimes can be controlled only by inculcating moral values.

(2) Gender Justice

There is no moral justification for gender discrimination; yet, there exist a variety of crimes committed on the basis of gender. What about the transgenders and hermaphrodites? Any rational or intelligent interpretation without taking into account the **Morality** of the issue means nothing. More than the intelligence, sometimes the morality matters. Morality and its principles are universal, absolute and time immemorial. Inculcate the moral values and principles in the new born so that crimes against gender justice may be controlled or reduced.

(3) Victim Justice

Criminal justice is administered from time immemorial in some way or other. But, what about the victim justice? There is no moral justification for the denial of victimological justice to people who suffer the consequences of crimes committed against them. Inculcation of the morality of victim justice has now an impact on the control and reduction of crimes against the victim justice. The absolute moral principles is ignored by the powerful on the basis of subjective morality which is understandable only to those who adhere to such unjust principles. Victim morality is a powerful weapon to control and reduce crimes against victims.

(4) Social Justice

Man is a social being and the resources of the world belong to all people alike. Nevertheless, some people enjoy them—denying them to many in society. It is found that the wealth of the world is possessed by a few and the people are exploited. In order to commit crimes against social justice, one finds a lot of discrimination made on the basis of caste, creed, colour, community, sub-caste, wealth, position, status, language, regionalism, sex and what not? Morality, moral principles and values can ensure social justice by controlling and reducing crimes against the weak or so-found weak sections of the society.

(5) Sex Justice

Sex is biological and often becomes a cause of many types of sexual offences. Moreover, there are transgenders and hermaphrodites and they involve in sex-crimes and they are made victims of sex crimes. They are discriminated in many areas like employment, education etc. and their human rights are not given due recognition. Certainly, there is the urgent need to inculcate sex values in the developing children. Women, owing to their physical weakness, should not be sexually exploited. The number of rape cases reported goes up alarmingly and they include gang rapes, raping of children of tender ages, rape by the near and dear ones including the father of the girl children. Raping the aged too is reported. The problem can be solved if and only if sex morality is injected to growing children.

(6) Juvenile Justice

Children under 18 years of age are vulnerable to many pressures and temptations in society. There are children (i) who are in conflict with law (delinquents) and (ii) who need special care and protection (the neglected, the destitute, the uncontrollable, the incorrigible and so on). The problem children can be identified fairly at their infancy and they can be given special attention inculcating moral values. My studies show that the children who are given special instructions in developing moral values in an upright way in the right direction, do not generally become delinquents. They experience guilt-feeling when they commit illegal or immoral acts. Good parents, good family, good schools, good teachers, good environment, good neighbourhood and good colleagues will teach good moral values which in turn help them to abide by the rules, laws and regulations.

(7) Bureaucratic Justice

Bureaucracy means a government characterized by a rigid hierarchy of bureaus, administrators and petty officials. A corrupt bureaucracy is dangerous; a politicized bureaucracy is a curse. They commit a lot of crimes and the injustice committed by them is beyond human imagination. A study conducted by me about the crimes committed by the bureaucracy revealed that—

1. Some of them lack moral conscience and ethical consciousness.
2. Some are controlled by instincts which come under greed and possessiveness.
3. Some of them have values detrimental to social welfare and human service.
4. Selfishness plays an important role in their behaviour.

Certainly such people can control their animal instincts only through an inculcation or infiltration of moral values and ethical principles.

(8) Domestic Justice

Crimes against family and domestic life are plenty. The old and the aged are persecuted; the young and the innocent are exploited. There take place family suicides, family murder-suicides. One of my studies showed that almost 70 per cent of the crimes take place within the family or within the vicinity of the family. No home life pregnant with desirable emotions may be seen in the family. Disorganized, broken or problem families are many. Divorce, desertion and judicial separation are going up in an incredible way. Parents neglect their children and the children neglect their old parents even by throwing them to 'temple care' or to old age homes. Some parents are thrown at the doors of the temples and the old age homes are constructed everywhere. Why? The answer lies in the moral weakness of family life. The sacramental interpretation of marriage [in certain religious groups] is weakening. Marriage is a contract and people have a tendency to wind up the contract as and when they like it to be terminated. Today one sees 'living together' and the number of unwed mothers get increased day by day. There is abortion of unborn children and sometimes, children are killed and thrown to gutters. Children go away from their parents and sometimes, their dead bodies are seen in railway tracks or flowing water. What to do? In order to control crimes and reduce domestic injustice, the only way is to develop moral sense and inculcate moral values among family members. Family is the basic unit of any society and if it is damaged, the entire social structure is destroyed. Maintain the sanctity of family life.

(9) Administrative Justice

Any administrator has power and authority. There is a saying: 'Power corrupts and absolute power corrupts absolutely'. The one who has the power and authority can abuse his power, misuse his authority, exercise pseudo-power and authority. Instances are plenty to show that those who enjoy power and authority simply refuse to exercise their power. Resultingly, people become helpless and sometimes, they feel that they are condemned to suffer the injustice done to them.

Administrative power/authority means *'de jure'* power/ authority. The one who has the *'de jure'* authority/power fails or refuses to exercise his power/authority, then the entire administration goes to chaos. It is nothing but the commission of grave crimes. This sort of administrative injustice is seen mainly against the poor, downtrodden, helpless, handicapped and powerless. Vested interests may play their role and the diabolic way they manage and manipulate matters are beyond human imagination. Why do the administrators behave the way they do? Among many reasons or factors for their unjust behaviour, one may see the moral breakdown. The entire administration is in moral wreckage and the ruin or destruction of the moral values can be recuperated only by nurturing moral principles among the *de jure* administrators.

(10) Political Justice

Political crimes are not defined or described in the penal statutes. Yet, there are political crimes. Political criminals want to overthrow the present Government in power. They may even aim to change the political system or a Government policy. They may commit murder. President John F. Kennedy was assassinated. Smt. Indira Gandhi and the former Indian Prime Minister Rajeev Gandhi were killed to achieve political aims. Likewise, there are innumerable instances in world history to show political crimes. Political crimes may be 'pure political crimes' and 'complex or connected' political crimes. Treason, sedition, espionage, other acts of endangering the security of the nation, rebellion and incitement to civil war etc. are political crimes exclusively against the sovereign authority and therefore they are treated as 'pure' political crimes. Other offences that endanger the life and property of individuals, but are carried out in connection with and in furtherance of a crime against the State are considered to be 'complex or connected' political crimes.

Is there something called political morality? 'Everything is justified in war and politics' is the approach and attitude of some people and precisely therefore, they justify everything they do to capture authority and power in politics. Political crimes may be seen so long as people lack political morality. Political leaders or the so called 'political leaders' are sometimes moral wrecks so much so that they commit various types of 'pure and connected' political crimes to achieve their political interests.

(11) Democratic Justice

Democracy is the Government by the people. In other words, it is a form of Government in which the supreme power is said to be vested in the people and exercised directly by them or by their elected agents under a free electoral system (Webster's). In such a system, there will be political leaders or so called 'leaders' who enjoy a lot of '*de facto*' powers and authority. They sit, sometimes, above the bureaucrats who enjoy '*de jure*' powers and authority. Such leaders pressure the officials and threaten them to manipulate their '*de jure*' power and authority so that their aims and objectives are achieved. Many such political 'leaders' become exhorbitantly rich within no time and they become so only by violating the law to their favour. In a democratic Government, many of the 'leaders' are above the law and no law can be, as a rule, enforced against them. These political *fews* decide what to do and how to do everything. They have *goondas* and extremist followers. They think that everything they do is just and fair. People cannot but suffer the injustice and crimes committed by these moral 'morons'. They have no moral values and they create chaos just to satisfy their political interests. They murder their opponents and it is seen that some of the so named 'people's representatives' in the Parliament/ Legislature are offenders facing charges like murder, dacoity, corruption, rape and what not? So long as they rule a nation, there cannot be any reduction or control of crimes in society. In a democracy, the crimes committed by politicians or by their instigation are on the increase and the trend will continue so long as there is lack of moral sense among the politicians.

(12) Just Justice

'Justice must be just'—this is what moralists say. In current parlance, people say: "Justice should be done and it should appear to others that justice has been done'. No doubt, justice is a nebulous—i.e., hazy, vague, indistinct or confused term. Precisely therefore, one can interpret it this way or that way. The cloudy or cloud-like concept may be made clear and clean only by an upright conscience rightly formed. Justice must be administered by the law of the conscience which is nothing but the 'moral uprightness'.

Some people are inclined to think about justice as 'subjectively' decided. They have many justifications and rationalizations for their otherwise unjust acts. Morality and moral principles are objective and absolute. Of course, people may apply such sublime and lofty principles to individual cases. If they do not feel 'guilt' even when they do an act in a particular way, then they feel mentally happy. That is not enough. Their act should be evaluated by others in the light of moral principles and they justify the act—at least, majority of them—then, we may endorse the view that the justice is just. In such a situation, the nebulous justice becomes clean and clear justice. Subjective decisions need not always be objectively just. In order to control and reduce unjust justice, be moral in thinking, speaking and acting*.

(13) Judicial Justice

Justice must be judicious and it means that the justice should be characterized by the worth of a good judgment. A good judgment means a judgment based on morality and moral values. Judicial means pertaining to judgments in courts of justice. Courts of

* When I did my Ph.D., I found that justice was a 'MYTH' and therefore I named my daughter 'NEETHIE' [Justice] just to see justice personified in my daughter.

justice means **judges**—people with flesh and blood—who take decisions. In other words, humans making judgments on humans. The question here is: 'Is the judicial justice just and fair?'. The answer is '*Doubtful-Suspicious*'. Why? Studies show that the judges are not heavenly beings. They are very much human in their thinking, speaking and acting. Their personality, aptitude, attitude, inclination, experience, education, expertise, reasoning, analysis, values, morality, training, proneness etc. affect the quality of judgments pronounced by them. In some cases, their judgments are not judicious although they are judicial in words. Injustice committed by the judiciary becomes a topic of discussion among the people and the media today. Why? The judgments are not judicious. How to reduce and control judicial injustice? The recruitment of judicial officers must be redesigned and it should contain personality and aptitude tests. Only those who possess moral values should be enlisted. They must be given value-based training and they must be supervised by a hierarchy having moral uprightness and values. Their activities must be transparent and they must be accountable to what they say and do. Today, there exists an appeal system and the judgments of the lower courts are accepted or rejected. This is not enough. There should be accountability too.

(14) Correctional Justice

Earlier, correctional justice was not there. There was only prison justice. Prison was almost a hell then and the justice administered in prisons was hellish. A hell means any place or state of torment or misery. The prisons made prisoners' life a hell on earth. It was not justice and therefore, concepts of reformative and correctional justice came into being. The officials always thought that they were O.K. and the correction was needed only to convicts. Many prison officials were not trained in Correctional Sciences and what they did were only custodial functions. The prisons were torture cells and some died in prison custody. Some, of course, survived their prison life, but were unable to live in dignity in society. Some committed crimes again and went back to prison as recidivists. Police caught hold of some branding them as recidivists. In many States, no correctional staff is appointed. In some States in India, they come less than 3 per cent of the total staff. Most of the prisons are overcrowded and the prisoners involve themselves in the commission of many types of crimes including homosexuality and lesbianism in the prisons during their life there. Why do the prisoners commit crimes? It means that many of the so-called correctional centers are not correctional or connection oriented. Morality and moral values are not given much importance so much so that the staff and the inmates continue to involve in many kinds of crimes even when they live in prisons.

(15) Communal Justice

Communal means pertaining to a commune or a community. Communalism has many meanings and one of them is strong allegiance to one's own ethnic group rather than to society as a whole. In India, by 'communal', I mean 'belonging to or deriving from the religious traditions of all people'. Accordingly, there are many communal leaders in India. Communal conflicts are recurring every now and then in various parts of the country. Sometimes, communal conflicts and religious bigotry (i.e., stubborn and complete intolerance of any creed, belief or opinion that differs from one's own) become a source and cause of many types of crimes. The actions, beliefs, prejudices etc. of a bigot creates law and order problems resulting in arson, murders etc.

'Communalism' is very powerful as many political parties in India are formed on the basis and strength of the community. It is a vote bank and sometimes, a communal party becomes a party in the ruling Government or in the opposition. The communal parties can mobilize their communes to agitations, organized defiance to authority and violence. People are afraid of communalism and communal conflicts which cause serious law and order rupture creating crimes of many kinds. Why? The communal leaders do not honour morality and moral principles. They do not tolerate others and their views. Intolerance to others' opinion and strong adherence to one's views are against morality and moral values.

(16) Religious Justice

Religion is nothing but 'a set of beliefs concerning the cause, nature and purpose of the universe, especially when considered as the creation of a superhuman agency or agencies, usually involving devotional and ritual observances and often having a moral code for the conduct of human affairs'(Webster's). Religion also means a specific and institutionalized set of beliefs and practices generally agreed upon by a number of persons or sections. Examples are the Christian religion, the Buddhist religion, the Islam religion etc. Every religion has its sacred books and they give guiding principles for every believer to follow. Most unfortunately, they become the cause of many crimes. It is said that more people were killed or murdered by various religious bigotry than by war or any disease like cancer, cardiac arrest etc. Religions want to save the human souls and miserably indeed they become powerful causes to promote and propagate crimes in various forms and injustice in many intensities. Horrible indeed! Most religions are 'rituals based' and not 'value based'. There may be a cure for caneer, but no remedy, relief or cure for religious intolerance.

Religions based on moral principles and values have tolerance, but most unfortunately they do not have them. They have fundamentalism, fanaticism, terrorism etc. and therefore, it is felt that any religion without a moral base is a havoc for human coexistence and society's welfare. There is no meaning in becoming religious, for a religion without a moral foundation is dangerous. Religious men claim that a religious man does not commit crimes, but one doubts very much whether or not that statement is true. Today, religious fundamentalism and communal fanaticism are found to be a great threat to peace and harmony in society. Religion with morality is what is needed today. 'Religion' tells lies after lies to their adherents.

(17) Extremist Justice

Extremist is a person who goes to the extremes, especially in political matters or in religion. The moral principle is that *virtus stat medio*—i.e., the virtue stands in the middle and never in the extremes. The extremists do not accept such a morality. The religious extremist adheres to the view that there is no salvation beyond and besides his religious belief. A political extremist thinks that his political beliefs are the best and all other political thoughts are unacceptable and intolerable. The extremism develops further into fundamentalism which further develops into *fanaticism* which again develops into *terrorism* and insurgency. This radicalism paves way to very many crimes in an atrocious and cruel way and certainly, it is not justice but is inhuman injustice. How to control or reduce such radicalism? This has become an international issue and many countries are at it. There is cross border terrorism and the enemy countries are promoting it. The crimes which come under extremist activities may go from abduction, hostages, air sabotage and plain hijacking etc. The religion and politics, when clubbed together become an international menace—something that threatens to cause evil, harm, calamity, threat etc. to the whole world. Only morality can save the people from this threat.

(18) Equal Justice

This is period of distributive justice—i.e., justice due to everyone must be given to him. Equal justice due to Caeaser should be given to him and to God must go to Him. The crime-doer, the victim of crime, the victim of abuse of power/misuse of authority, the society and the legal system must get justice due to each one of them. When criminal justice (justice due to the crime-doer) is administered, the victim must not be forgotten. He must get victimological compensation/restitution for the sufferings he had. The victims of the abuse of power/misuse of authority, if they exist, must get what is due to them. The society which invests very much money and labour must be ensured of justice due to it to the society's satisfaction. The justice system should feel that the system ensures justice to all. The undue delay in administration of justice, the unnecessary adjourning of cases, the unwarranted harassment and transfers of judges etc. are infamies to the justice system. They must be eradicated.

What is the problem in administering equal justice? The problem lies in the fact that the agencies responsible to administer justice to all are not concerned with everyone seeking justice in the matter. They do not think from the morality of the issue, rather is concerned only with the legality of the matter. The crimes in this area can be controlled or reduced only if moral principles are adhered to. Justice is above law and it must be administered.

(19) Wholistic Justice

The traditional definition of crime is that a crime is a violation of law and the law may be State-made, social, cultural, moral, ethical or religious etc. In my view, the crime is an act or omission against justice. Why do I say so? The law may be just or unjust. The law today may not be the law tomorrow. On the other hand, justice is time eternal, universal and unchanging. Justice contains morality which is absolute and eternal.

Wholistic—i.e., comprising the full quality, amount, extent or number—justice may be an utopian idea. For, there is nothing like wholistic justice. Nevertheless, one may make an attempt to provide justice to the maximum extent possible. A judge may award maximum punishment to the offenders, another judge may give a nominal punishment and a third one may acquit the accused. An appeal court may convict or acquit any accused. A second appeal may turn down any judgement of the lower courts. Ultimately, what is given is justice?—Injustice?—Wounded justice?-Less justice?—No justice? No one can answer the question and the time taken may be unimaginably long. In my view, justice comprising the full quality is only in imagination. Wounded justice, injustice, miscarriage of justice, no justice, less justice—all contain crimes in one form or another. An acquittal means miscarriage of justice—i.e., either a guilty escaped or an innocent is falsely accused of and persecuted. This is an immoral act and should be eliminated at any cost.

(20) Justice to the Old

60 + is the age of the senior citizens. 60-65 years of age means, the young old, 65-70 means the middle old, 70-75 means the old [old old] 75-80 means the older old and 80 + are the oldest old. Whatever may be the arguments which the psychologists advance, old age is a disease which requires treatment. Their income comes down and dependency becomes a necessity. Nursing care is needed and expensive medicines become a part of life. The old are the neglected and it is seen that the suicides among the old in India are going up. Even those who have a regular income by way of pension too commit suicide. They do not get emotional support. Nobody talks to them and the children/grand children do not get time to spend with them. They do not talk and some are found to be depressed. The old age homes are constructed to accommodate them. There are 7 star, 5 star old age homes on one side and destitute homes on the other side. In both homes, depression is found in an incredible

way. This sort of neglect is a crime and the moral sense of the dear and near ones, kith and kin do not work. It is sterile so much so that the crimes against the old go up abnormally high. It is reported in the media that the old are, as shown earlier, taken to some temples and are thrown there like wastes. Some temples construct old age homes to accommodate those who are just victimized thus by their own children. How to control this attitude and approach to the old? No law can solve the issue; no punishment will find a solution to the problem. Only morality and moral obligation will save the old from their misery and neglect by the 'close ones' around them.

(21) Justice to the Infirm

Go to a government hospital and see the poor and the downtrodden gathered there. It is a crowd and it shows that the people are sick. The long queue of patients before the medical officers' desk and the way the consultation is done for diagnosis may show the speed with which the sick are attended. The pharmacy tests are to be conducted outside and scanning is done elsewhere. Allegations are there that many medical officers have unholy nexus with private pharmacy labs. Medicines available in the hospital are not given to the needy and the poor people. The prescriptions are to private medical shops from where the medical team may get regular kick back monthly. What about the in-patients? In order to get a bed in the hospital, the medical officers need to be humoured. If a surgery is to be done, there is a fixed amount for the surgeon, for the anastasiast, for the nursing staff and others. Even the trolley pullers demand money. Why do they do so? The food for the patients are not fully served to them and thus goes the litany of injustice committed on the sick in the country. Treatment in private hospitals is run as a business and that is very expensive and the expenditure incurred is exorbitant. In ICU, the medicines are highly expensive and the treatment in the ventilator is done with ulterior motives. There have been allegations that the dead bodies treated in the ventilator is a source of good income in private hospital business. The target-fixed appointment of doctors make them to extract money from patients by loot under many counts. Let the moralists answer the question: "how to control and reduce hospital crimes".

(22) Justice to the Differently Abled

People with all organs functioning reasonably well cannot survive in a society contaminated with crimes of many kinds! In such a situation, what about the physically handicapped? The blind, the deaf, the crippled, the transgenders—all of them are denied opportunities of a life in dignity. They do not gets employment. There are countries where people differently abled have reservation for employment.

Crimes committed against those who are differently abled are many. Sometimes, they are mocked at and isolated. Instances are reported that the blind are sexually harassed and exploited in many ways. They cannot see the victimizer. Transgenders are misused for homosexuality and lesbianism. They are otherwise called male prostitutes. The crippled can do almost all jobs which anyone can do. But, they are avoided or kept away in the employment market. They are not given vocational training as institutions for the same are not enough. There may be schools for the blind, deaf and so on here and there. But the expenditure for their education may be very heavy. They need special hostels to stay. Neglecting the physically handicapped is a crime indeed. They need scholarship and educational assistance. They need more special schools and employment opportunities. If the moral responsibilities towards such handicapped people are fulfilled, certainly crimes by them and against them can be controlled/reduced.

(23) Disciplinary Justice

Discipline has many meanings. Punishment inflicted by way of correction and training is discipline. Parents and teachers do it. Sometimes, the punishments become very cruel that criminal cases are registered by police against parents/teachers. Forget about such harsh punishments. Disciplinary justice here means the justice administered to the delinquent (so-named) employees of Government or otherwise. Studies show that the authority and power to initiate departmental inquiries are misused or abused by some of the higher ups so much so that many employees suffer the ill-effects of such 'disciplinary' actions. The inquiry officers in many cases are so selected that they execute the desires of their higher-ups. Many of the inquiry officers have little or no knowledge in disciplinary jurisprudence so much so that the inquries are conducted in the way they like. The Manual for Disciplinary Inquiries is not taught to many inquiry officials. Resultingly, the disciplinary justice administered by them is nothing but miscarriage of justice. This is a crime committed against the employees. I made a study in the police department in Kerala State and I could note that maximum number of officials facing departmental inquiries in Government service comes from that department noted and known for discipline. Out of the total number of inquiries, 6 per cent are recommended for punishment. On appeal it comes down to 2 per cent. On further appeal to higher authorities/Administrative Tribunals/High Courts, the decision to punish the officials are coming further down. The question is: 'Why is this futile exercise?' The answer is: 'Initiate disciplinary inquiries if and only if the inquries can be justified on moral grounds' too.

(24) Divine Justice

'Divine' means pertaining to, proceeding from God, esp. the Supreme Being. **Divine Right** of Kings means the right to rule derived directly from God and not from the consent of the people. **Divinity** means the quality of being divine. It also means a 'deity'; 'godhood'. There are 'Avathars' and 'human gods' flourishing in society and they mint money in crores. They have devotees and 'ashramas' in India and abroad. Whatever they say are considered as 'Divine Law' and the devotees meticulously follow them.

They are godmen who claim that they are the gods and they give laws and such laws, they say, are revealed truths. People are to abide by such laws. Otherwise, there will be divine punishments or god's curse on them in the form of 'hell', purgatory, rebirth as animals, wandering souls etc. and people are afraid of such godmen and their revealed 'truths'. They exploit the people and mint money. They run institutions of charity and such institutions too are means to exploit people and precisely such institutions and their activities are called "Charities with a Hook" and the hook is to take away money from others' pockets or to plunder them. A 'noble and moral purpose' and various exploiting methods are found to be their ways to amass wealth. They cheat the public. Their 'noble crimes' are praised as noble acts performed to please 'human gods'. These godmen and their nefarious activities must be condemned in strongest words. But, no one does it as people are afraid of their 'curses' and divine punishments.

(25) Marxist Justice

Marxism is a system of thought developed by Karl Marx (1818-83), a German socialist and political theorist, along with Friedrich Engels. It is a set of economic and political doctrines characterized chiefly by the theories of dialectical materialism, surplus value, and class struggle. In Marxist criminology (it is also called radical criminology, critical criminology), the major elements are: (i) Members of the ruling class can violate the laws with immunity. On the other hand, if the laws are violated by the members of the subject classes, they will be penalized. (ii) Penal laws expand to coerce the proletariat into submission, (iii) Crimes divert the attention of the lower class people from exploitation of them by capitalists or the economic system that prevails in the country. As a result, crime directs the attention of the lower class people towards other members of their class. (iv) Crime is a reaction to the life conditions of a person's social class and it varies from society to society depending upon the political and economic structures of the society. (v) In socialist societies, crimes will be less because there exist little or very little class struggles. (vi) Less class struggles will reduce forces which are at work behind the commission of criminal acts (cf W.J. Chambliss, *Towards a Political Economy of Crime*). Countries where Marxist Governments are in power, the injustice and crimes go up like anything in an incredible way. Any Marxist Justice without morality and moral sense is like a gong booming or a cymbal clashing. The crimes committed by the Marxists are many and the injustice done by them is very many/much. Morality alone can save a Marxist Country from crimes and injustice.

(26) Police Justice

Police justice is a special kind of justice understandable only to those who wear police uniform. *Legal Sanctity* and *Moral Sanctity* are two terms used in police circles. *Legal Sanctity* means 'do things as the law says'. Moral Sanctity means 'do things as morality and as moral norms say'. The question here is: 'Can the police resort to any means for investigation of crime, detection of criminals, and maintenance of law and order'? Policemen may say that they are concerned only about the legality of police action. The British taught the 'Rule of Law' and they did not say anything about the 'Rule of Justice'. The 'Rule of Justice' implies 'morality' too whereas the 'Rule of Law' necessarily does not. Today, the 'Rule of Law' theory is almost rejected and the presently accepted theory is 'Rule of Law coupled with Rule of Justice'. In other words, enforcement of law without taking into account the 'Rule of Justice' (i.e., morality) is no law enforcement at all. Both the end and the means adopted must be justified legally and morally. The people criticize the police because they see violation of moral values in police enforcement of law. Searching a house several times during a night to catch a suspect, keeping a person without providing quality-food to the detainees in police custody, taking into custody the father or wife of the suspect to pressure the wanted to surrender before the police are immoral although the police may succeed to reach the end to some extent. In other words, this sort of police justice is a crime in every sense.

(27) Judicial Justice

'Justice is what the judge says'—this view is challenged as the justice given by some judges is found to be far away from being satisfactory and judicial. The Chief Justice of India once said that 20 per cent of the judicial officers were corrupt. The question is: 'what good can come from such officials lacking integrity?' The Bar Council of India once accused a section of judicial officers as people having suspicious integrity. The judicial officers are sometimes criticized in the visual media so much so that a judge in the Supreme Court of India expressed his anguish by expressing his anxiety—'Never destroy the institution called judiciary by criticisms—and he said so looking at the lawyers practicing in the courts in India. No doubt, there is a lot of truth in everything and people take note of the fact that judicial justice is not that judicious. When I write this, news comes in the TV accusing a candidate for the election for offering crores of rupees to get a judgment favourable to him. The telecast contains video clipping as well. What is happening here? What is rotten in the city of Denmark? The morality and the moral principles of the judicial officials are rotten and there is a growing feeling that justice can be purchased.

The commodity is for sale in the market and the one who pays the maximum price will get a judgment to his favour. Judges in the Supreme Court hold press conferences to expose the type of judicial justice and they lament at the fate of the judicial system without morality. Alas! What to do? Undue goverments mid-night transfers of judges, seemingly ungust verdicts etc. create further problems adding insults to ingury.

(28) Labour Justice

Labour means productive activity, esp. for the sake of economic gain. Accordingly, labourer means one who is involved in such associations—i.e., the body, class, or such activity esp. as distinguished from management and capital. There are trade unions sponsored by various political parties and they work for the welfare of the workers/labourers.

The labourers in many trades are well organized and they abuse their strength and muscle power to exploit the people. Head load workers extract money in an exorbitant way from the people. The *Nokkukooli* which is otherwise called *wage just for seeing or looking at* is very notorious in Kerala State. The labourers do not do any work, but demand wages or money for seeing or *looking at* others, work and the wages extracted are unimaginably huge. Recently, the Government of Kerala has banned such extortions. Head load workers demand exorbitant wages for their work and it is like robbing the people. They threaten the people and very rarely police register cases for robbery. During a day of *Hartal* or *Bandh,* they do not allow the labourers who are willing to work to do their job. The right to work is denied to labourers. They declare strikes for anything and paralyse the work atmosphere. The general public are put into extreme difficulties by the striking employees. Labourers in the organized sectors are misused by selfish politicians to achieve their political interest. Morality is lacking so much so that their activities result in many types of crimes. Organized strength is their consideration given to people's rights.

(29) Agrarian Justice

It means 'relating to land' and there are agrarian laws. It also means pertaining to the advancement of agricultural groups. India is basically an agricultural country and precisely therefore, one sees agrarian unrest everywhere. To quote National Police Commission (IVth Report, Government of India, June, 1980). "In 1946, Communists organized a large scale peasant uprising in the Telangana area of Andhra Pradesh. West Bengal witnessed a violent movement organized by the Naxalites in 1967 for eliminating the *Jotedars* and forcibly capturing land for occupation and use of by the tillers of the soil. Activities of extremists in formenting agrarian unrest and organizing agitations have come to notice in several States, notably, West Bengal, Andhra Pradesh, Tamil Nadu and Kerala". Although agrarian unrest was seen as a phenomenon since the days of Mughals, it received accelerated momentum after India became independent in 1947. Exploitation, exploitation and exploitation everywhere and we observe large scale riots accompanied by arson, murder, tension etc. There have been constant fights between the depressed landless rural poor and the land owning farmer community. The landless poor are denied of a fair share of the economic benefits. The landless poor are attacked back ruthlessly by land owning community. The injustice committed against the depressed is a powerful cause for many types of crimes. How can the crimes be controlled and reduced? Of course, the Government, agrarian legislations, police, media and the courts can do a lot in this area. But, they do not do anything much. Why? There are unholy nexuses, pressures, corruption, political patronage, helplessness of the poor and the landless etc. seen everywhere. Let the moralists answer the issue and find a solution for the same.

(30) Murder Politics Justice

There are two expressions now heard often. They are (1) Political Murders and (2) Murder Politics. Political murder is counted as a crime under 'political crimes' which has a different meaning. Murder politics is an expression used to mean the murder of politicians owing to enmity, vengeance, retaliation etc. The intention in such murder politics is not overthrowing a Government in power. It is not like treason or espionage etc. It is just a calculated murder and the politicians (political parties) want to justify their killing the enemies by politicization of crimes. One notices a series of such instances in the recent past and the intention is to eliminate an enemy from this earth. As the political party favours and encourages such murder-politics, it is seen that the culprits are patronized by the political party and its leaders. Allegations are there accusing the political party exerting influence on police, prosecutors and so on to manipulate the cases in a way favourable to the political interests of the party. The party gives a list of people and the police is pressured to make them the accused. The party looks after them and their financial needs during the period they are confined in prisons and ultimately, the party sees to it that the listed accused get acquittals from the courts of law. It is done without any prick of conscience for political advantages and the politicians feel proud of having done such 'murder politics'. So long as there exist no political morality and moral politicians, 'murder-politics' is likely to continue and reduction or control of 'murder-politics' is a difficult task, if not impossible.

(31) Migrant Justice

Cities—major or minor—are today undergoing drastic changes in the composition of their population. The migration of the unemployed youth from the rural areas to cities and towns, from one State to another State (unemployed youths are migrating to Kerala from other States and the large scale migration causes very many and any number of problems including crimes in the State) alone or along with their families and children. To quote the National Police Commission: "Some drift fortuitously among the low paying jobs. Others try crimes, and if successful make it their regular livelihood; others lacking aptitude become failures in the illegal as well as the legal world—habitués of our jails and prisons. And there are those who give up, retreat from conventional society and search for a better world in the private fantasies induced by drink and drugs" (cf *Human Relations: Law Enforcement in a Changing Community*, Allen Coffey *et al.*). A study conducted in Kerala State, it has been found that '*ganja*'—a natural drug is transported from other States, (in huge amount) and is distributed to people including school going children. Now, there is a campaign conducted at the school levels in anti-drug activities. Teachers, parents, media and NGOs, are at it and they inculcate morality and moral values to school going children to save them from drug abuse. Good and let it continue.

(32) Nexus Justice

In my book, *Indian Police and Nexus Crimes*, I have enumerated a number of such crimes committed by partners in the Nexus. The unholy nexus among the **Neta-Babu-Dalal-Dada** [Leader-Bureaucrats-Middle men-Bandits (*Goondas*)] commit a lot of crimes. Such partnership consists of police officials, judicial officers, lawyers, politicians, highly positioned bureaucrats and so on. They mint money like anything and nothing much can be done against them as they are the officials executing, interpreting and evaluating crimes and criminal activities.

Most of the media crimes, syndicate-crimes, organized crimes may have nexus partnership. The Nexus Nucleus—i.e., the one at the Center—who lavishly humour the leaders, bureaucrats, middlemen and *goondas* become immune to all sorts of legal and penal actions. As such, the Nucleus flourishes in society exploiting the people. Even religious leaders have such nexus partnership. In short, all suite crimes/meat eater crimes need nexus partnership. How to control and reduce **Nexus Crimes**? It is difficult, though not impossible, to do so. It is so because the moral fabric of the leaders and the bureaucrats is so weak that crimes will flourish in society. For, the **Nexus Crimes** have a fertile soil in the society.

(33) Mafia Justice

Mafia is a secret organization of persons, generally assumes to be of Sicilian and mainland Italian origin, engaged in criminal activities. It has a history and in the United States, the *Mafia* engaged in very many types of criminal activities including illicit production and sale of liquor during prohibition. It has a second meaning—i.e., a popular spirit of hostility to legal restraint and to the law, often manifesting itself in criminal acts. (see, Webster's). In India today, *Mafia* activities are seen everywhere and they include, (i) Land *Mafia,* (ii) Liquor *Mafia,* (iii) Investment *Mafia,* (iv) Money chain and Multimarketing *Mafia,* (v) Travel and Tourism *Mafia,* (vi) Pilgrimage *Mafia,* (vi) Relics and religious *Mafia,* (viii) Retreat and Charismatic *Mafia* and the list is very long. They commit crimes of various types to cheat, extort, rob money from people. The drug *Mafia* is notorious and the religious *Mafia* is very old. The first known *Mafia* is the sale of relics of Padre Pio, a

Catholic priest who had bleeding from 5 holy wounds. While they involve in criminal activities, they claim that they are doing certain good activities and they justify their nefarious acts. Now, the word *'Mafia'* is used in all kinds of organized crimes. The criminals involved in *Mafia* activities lack morality and moral sense. They have *goondas* of every description and they commit all sorts of crimes. They are supported by the law enforcement officials, lawyers and bureaucrats. Some *Mafias* have nexus partnership with politicians and religious leaders. The situation goes from bad to worse in India and it will continue to be so as long as the moral atmosphere remains to be the same.

(34) Journalist Justice

Journalism is the occupation of reporting, writing, editing, photographing, or broadcasting news or conducting any news organization as a business. A journalist is a person who practises the occupation of journalism. There is yellow journalism and they promote and propagate unreal or half-real matters to earn money. Forget about them. The journalists now mix news and views together so much so that the readers cannot distinguish news from views. They believe everything. If one wants to have a correct picture of truth or facts, he needs to read half a dozen of news papers and seldom people do it. The media may be run by political parties, religious groups, communal forces, extremists and so on and precisely their views are put along with the news. There is competition in the sphere of journalism and it is found in print as well as in visual media. The discussions held in the visual media and articles printed in the print media are often biased and prejudiced. Objectivity is lacking and the journalistic justice today means the justice given by journalists and not by objective truths and facts. The media has very powerful influence in people and the wrong journalistic promotion and propagation of untruth or half truths cause serious law and order issues and crimes. Today, one notices a number of on-line journalism and they have no control. They publicize many things in their own way. Added to such on-line publishing, the social media play an important role. Everyone promotes and propagates his views and sometimes such views become viral. People all over the world get such views and they share the information. Resultingly, crores of people read them within no time. The justice administered by the journalists are, sometimes, in the nature of miscarriage of justice. It is difficult to control them. Journalism with an upright morality is what is required now.

(35) Social Media Justice

Social media—i.e., Facebook, Blog, Twitter, You Tube, Instagram etc. are three dimensional and are really good if they are used for noble purposes. They have an incredible impact on people. Nevertheless, they are misused and abused with criminal motives. Sexual harassment, indecent exploitation of girls and women resulting in their suicides, propagation of false and immoral matters against enemies, expressing filthy words and foul expressions to express one's vengeance, showing immoral videos and photos etc.—all with a diabolical mind to damage people and defame them in public. The photoshop techniques are widely misused and morphing is going on lavishly to caricature people ludicrously exaggerating the peculiarities or defects of reputed persons or things. The injustice committed via social media is beyond human imagination and cases registered in such matters do not reach anywhere. Anyone can do it from anywhere in the world and the investigating agency in one country has limitations to inquire into such matters in other countries. The laws are helpless and precisely therefore, the criminals in social media-misuse are relatively in comfort zones enjoying immunity. Who can initiate action and how can the criminals be punished? This is a real problem and the problem can be solved only by inculcating moral values to social media users. That too is not that easy as there exists no method to do it effectively. In my view social media crimes are likely to go up and enactment of legislations against social media misuse/abuse may not easily reach its destination.

(36) Cultural Justice

People minus culture is animals or animals plus culture is man—this is what sociologists say and those who accept the Darwinian evolution will have no difficulty to accept the sociologists' views. Culture means inculcation of values including moral values. Culture in sociology means the 'sum total of the ways of living built up by a group of human beings and transmitted from one generation to another'. The group of human beings is made on the basis of caste, colour, creed and community etc. The casteism in India has been a perpetual cause of various types of crimes. The lower castes were not counted as human beings and there was untouchability. The colour was a source of very many crimes and the fights against discrimination on the basis of colour are going on still. The injustice in the area is very severe. Creed is another powerful cause of crimes. The sects, denominations, groups and subgroups have their cultural norms and rules. The cultural discrimination on the basis of sex and prevalence of patriarchal/matriarchal system creates havoc in man-woman relations. Looking at the atrocities committed by man against man, people want human rights to all people without boundaries. They say that the human rights are the universal and inalienable birth rights of people without considering the cultural differences. Yet, we notice human rights violations everywhere and the administration appears to be blind to such injustice committed by man against man. There are Declarations, Covenants, Conventions, Principles etc. on papers and the crimes continue to dominate the people and their culture. Can morality and moral values find a solutions? Let us see.

(37) Lawyers' Justice

What is lawyers' justice? Let the lawyers answer the question. What are the crimes committed by lawyers during the course of their profession? No doubt, the lawyers form a subsystem in the justice system and the crimes committed by them during the course of their profession cannot and should not become a menace to the society. Researches show that the lawyers' crimes, sometimes, become really a menace to the society. How?

Some people say that a lawyer 'profession is a lier's profession and he wins the cases by that profession. Is it administration of justice or is it miscarriage of justice? Do the defence lawyers make secret understanding with the prosecutors? Do the lawyers bribe the prosecutors and police? Do the lawyers create evidence? Do the lawyers produce false witnesses? Do the lawyers produce untrue documents? Do the lawyers manipulate records? Do the lawyers have unholy nexus with the judicial officers? Are the lawyers honest to their clients? Do they have morality and professional ethics? The honest answers to the above questions will show the extent and intensity of lawyers' justice or lawyers' crimes and criminal activities in society. What do the judicial officers think about the lawyers? Do they think about the lawyers practicing in the court are people of integrity? Do they lack morality? If they lack morality and professional ethics, they are the agents of miscarriage of justice. They do not control crimes; they cannot reduce crimes as well.

(38) Health Justice

'If health is lost, many things are lost'—This is a village saying. Yes, there is a lot of truth in it. Since the health is the 'health' of the person, the hospital exploit the patients. The expenditure incurred for treatment, nursing care laboratory tests, scanning, I.C.U., ventilator service etc. is unbearable for anybody—even for those who are in the upper middle class (financially). Different hospitals have different charges. Of course, there is insurance (mediclaim) schemes and many people complain that they do not get expected benefits. The terms and conditions for the insurance mediclaim policies are printed in such a way that one cannot read them even by using a very powerful magnifying class. The private laboratories seen all over the country cheat the people in different ways. A recent media report is that they give examination or test results without conducting any tests. Chicken blood given to a few laboratories gave a high cholesterol result and the blood of a dog had very high sugar readings. The test is done by unqualified or under-qualified personnel. The secret and clandestine understanding between medical officers and the laboratories are other ways of cheating the public. Medicines are given in Ayurveda, Allopathy, Unani, Siddha, Nature Cure, *Murma,* Homeopathy and in every system of medicine, the patients are given adulterated medicines. Instances have been reported that fake doctors and fake medicines are plenty in society. The treatment for mental patients is given by people who are ill qualified. They treat the patients with exorcism, black magic, *Mandravada, Koodothra, Elas treatment,* magical remedies, prayers and what not? The entire health field is under criminality and morality/moral principles have no place or scope in the health sphere today.

(39) Educational Justice

Education is a lucrative business today. An admission for medical course means several lacs [crores] of rupees. There are genuine institutions and fake institutions. Fake universities issue certificates. The bogus certificates are plenty and anybody can purchase them from the market. Even Ph.D certificates are sold. Recently, it has been brought out that some who practise law in courts had bogus certificates.

Self-financing colleges are plenty and self-financing courses are countless. They amass wealth even by providing qualitatively poor education. The faculty may be underqualified. The recognized schools and approved educational institutions accept capitation fees openly and secretly for admission. Some of them accept compulsory donations for admissions. The interest-free loans are notorious and at the end of the course, the loans are not repaid.

The politics play an important role in educational institutions. Many of the political leaders today had a past in educational institutions and they were student leaders involved in strikes, boycotting of classes, stoning at the police, burning private and public property, destroying State Transport buses and government vehicles, gheraoing teachers, involving in many criminal cases including arson, throwing country-made bombs, using cycle chains and daggers against fellow students etc. Educational institutions have become the breeding ground for later criminality seen in politics. Educational institutions which are supposed to inculcate values and provide value oriented education have become institutions of deterioration. They have become failures so much so that crimes and criminal activities flourish in society today.

(40) Environmental Justice

Environment means the aggregate of surrounding things, conditions or influences. Today, there are many who claim to be environmentalists—i.e., people who advocate and work to perfect the air, water, animals, plants and other natural resources from pollution or its effects. There are many fake environmentalists who register a paper-society or NGO for protecting the environment. They do not allow any developmental activity and they do so in the pretext of protecting environment. They raise their voice, organize protest meetings, *jadhas, hartals, bandhs* just to make an income—small or big by clandestine understanding. When they are paid, they issue 'their clearance certificates'. All said and done, one sees massive environmental pollution. The rivers are contaminated by poison, the forests are destroyed, the trees are cut, sand is taken away, rock mining is lavishly done and thus to say, there are many *Mafias* exploiting the environment for their benefits and lucrative activities. There are nexus crimes too in this field. The enforcement crimes and corruption are seen and the pollution is done with the connivance of the government officials and political leaders. Genuine environmentalists who voice against the environmental crimes are put down. Sometimes, their dead bodies are seen on railway tracks or flowing water. Those who destroy the environment are corporates and millionaires. They lavishly contribute money for political elections and are sponsoring the candidates. The damages caused by such hard-core criminals to the forests, water, air, animals, plants and other natural resources are beyond human imagination, yet they flourish in society because there are political sponsors for such venomous creatures. No morality or moral principles work with them. They do things as they want them to be done.

(41) Students' Justice

The dictionary description for a student is that he is a person formally engaged in learning, esp. one enrolled in an institution of secondary or higher education (Webster's). Good. The concept is that a student is a person who studies, investigates or carefully examines a subject. Now let us see what is going on in the society? Students are of many categories. They are (1) very serious students who spend their time and energy for studies. They make use of the services of tuition masters, tuition centers and spend any amount of money for education; (2) Students who come to an institution for studies and they study seriously to earn a certificate, diploma or degree. They do not have greater ambitions. They want a job after the study; (3) Students who come to the institution not for study, but for achieving other purposes. They form students' unions and associations and play politics and thereby want to become political leaders. These few students manage the student-activities and functions in the institution. They want an organized strength to fight against the university or management of the institutions. Many students join with them so much so that the institution is closed for several days in a month owing to strikes. The teachers, in many institutions, favour, encourage, promote such student activities so that they can earn their salary without working. What is going on in the educational field? Students declare educational *bandhs* and *hartals* and the institutional instructions are paralysed. Instead of inculcating values, they are inclined to accept anti-social activities. After the institutional education, they become unemployed and some of them drift into criminal activities including organized criminality.

(42) Criminal Justice

Who is a criminal?—a crime doer?—and offender? Everyone violates law—may be social, cultural, institutional, moral, ethical, State-made etc.—and necessarily he deserves punishment if administration of justice is what is aimed at. Let us take the violation of State-made laws. Imprisonment is the usual punishment (fine too may be seen). Who goes to prisons? The prisons are predominantly packed with poor people who do not have enough money to purchase 'justice' for them. Some are innocent as well. What is the impact of punishment?—Is it correction, reformation, resocialization, rehabilitation and reintegration to society back? Recidivists are plenty in society and they are called jail birds. If one is rich, he can boldly commit crimes provided he is prepared to pay the fine and many traffic law violators take such a liberal attitude. Punishments do not have that much deterrent effect as expected by the law makers. What about those crime-doers who violate the social laws? As they are anti-social people, they should have a feeling of humiliation. Shockingly enough, they do not have any such feelings. Instead, some of them feel proud of it. Sound pollution caused by the misuse of mikes by temples, churches, mosques, advertisements, election campaigns is really horrible and the violators have the muscle strength of an organized criminal group. How are the criminals who violate the moral and ethical laws? Very many in that group do not have any guilt feelings. They justify the moral wrongs by arguments which they only understand. No social or moral punishments to the crime doers are given and today's anti-social and amoral/immoral people become tomorrow's leaders and 'honourable men'! Money matters a lot and it washes away the discolouration caused by moral wrongs and anti-social activities. Muscle power and money power are found to be, sometimes, above mind power. What a deplorable situation indeed!

(43) 'Legal' Justice

Is there something called 'Legal' justice? Criminologists will subscribe to the view that there is 'Legal' justice. In other words, what is considered as justice may not be 'justice proper' under the social or moral laws. State-made laws are the laws made by a few elected people in a democracy and by a ruler in other kinds of administration. In a democracy, who are the elected members? Many are those who belong to a political party. It is seen that the same people are elected repeatedly so much so that some are the elected representatives for 40-50 years or more. Their children, grand children, kith and kin are elected. A sizable number of the elected representatives in India face criminal charges. Many are suspects in crimes. The crimes they commit may be murder, kidnapping, *rape, corruption, mafia,* organized racketeering and what not? The corporates send their representatives to the Legislature/Parliament. They spend lavishly money and many political parties are sponsored by such corporates. They make the laws and some laws passed by them favour them a lot-more than the general public. The justice administered by the laws made by them is called legal justice by them. Where is the morality/ethics in such enactments?

The law is what the judges say and the 'justice' is what the judges award. The justice awarded by the judges is called 'legal justice' and some of the judges are found to be the 'yes' men of political parties, leaders, legislators, 'religious' leaders, vested interests so much so that the justice they award is, at times, technically 'legal justice', but really 'moral injustice'. Media and the citizenry criticize the judges and in some situations, the judges themselves find fault with other fellow judges who administer 'legal' justice which in reality is injustice or miscarriage of justice.

(44) Justice to the Insane and People of Unsound Mind

Go to a mental health hospital and see the insane or the people who are of unsound mind there. If media reports are true, they are 'sub-human' people who are condemned to pull on their lives in deplorable conditions. No one wants them and those who are near and close to them by blood forget them. The criminal laws give complete immunity for the offence they commit. "Nothing is an offence done by them" —this is what the law says.

What is discussed here is about the crimes committed by those who are insane or are people of unsound mind politically, communally, religiously, morally etc. Political insanity makes many to commit any sort of crimes including repeated murders, arson, corruption and malpractices. The communal insanity makes them to annihilate people who belong to another community. The number of people killed in communal violence may be millions. What is genocide? It is nothing but any acts with intent to destroy in whole or in part, a national, ethnic, racial or religious group; killing or causing bodily or mental harm to the members of the group; deliberately inflicting on the group conditions of life calculated to bring about its physical destruction in whole or in part; imposing measures intended to prevent births within the group; forcibly transferring children of the group to another group etc. There is moral insanity as well. Such people consider immoral acts as moral and they are brainwashed to have such feelings and thoughts. The terrorists, fundamentalists, fanatics, insurgents and so on belong to this category. Moral preachings do not have any meaning or impact with them.

(45) Market Justice

Market justice is related to the crimes seen in markets—in buying and selling commodities. Let us start with purity of the items sold. Duplicates are plenty and the purchaser is cheated. There is under-weighing everywhere and it is seen not only in the retail fish markets but also in the wholesale hyper markets. Adulteration in everything including food items is seen. Chemicals are used to ripen the fruits and many chemicals used as preservatives are harmful to health. Some cause cancer and the colours used in soft drinks, pickles, bakery items, full-jar soda, shake-drinks etc. cause many incurable diseases including cancer. Sale of goods without sale tax, without warranty, without guarantee may be seen everywhere. Medicines are no medicines and the patients are cheated in all systems of medicines. The advertisement market gives undue publicity to all sorts of medicines and thus the patients are plundered. The enforcement agencies sleep over the injustice as they are given kickbacks regularly by the plunderers. The booty is shared. The nexus transactions are seen in gold markets, liquor shops, bars and restaurants, big bazaars and supermarkets, textile shops, hyper markets, margin-free-shops and in the sale of automobiles to list a few. The crimes committed by the head-load workers and lorry transport agencies are innumerable in the markets. Price is fixed by the sellers and the purchasers have no voice in such matters. 'If you want, you purchase. Otherwise, go away'—is the attitude of sellers and the same item is sold at different prices in different shops. In my research, I have seen the markets to be a world of crimes and criminal activities, malpractices and corruption, atrocities and plundering, looting and extortion, cheating and misappropriation. The trade is flourishing and the traders dictate the rules in the market. They administer justice and the people suffer them helplessly. Everything is justified in trade and market is the principle now followed. No salvation! Horrible!

(46) Enforcement Justice

Those who are close to churches, temples or mosques are far away from God/gods—This is a village saying which is found to be a reality by researchers. They sell the God/gods for their self-interest by giving promises and hopes which they certainly know will never happen or take place ever. Forget about it. As far as enforcement justice is concerned, it is found that those who are close to administration of justice is far away from the goddess of justice. The eyes of the deity (goddess) is covered with a black cloth and precisely therefore it cannot see anything—even the balance in her hand. When you google for the goddess of justice, you get more than a dozon goddesses in different shapes. Law enforcement officials, the Bench and the Bar commit a lot of crimes during the course of their profession and many of them do not have any guilt feelings or moral pricks. Using third degree methods, concocting evidence, manipulation of facts and records, production of false witnesses, purchasing of witnesses for tutoring, arguing false and fake cases in courts, corrupting the prosecutors, entering into clandestine understanding between the prosecutors and defence counsels to torpedo the cases, keeping purposeful silence in courts, refusal to produce genuine evidence and witnesses during trial, bribing the judges, purchasing justice, acquitting the case on the grounds of benefit of doubts etc. are just a few crimes coming under enforcement crimes. Enforcement crimes smell everywhere and the goddess of justice senses everything silently with eyes covered and a tongue locked in the mouth. Morality of enforcement crimes is not a topic taught or discussed in the area of justice administration and the entire system becomes rotten and smelling. What to do? How to go about?

(47) 'White Collar' Justice

The simple dictionary meaning of 'White Collar' is 'belonging or pertaining to the salaried or professional workers whose jobs generally do not involve manual labour'. One sees white collar with lawyers, clergymen and so on so much so that the white collar people are thought to be 'respectable' persons in society. Precisely therefore, the crimes committed by them during the course of their profession do not normally come to the notice or attention of the common man. The crimes committed by the white collar 'gentlemen' are: (i) Personal crimes, (ii) Abuse of trust, (iii) Business crimes, (iv) Con games etc. (see, Edelhertz, Herbert, *The Nature, Impact and Prosecution of White Collar Crimes*) O.K., I want to add more white collar crimes to the categories given above. Earlier, the enforcement crimes and their extent in the present society have been discussed. The crimes committed by the justice personnel are numerous and they enjoy life with others who are notoriously 'reputed' in their area of specialization. Most of them are real experts in the commission of crimes in justice administration and they interpret their crimes as '*Justice Proper*'. The media until recently used to eulogize them. After the advent of the social media, the cat comes out of the sack. 3D defence methods proposed and propagated by me in criminology pay rich dividends now. People come to know how the law and justice are prostituted by the very same persons who are expected to uphold justice in its real sense. Police, prosecutors, defence lawyers, media, personnel in correctional services—all do commit white collar (enforcement crimes) crimes during the course of their profession. There exist professional Codes of Ethics for each one of them, but seldom do the justice personnel bother about the ethical principles enumerated in the Code. Very sad, indeed!

(48) Justice to the Mentally Challenged

The mentally retarded are those who have a low I.Q. According to DSM, they are (i) Mild (50-70 I.Q), (ii) Moderate (35-49 I.Q), (iii) Severe (20-34 I.Q) and they commit crimes of emotional nature. The animality in them is not under their strict control and they commit acts which are said to be crimes. People are not generally considerate to those 'human beings' and therefore whenever they commit instinctual acts which are legally treated as crimes, they are physically assaulted by most of the people. Crimes committed by the mentally retarded or crimes against them are not the issues under discussion.

There are 'legal morons', 'political morons', 'religious morons', 'communal morons' and so on—and they commit a number of crimes against humans and humanity. They are people lacking good judgment. 'Morons' are found in the legislature, among the executives and amidst the judiciary. What is happening in some State-Legislatures/Parliament? The representatives of the people do not allow the Legislatures/Parliament to run. They boycott, they shout slogans, they attack the fellow representatives, they organize sit-in-strikes, quickie, hunger strikes, gherao etc. in the Houses and thus incredibly waste the money of the tax-payers. The executives abuse their power/misuse their authority, exercise pseudo-authority or refuse to exercise their power and authority. The judiciary too is blamed for their poor judgment and the 'moron administration' cause havoc in society and people suffer them helplessly. The 'moron judgments' of the politicians, so-called religious men, communal leaders have created law and order problems and massacre. The unnecessary, indiscriminate killing of a number of human beings as in a barbarous warfare or in persecution or for revenge or plunder take place as a result of moron judgments. There may be massive destruction of property and the morality/moral principles are stilled in such situations.

(49) Consensus Justice

Consensus means a general agreement or concord. Majority

opinion matters here. Consensus of opinion is felt by many grammarians and teachers to be redundancy, but it is so only if consensus is taken in sense of 'majority of opinion', rather than its equally valid—and, according to available evidence, earlier—sense of 'accord or general agreement' (Webster's). The evils are tested by the people in society, but there is no law to put them down. Many economic crimes now seen in the society are not crimes under the law. As such, no legal action can be taken against them. Nexus crimes, *Mafia* crimes, bureaucratic crimes, political crimes, crime syndicates, white collar crimes etc. are real crimes, but the law does not legally define them to be offences. Corporate crimes, social media crimes, banking crimes, cyber crimes emerge and they damage and destroy the people. There exist no legislation defining, describing or punishing such newer and newer crimes. The patch works made in the ancient, old or modern, legislations are not useful or effective to curb down the contemporary and current crimes in society. These new crimes serve the interests of the social-political-religious-bureaucratic higher ups and therefore they slumber over many of the consensus crimes. They are in a state of inactivity, quiescence or calm. The slumberous attitude and approach to consensus crimes in society make the criminals to be very active in the field. Even the Law Commission of India, the Supreme Court etc. are felt to be unfortunately slumbering over the aching issue.

(50) Justice to the Unborn Children

An unborn child means a child yet to be born. Studies show that abortion or miscarriage of unborn children take place in large numbers and the colon in the fetus is sold at exhorbitant price to manufacture cosmetics. Girl children are killed in the uterus itself after a sex scan and there is a law against such atrocities to unborn children. The issues to be discussed here under are:

1. Environmental pollution and destruction harmful to unborn children
2. Inculcation of extremist thoughts to pregnant women
3. Lack of nutrition and health care to pregnant women
4. Use or abuse of drugs by pregnant women
5. Family discord and connected psychological problem to pregnant women

6. Adulterated food and food containing harmful chemicals to pregnant women
7. Country's economic dependency and pauperism on every new born child.

Thus, one sees a series of dangerous issues affecting unborn children. See the children in poor countries and the same in rich countries. Wealth belongs to the people and they have a responsibility and obligation to all children to develop their personality in the best atmosphere. Does it take place?

(51) Economic Justice

There was a time people thought economic crimes were the crimes committed by the economically poor people, by the unemployed or underemployed persons or by individuals who suffer financial problems. Accordingly, we find attempts made by Xenephone, Plato, Aristotle, Vergil and Horace to explain criminal behaviour in terms of economic conditions. The 'economic determinism' of Karl Marx argued that private ownership of property resulted in poverty. Consequently, the exploited class of the society turned to crimes owing to their property. Forget about such old and dilapidated explanations of economic crimes and justice. The society today is contaminated with the economic crimes of the affluent, of the corporates, of the sharks in society and of those who are involved in suite crimes. The offenders here are 'meat eater, criminals—the carnivorous mammals of the order carnivora, comprising the dogs, cats, bears, seals, weasels etc. against whom the laws are powerless. They are people of affluence and their crimes are crimes of affluence. They plunder money and invest in foreign countries. They escape to other countries when caught and legal action against them is time consuming, laborious and meaningless. The corporates commit crimes and they rob the country and its economic resources. The ruling government may be on their side and all laugh at the plight of the common people in a democracy. The money accumulated with the political parties may be incredible and the money thus amassed by corruption and malpractices rules the people in its own way with vested interests. Poor people commit crimes resulting out of poverty/ unemployment etc. Such grass-eater criminals are mercilessly pulverised by the enforcement machinery. Why? No answer. The powerful-affluent politicians are engaged in legalized plunder and organized loot.

(52) Management Justice

The 'manager is always right'—this is what is seen today. The nurses are not paid or paid very low wages that may not be enough for their subsistence. Teachers working in recognized schools are paid nominally and those in self-financing institutions are given inadequate pay. Even the wages in prisons—atmosphere controlled by strict discipline—are not wages worth their name. The poor wage structure in prisons is falsely said to be a means and method for their correction. This argument is stupid. Doctors are paid lavishly on condition that the huge targets fixed for each one should be achieved. A doctor who is paid 3 lakhs rupees per month will have a target of making 50 lakhs of rupees every month. The impact is that the patients are extracted. The Hire and Fire policy adopted by the management makes everyone to work under heavy stress. They become sick very soon. The employees are pressured to work overtime without any overtime allowances. Little children and juveniles are appointed to work even in hazarduous atmosphere. Girls and women working as domestic servants are exploited even sexually and by many other ways. The employees are given no good working environments and the accommodation given to them does not have even creature comforts. The food is qualitatively poor and in some spheres, they are not allowed to answer their nature's call in a decent way. No toilet facilities are provided and many become kidney patients. The litany is very long and the sufferings continue.

(53) Law and Order Justice

What is law and order? It means that the law is enforced strictly and the order is maintained properly. Statistics on crimes shows that the law and order crimes are on the increase. Why? Many such crimes have political patronage as we see politicization of criminals. If the offenders are members of the ruling political party, then they are treated with favours. Their crimes become no crimes at all. There are *goondas*, hooligans, unprincipled men and they use their muscle power to subdue their opponents. They attack them, stab them, kill them and so to say, the law and order crimes are plenty. Police patronage and political god fathering make them to commit any kind of crimes and instances have been reported that the political party prepares a list containing the names of those who ought to be made the accused in crimes. The police execute the political decision as their most obedient servants.

In a democracy there will be opposition and the opposition parties organize protest and conduct protest meetings, processions, *hartals* and *bandhs*. The success in the protest depends heavily upon the amount and intensity of law and order violation crimes. They burn government vehicles, damages public property, block the vehicular traffic, forcibly pressure the businessmen to shut down their shops etc. In certain cases, the police may have to have recourse to *lathy* charges and even firing at the crowd or mob as the case may be. The policemen have their political affiliations and such policemen may commit atrocities on the protesting people. There will be casualties and inquiries conducted. The criminal policemen (if there are) will behave worse than *goondas* and hooligans. They may stone at the mob or damage public/ private property. Any law and order established by the police without morality invite public criticisms.

(54) Investment Justice

Investment in gold, real estate, shares, business etc. may bring money and fortunes to people. People in general want to become rich-richer-further richer within no time and that too without any labour or hardship. Making easy money is what the people want. This weakness of the man is exploited by people who have vested interests on those who have a criminal mind. They offer very attractive projects to trap those who wish to invest. Money chain and multi-marketing is one such scheme to invest money. Con-games are notorious and they include charity and religious frauds, personal improvement scheme, money order swindles, securities fraud and commodities fraud etc. Of course, they come under white collar crimes. Investment injustice means injustice offered to investors who invest money for exhorbitant profits. The criminals involved in such crimes make use of advertisement to attract people. Almost 30-40 per cent of the money invested with them may be spent for advertisement. After amassing wealth, they vanish into the thin air and the investors spend their time in crying. Some commit suicide and cases registered take several years to reach a final decision after revision and appeals in the cases. My researches show that many cases have a hue and cry in the beginning and as days are elapsed, people forget about the crimes connected with investment. They have no option but to suffer the loss. Immediately, new investment schemes appear in advertisement and people invest their money in the new schemes. The drama is repeated. In one of my research studies, I could learn that the schemes for fixed deposits (with exhorbitant interest) has gone to investment on teak, mangium and goat and from it to investment on shares and from there to investment on tourism and thus the investment crimes have become recurring crimes in different nomenclatures in society. Morality keeps silence against this sort a crime chains.

(55) Cyber Justice

Cyber justice is a newcomer in criminology. It was not born about two decades ago, but today, it is seen everywhere. Actually the police have no praiseworthy expertise to investigate cyber crimes. Cyber world grows and the growth is in geometric proportions. The allegation today is against voting machines. According to some political parties, the voting machines are misused and manipulated in such a way that all votes will go to a particular political party programmed in the voting machines. True or false, the allegation is yet to be proved and decided. Nevertheless, the money deposited in banks are lost to people and it has been noted that there are international cyber crimes-syndicates and they loot even the governments. The Websites are hacked and the professional hackers provide their services to anyone who pays them.

Social media crimes are many. The friendship established via the social media is exploited and the children are found missing as a consequence. Fake love creates a lot of problems and the victims are found dead and some commit suicide. Sexual abuses in the cyber world are beyond imagination. There are ATM frauds and the money is taken away. Defaming people through cyber techniques and the trolls seen in social media have become a menace to many. The language used in comments are vulgar and sometimes very filthy and indecent. Morphing is done and anybody can be victimized. The fake profiles in the cyber world help many to escape legal action. Some cyber crimes are international and therefore initiating action against cyber criminals is indeed very difficult. There is no cyber code of ethics and no one knows much about cyber morality.

(56) '....isms, ologies and sophies' Injustice

Naxalism, terrorism, fundamentalism, fanaticism, rationalism, empiricism... and thus the '*....isms*' are many. People are attracted and some such '*....isms*' like Maoism, fundamentalism etc. become causes for many types of crimes. Marxism, Leninism, Communism are '*....isms*' which uphold the principles that the end justifies the means. The principle is questioned by many who hold different '*...isms*'. What about the '*....ologies*'? Theology and moral theology of the religions attract many and there take place conflicts and massacre on the basis of the theological doctrines and '*...isms*' held by various denominations and sects. The ideology of the Maoists, extrimists, fundamentalists and the political ideology of some are found to be a perpetual cause for disharmony and fights. The '*....sophies*' held by some become the causative factors for crimes. The theology plus sociology and philosophy plus criminality prone '*.....isms*' are put together to coin a new word called **Theosophism** which means all '*...ologies*', '*...sophies*' and '*....isms*' which cause crimes in the present society. Criminal **Theosophism** does not have a moral basis. It accepts, approves, promotes and prompts all types of crimes to achieve its objective—legal or illegal, moral or immoral, ethical or unethical.

(57) Mic or Rhetoric Justice

Misuse or abuse of mics becomes a crime in these days. It causes pollution which affects the hearing capacity of people adversely. The religious micism—i.e., abuse of the mic causing sound pollution by churches, temples, mosques, gurudvaras etc.—is indeed unbearable. The road campaign through mic propaganda and announcement during elections is indeed a social evil to which the people are helpless. The *Rhetoric*—i.e., the ability to use language effectively—is an art. People who are good in rhetorical art will be able to manage and manipulate people in any way they want. The oratory capability coupled with rhetoric capacity make one's speech highly influential. The speech of Mark Antony, Martin Luther King, John F. Kennedy are examples in point. Today, the rhetoric capacity and oratory capability are criminally abused and misused by politicians and 'so-called' religious men to tell lies, repeated lies; to give false promises and vain hopes; to ensure impossible achievements and happiness etc. They want power, authority, money and pleasure. They mint money by exploiting people and all of them misuse or abuse mics for the purpose. The mic, the voice, the sound, the actions, the non-verbal language, the body posture, the expressions, the lights etc., etc. of these orators create a sort of euphoria—i.e., a feeling of well being, esp. an exaggerated one having no basis in truth or reality. These politicians and 'so-named' religious men have no respect for morality and moral principles. Preach and plunder people may be their objective and thereby enjoy power and authority. This is nothing but verbal diarrhea.

(58) Third Degree Justice

Third degree methods during an investigation of crime is doubtlessly third rate methods; still the police employ them lavishly. In India, a Commission known as the Torture Commission was appointed to inquire into the nature, extent and intensity of torture employed by police in 1855. The Commission brought out third rate methods which only human imagination could conceive of. The situation continues even today as it was in 1855—or even worse in a wider and deeper way. Third degree justice is not justice, rather it is an atrocity committed on people and their lives. When I write this, I hear about 6 such cases in which third degree methods were used. Out of the 6 cases, 3 people were killed and the Government has ordered an investigation of them by appointing a Special Investigation Team (SIT).

What are the various third degree methods? They are thousands in number and they are employed to get a confessional statement from the interrogated. The animal policemen employ very cruel methods of torture even on innocent people and the false confessions recorded by the police are misused to obtain punishments for them from the courts. What an injustice indeed! Yes, one who commits a crime (even innocent people) get many types of punishments—namely, torture, harassment, extraction of money, ill-fame and humiliation and a court sentence of punishment. If acquitted, the pain connected with all except the court pronounced punishment is suffered by the victims of police action. No doubt, this sort of justice administration is called 'Wounded Justice' administration containing many kinds of crimes committed by the sub-systems of so-named justice administration. Horrible indeed and a sort of justice administration without morality and ethics.

(59) Adulterated Justice

Justice is adulterated everywhere and that is the cruelest crime today. Justice can be purchased and the adulterated justice can be purchased at a cheaper price. Police administer police justice in various forms. Muscle justice and money justice may have a role to play when the police justice is administered. There is something called the *Mind Justice* and do the police administer it? *Mind Justice* means the quality of conforming to principles of reason (i.e., Intelligence), to generally accepted standards of right and wrong (i.e., moral and ethical) etc. and to the stated terms of laws, rules, agreements etc. in matters affecting persons who could be wronged or unduly favoured. Do the police perform their duty as expected? Complaints are not rare and all of them tell about police abusing their power, misusing their authority or exercising pseudo-authority etc. Police justice becomes crimes for many in society.

What about the 'Prosecutor's Justice? 'Defence Lawyers' Justice? Judicial Officers' Justice and Prison Justice? The prosecutors offer justice in their own way and the justice they administer is adulterated by money in kind or in cash, by positions and fortunes, by politics and privileges, by women and sex etc. Do the prosecutors succeed in winning cases in which the affluent, the influential, the powerful and the privileged are involved? How many political leaders, social higher-ups, religious leaders were punished till now? There is adulteration and some of the defence lawyers, more often than not, make all attempts to adulterate justice by conniving with the unscrupulous prosecutors and the police. All of them join together to fool the court of law and the judicial officers knowingly or unknowingly adulterate justice and administer it in their own way. Go to the prisons and see the convicts and there too one sees adulterated justice in many ways. Morality is and should be above everything in administration of justice.

(60) *Ad hoc* and ad *Hominem* Justice

Ad hoc means 'for this (special purpose) only or with respect to this (subject or thing)'. No law generally applied in similar situations will be applied there. *Ad hoc* decisions should be evaluated from the point of view of the special or specific purpose or subject. *Ad hominem* which means 'appealing' to a prejudice, emotion or a special interest rather than to intellect or reason; against an opponent rather than his arguments'. People often say: "Tell me the man and I shall tell you the law". This is seen in politics, religion, in culture, in social interaction, in human transaction etc. Man matters a lot.

Just listen to the T.V. Channel discussions and talk shows. If a politician participates in a discussion, he justifies and rationalizes any injustice done by his political party leaders. He does not think about the morality and principles of justice. He has *ad hoc* justice principles and he interprets everything basing on *ad hominem* approaches. The same *ad hoc* and *ad hominem* justice principles are applied by religious speakers, communal speakers and so on. Even the terrorists apply the principles in an *ad hoc* manner. Women do the same thing when women's issues are discussed. The same approach is seen in social media discussions. No philosophy, no principles, no jurisprudence, no '....*ologies*' and '....*isms*', no natural justice in such *ad hoc* and ad *hominem* justice delivery. The most unfortunate and saddest part of such *ad hoc* and *ad hominem* justice is that the advocates and adherents of such an approach commit any sort of crimes for their so-called success or victory. Such crimes are in abundance. No morality worth its name!

(61) Mob Justice

A mob is a disorderly, riotous or lawless crowd of people. In criminal sociology, it is a group of people stimulating one another to excitement and losing ordinary rational control over their activities. A mob violence is often preplanned in these days and the calculated move is to create problems and issues for another religious groups, communal groups, racial groups, ruling government, management, school authorities etc. They commit crimes purposefully damaging and destroying people and their property. Once the mob violence is initiated, it is not that easy to subside the emotionally driven—non logical destructions. The members of the mob see the policemen and other authorities as symbols of their hatred. Precisely therefore, the mob directs their anger to them. No rules or moral principles apply. There is no fair play. The behaviour is governed by mass hysteria, hatred and impulses of aggression. Today, the news about such mob violence and crimes committed by the members of the mob occupy good space in the media. Vested interests fish in the contaminated water for success and the crimes committed by them are not investigated properly. The members of the mob constitute the vote bank of some political parties and often the political parties pressure the government to withdraw the cases from the court. Many a mob violence and their criminal activities get immunity and they do not have any criminal liability. The criminals are in comfort zones and the damages/destruction caused by them become a private or personal injury for the people. They suffer helplessly the injuries sustained by them during a mob violence. No one is punished and many of the criminals enjoy life with added vigour and vitality. Morality has zero impact.

(62) Criminal Police Justice

Criminalization of police is a widely discussed topic in these days. According to the data obtained under the Right to Information Act in many States show that a sizable number of policemen/officers face criminal charges and the crimes they commit include murder, rape, enforcement crimes, corruption and bribery etc. These criminal policemen administer criminal justice to those who commit crimes. The irony is indeed very shocking to human conscience.

In my book *Police Criminology and Crimes,* I have enumerated almost 600 types of crimes committed by the police personnel in these days. Many of the crimes committed by them are not reported or recorded. Justice Mulla of Allahabad High Court said once: 'There is no organised group of criminals in the whole country whose record of crimes will come in any way near to that organized group which is called the Indian Police'. Oh, my God, how true it is although he said it long back! Criminal policemen administering criminal justice will be almost like a prostitute preaching against prostitution. The Crime in India [A Government of India publication] gives statistics about the number of policemen killed on duty and the figure is indeed frightening. But the reality is that the number of people killed by policemen sometimes outnumber the number of policemen killed on duty. The number of people who are made complete wrecks in the sea of life goes several fold higher than the number of policemen injured on duty. But the multitude of people so made does not figure in any official records [like Crime in India] as figures are not registered. Police crimes are frightening and terrifying indeed!

(63) Mobility Justice

The movement of people in a population, as from place to place, from job to job or from one social class to another is called mobility in sociology. There is vertical mobility, horizontal mobility, spatial mobility, social mobility etc. Mobility is found to be a causative factor for very many types of crimes. The alarming statistics of street sleepers and homeless people, gypsy like nomadic tribes and other denotified tribes indulging in crimes against property and person may be frightening. Some of them involve in the commission of sex crimes, prostitution, beggary and what not? Truancy and vagrancy among children and aimless wandering are other issues in a mobile society.

Individuals who move from place to place, group to group, status to status create many problems and they involve in the commission of crimes primarily because they become increasingly isolated from the continuous social control which is implicit in a settled society. The identity lost individuals can involve in any sort of crimes as they do not have any ties with the settled society. Their ties are severed from the settled society and they thus loose their sense of responsibility. They are found to involve in a variety of crimes including drug trafficking and flesh trade etc. A study showed that nearly 200 girls move everyday in India and they enter into the flesh trade. Girls between the age 10-16 are increasingly seen among the moving population. Vertical mobility causes further crimes and people of the lower economic strata, of the lower castes/sub castes, of the lower job etc. are exploited and victimized. What kind of justice is ensured to such people? What kind of morality is seen in this special area?

(64) Journalistic Justice

Media is the fourth estate in a democracy. Fourth Estate means a group other than the usual powers, as the three estates of France, that wields influence in the politics of a country. In a democracy, the Legislature, Executive and Judiciary are important, but, experience shows that the press and the media are sometimes more powerful than the three powers in a democracy. They generate public opinion and the people are more powerful than the Legislature, Executive and Judiciary in a democracy. It is an accepted fact that the (i) pen is mightier and sharper than the sword and (ii) 'seeing is believing' and the print media makes use of the (i) and the visual media makes use of the (ii) above. Today, there is a number of online news channels and they publish many things. They too have a pressuring force among the people.[1]

Journalism which does not have moral values publish half truths and falsehood with their views and cause damages to peace and order in society. Some journalists today are political extremists or religious fanatics. They publicize small things in a big way sensationalizing everything in a manner detrimental to peaceful co-existence. There is competition in journalism and the first one reporting a news scores higher than others. Recently, the injustice which would have been otherwise forgotten are brought to public visibility by committed journalists who make use of their pen and camera, their tongues and videos, their repeated telecasts to the maximum extent possible. While they do such praiseworthy things in a violent way, they may at times prostitute the journalistic ethics as one may see in the ISRO espionage case. This sort of journalistic prostitution without any morality must be condemned in strongest words.

(65) Raping of Juveniles Justice

A juvenile is a child under 18 year of age. The juveniles are classified as 'infants' (1 to 7 years of age) and children (12 to 18 years of age).

A study conducted in Kerala by me about rapes shows that in 30-33 per cent of rapes, the juveniles are the victims—most of them are raped at their residence and are raped by the 'near and dear' ones including the father, step-father, grandfather or brothers and so on. Why? The causes found out by me are (i) no forceful resistance from the victim, (ii) no reporting of the sexual abuse by them, (iii) no fear of contamination of venereal diseases and AIDs, (iv) no legal action if at all known etc. The sex abuses on children below 10 years of age are reported increasingly in these days and they come out owing to the positive role played by child line workers, school counsellors and teachers and so on. The number of people affected by pedophilia is noted to be alarming. Heterosexuality oriented males [Pedophilia] are found to abuse girls in the age group of 8-10 years old and the desired sexual activity usually being limited to looking or touching and manipulating the sexual organs for their sexual excitement. Most incidents are initiated by adults who are in the intimate inter personnel environment of the child (see, DSM). According to studies conducted, it is seen that homosexuality oriented males tend to prefer slightly older children (above 10 years). Thus, the act or phantasy of engaging in sexual activity with prepubertal children becomes a repeatedly preferred or exclusive method of achieving sexual excitement and it has become a serious issue now even though POSCO Act is in operation.

(66) Lier Justice

Liers and Liers everywhere and they are seen anywhere in politics. There was a Quiz programme and the question asked was: "Who tells more lies?"—The options given were: (i) Advocates, (ii) Journalists, (iii) godmen (priests, *poojarees*, *sannyasees* and *avathars*), (iv) Cine artists, (v) Advertisers, (vi) Politicians and (vii) Doctors. Prize was given to answer (iii)—i.e., godmen. They tell the maximum number of lies and they claim that they guarantee spiritual and heavenly pleasure and justice. Second prize was given to answer (vi)—i.e., Politicians who open their mouth to say lies after lies. They ensure heaven on earth. The third prize was given to answer (v)—i.e., advertisers who cheat the public by telling and showing lies after lies to sell their commodity or to obtain fortunes for them. The journalists, for their livelihood, cine actors and advocates, doctors tell lies and all of them know that they are telling lies for the lucrative achievement and benefits. Unfortunately, people do not react against their lies and Why?

Lier justice is a newcomer in criminology. The lies said, promoted and propagated by politicians during an election campaign are forgotten once the election is over. The lies repeatedly told by the godmen and the so named spiritual men are just ignored even when everyone is pretty sure that they speak lies after lies. Why? People are afraid to speak against them as they think that god will punish them. The lies said by the advertisers are not taken serious notice by the public as they think that they become part of their profession. The same logic is applied to the profession of advocates, lawyers, doctors and artists. They commit injustice without any accountability and morality is sleeping over such lies repeatedly seen and heard.

(67) Voting Machine Justice

In a democratic set up, votes assume a lot of importance. The franchise—i.e., the privilege of a public nature conferred on an individual or body of individuals by a governmental grant—is exercised by casting votes to favoured candidate contesting in elections. Earlier, in many countries the votes were by ballot papers. When electronics got developed, the ballot papers were substituted by voting machines. Many countries like the USA, Australia, Germany etc. use ballot papers for voting. Japan, which was a pioneer country in electronic researches use ballot papers for voting. Why? They say that the voting machines are not reliable and the results are at best suspicious. The machines manufactured by people can be manipulated by people who are capable of doing so. There is no infallibility—i.e., exempt from liability to error. In other words, the electronic machines are not absolutely trustworthy or sure. There are demands from many quarters—especially from political parties—to accept ballot papers instead of voting machines. According to them, the crimes committed by manipulations in the voting machines have far reaching consequences in a democracy. Unworthy candidates are likely to win the elections and they form the Government. The Governments thus formed are likely to commit several **theosophism-crimes** which people in general do not know. The most unfortunate aspect of the voting machine-frauds and crimes is that they are favoured by the political party in power and they are committed for their advantages and vested interests. Morality—i.e., the election morality is violated.

(68) JEL Crimes and Justice

JEL crimes are a different category of Nexus Crimes. If Nexus Crimes are committed by the Leaders, Bureaucrats, Businessmen, Middles men and *Goondas* as Nexus Partners, the JEL crimes are committed by the Legislators, Executives and Judicial Officers as a joint venture. The Legislature enacts the law, the Executives enforce and implement the laws enacted by the Legislature. The Judiciary interprets the law favourably and it happens as a result of a clandestine understanding or a hidden agenda among the Legislators, Executives and Judicial Officers. At the top level, the legislators, the executives and the judicial functionaries are of the same category. They can mutually help a lot if the creation of the laws, interpretation of the laws and execution of the laws are made after reaching an understanding among the three powerful wings of a democracy. Allegations are there against the bad laws enacted; against the wrong interpretation of the judiciary; and the overenthusiastic execution of the laws thus enacted and interpreted. The beneficiaries are the top level functionaries in all the three wings of the democratic rules. There are cases in which the laws are amended by the legislature to suit to the clandestine understanding arrived at the three wings. Thus, the JEL crimes come under heated discussions in the media. Now, judges are coming out criticizing the judiciary, executives and legislatures for their involvement in JEL crimes. The same is said by legislators and the executives. Where do we move to? That is the question and many questions are not answered yet.

(69) Horse Trade Justice

Horse Trade means shrewdly conducted exchange, as of favours, objects etc. usually resulting from or accompanied by very close bargaining. In a democratic set up, after each election, a political party or its coaliation—i.e., union into one body or mass; an alliance of political parties—should get at least simple majority to form a

Government. In some situations, it may not be possible to get such a simple majority. In such instances, there will be **Horse Trade** to form the Government and capture power and authority. If successful in the **Horse Trade**, the Government is formed. There starts all sorts of corruption and malpractices. It is found that the money spent during the elections and election campaigns form the basis of corruption and malpractices in a democracy. The energy provided by the money thus spent by the corporates, the affluent, the financially higher ups is so powerful that there is no option but to form the Government by **Horse Trade** or other foul and fair methods whatever. The crimes committed by the **Horse Trade** become topics of discussion in the media and among the general public. Once the Government is formed, people in a democracy forget the **Horse Trade** and it becomes a part of history in Government formation. No morality or moral principles may be followed in **Horse Trade** so much so that any and many crimes committed during, before and after the **Horse Trade** vanish in to thin air. The **Horse Traders** become the rulers and the leaders in society. They are 'honourable men' enjoying ministerial status and elevated positions.

I am really tired to enumerate the crimes seen in the present day society. Why? The crimes are numerous and they number in thousands. When I wrote the book *Contemporary Indian Criminology* (ISBN: 13: 978-93-5125-100-2), I wrote more than 60 crimes. The book was written from the point of view of *Push-Pull-Ego Factor* Theory of crime causation. Idea in that book was further elaborated in my later book titled *Advanced Criminology or the Why of Crime* (ISBN: 13: 978-93-5215-265-8). The purpose of this book is to find out an answer to the question: *How to effect Crime Control and Reduction?* And I find a development of a moral ego uprightly formed in the right direction is a good way or the **Best Way** to achieve the objective. Hence, let us talk about morality and ethics.

Morality and Ethics

Before we discuss the difference between *morality* and *ethics,* it is necessary to understand and appreciate the meaning of **Norma Normans** and **Norma Normata. Norma Normans** means norming norms; **Norma Normata** means the **norm that norms the norm.** The **Norma Normans** are universal and absolute. Examples are—

(1) Do not murder a human being; (2) Do not commit theft, (3) Do not indulge in adultery, (4) Do not show disrespect to parents and thus one thousand or more such norms are there. They are moral laws. There can also be cultural laws or State made penal laws. Every law therefore is objective and absolute.

The **Norma Normata** is not absolute. Why? Every law is to be applied to each situation which is unique. In that way the application is individualistic. Take for example, the law relating to the right of private defence. Example:

(i) 'Nothing is an offence which is done in the exercise of the right of private defence' (Sec. 96, IPC). Here, in a particular set of circumstances, a person legitimately acted in the exercise of the right of private defence is a question of fact to be determined on the facts and circumstances of each case. Likewise, in morality, act/omission should be evaluated and assessed from the point of view of the facts in each case by the conscience of the person. If he feels and decides that he had no option, but to kill the one for exercising his right of private defence, then there is no moral wrong. Consequently, he does not have any **guilt feelings.** He is ethically right [subjective] although he violated the moral laws which is universal and absolute. **Morality** is social and **Ethics** is individualistic.

(ii) A is attacked by a mob which attempts to murder him. He cannot effectually exercise his defence without firing at the mob, and he cannot fire without the risk of harming young children who are mingled with the mob. A commits no offence if by so firing he harms any of the children (Sec. 106, IPC, illustration). Here, the moral principle is 'Do not murder a human being'—that is universal and absolute. But, the ethics is that you can kill a human being in the above situation. Circumstances matter a lot when ethical decisions are taken.

Coming to the control and reduction of crime, we must admit that the animal instinct in a man can be—better—should be controlled, regulated or guided by morality/ethics.

The human conscience is **norma normata** and not **norma normans**. What does it mean? It means that every human conscience applies ethical principles and justifies its acts/omissions on the basis of moral principles which are objective. A human conscience which is uprightly formed in the right direction can apply the ethical norms and thus control his animal instincts which go beyond the permitted level/extent.

Example:

A man becomes aggressive and he utters filthy expressions and epithets to a fellow human being. Here, morality or moral principles inscribed in his mind says that such a behaviour is bad and it is a violation of the social and cultural law. The circumstances are unwarranted and there is no ethical justification to utter such filthy expressions. Realizing the ethical principles, his conscience controls him and thus he does not commit a crime. Hence it may be safely concluded that whenever morality and ethics say the same thing, the conscience does not permit a man to express his animal instincts in an undesirable manner.

Habitual Conscience and Actual Conscience

Right formulation of the human conscience is important in controlling the animal instincts. Every child should be told and taught by his/her parents about the external or absolute moral principles and values from its early infancy. 'Don't tell lie; don't show disrespect to elders; respect the teachers; obey the parents'—all these are eternal moral principles and they form the **habitual conscience** in a man. Really, it is this **habitual conscience** which contains the moral laws—otherwise called the **laws of the conscience.** Man applies these laws of the conscience when he is disturbed by excessive attacks of animal instincts.

Actual conscience is the practical judgment of the intellect about the ethics (i.e., morality applied to individual situations—or—individualistic morality) of an act which one is contemplating to perform. Here, his conscience is reduced to an act of value judgment, very much an exercise of the intellect. Really, the actual conscience based on habitual conscience gives concrete moral/ethical guidance—to do or not to do the contemplated action—through his judgment. For example, a person experiencing excessive *acquisitiveness* (accompanying **emotion** is feelings of ownership) takes a decision (judgment) not to involve in economic crimes. It is because of his **actual conscience**. Here, his **actual conscience** controls his animal instinct and it reduces economic crimes in society. **Actual conscience** is the concretely guiding conscience. In short, the **habitual conscience** is fundamental and the **actual conscience** is the final concrete command or prohibition.

Development of Habitual and Actual Conscience: Animal Instincts

Habitual conscience is otherwise called the **moral conscience** and the **actual conscience** is otherwise known as the **ethical conscience**. In order to develop the **moral conscience**, there should be a **habitual conscience** uprightly developed in the right direction. How? For this, the moralizing agents—parents, teachers, value preachers and so on should have upright moral values. Remember that the blind cannot lead the blind.

The developing child in its early infancy may not know the moral implications and meanings of what is right or what is wrong. It listens to what is told to it. As it grows older and older, it starts appreciating the meaning and relevance of moral teachings. It understands the values of morality and ethics. Precisely therefore, the animal instincts are controlled and he wants to observe the rules of behaviour. If he does not, then he violates the norms. A child in his teens should have a **mature conscience** and a person observes moral laws and controls his animals instincts. The formators of conscience must inculcate in children an evaluative/ appreciative moral knowledge. Evaluative/appreciative moral/ ethical knowledge supposes one's ability to understand and appreciate moral/ethical ability to think, judge and behave in the light of them.

Controlling of Animal Instincts by Moral Principles and Values

I have keenly observed children with a purpose to study the process and progress of developing moral values in them. I divide the stages of moral development into five stages and they are—

1. **Up to 3½ years:** 'Home-centric'—i.e., when the child is taught moral values by the mother (principal moralizing

agent), father and other members of the family. Here, the infant does not control its animal instincts consciously by taking pain or efforts. Affectionate mothering is important here. The denial of the affectionate mothering during the very early stages (up to 2 years of age) during the Home-centric period and the show of disapproval by other members at home during the later stage (2-3½ years) may be considered as fine moralizing methods. In my studies, I understand that the infant develops unconsciously (consciously at the later stage) a basic sense of morality and moral values—i.e., the right and wrong. This awareness or the sense controls its animal instincts to a certain extent however insignificant it is.

2. **Home-school-centric:** This is from 3½ to 7 years of age. During this period, the child is rebuked, disfavoured and his instinctual behaviour beyond a level is disapproved and sometimes punished not only by the parents but also by other members at home and teachers in pre-primary/ primary schools. The child then learns that its behaviour which invites/necessitates punishment is bad. On the other side, what brings rewards and appreciation are good. Pain and pleasure or punishment and reward are the controlling factors. The child realizes that he/she is a separate person. Of course, the child can decide what to do and what not to do in many situations. The decision is taken basing on the pleasure-pain/reward-punishment principle. Here, he/she may be immature in the area of self-determination. The family and school must control, guide and protect the child from exceeding the limits of self-determination on the basis of the pleasure-pain approach. The interaction between the child and the parents/teachers and so on decide how good or bad the sense of autonomy in matters of morality which develops in him/her.
3. **Home-school-others centric:** This is from 7-10 years of age. The others here mean the friends and peers. The child develops sentimental relations with parents, family members, teachers, friends and peers. During this period he/she behaves morally in an upright way. This is a time when parents, teachers, friends and peers exert great

influence on the moral thinking. Lack of encouragement or support from the parents, teachers and so on for the moral acts he/she will have very bad impact/effect on his/her moral personality. By the time, the child becomes 10 years or more in age, he/she becomes more social. He/she learns the rules, regulations, customs and laws of the social life. He/she understands that what is considered to be morally good get applause from the people—i.e., those who are outside the family and school. The neighourhood and the community take note of the child's behaviour. They too contribute to the development of the child's moral thinking. He/she tries to avoid social evils as far as possible. If everything is fine, the ground work for a moral life is well laid down for proper development.

4. **Home-school-others and community-centric:** This period is from 10-14 years of age. No doubt, the child asks to himself/herself: "Who am I?" He/she finds an answer to his/her question from himself/herself and from others. He/she wants to show to others that he/she is a good person. If his/her character is good and praiseworthy, the child sees himself/herself as a good member of the society with good moral values.
5. **Home-school-others-community-society-centric:** The period is from 14-18 years of age. The child becomes a senior child and that is the reason why the Juvenile Justice Act all over the world consider 18 years of age as the upper age of the juveniles. A child who is in conflict with law is treated leniently till that time by the State-laws. The child who needs special care and protection too are treated with concern and consideration. It is presumed that the juvenile should have maturity in emotions when he/she reaches 18 years of age. A give and take attitude must be seen. There must be human co-existence in society and morality, moral values, moral thinking, ethical behaviour etc. become necessary and inevitable. Thus we notice that there is a progressive 'interiorization' and 'personalization' from birth to 18 years of age in a child/juvenile. People who express excessive animal instincts and show unacceptable emotions in life tell us that they

did have inadequate moral development somewhere during the sequence of various moral stages.

Defective Development of Moral Personality and Crimes

Mother's failures or refusal to give breast feed will make the infant to become aggressive in later life. Cruelty and aggression make their appearance during the oral stages—when sucking stages goes to biting stages (8th month after birth)—says Sigmund Freud. This is the reason why it is said that the history (like war, genocide, mass-killing etc.) occurs when the child is at the mother's breast.

If the parents train their child by severe punishment, then there is a strong likelihood of making the child to react strongly against such cruelties. Children must be punished gently and the purpose must be the development of right morality with enviable values. Cruel punishments will, in all probability, make the child to become very cruel. There is no meaning or sense in developing a kind of 'fear morality' in children. What happens in some of the orphanages and destitute homes? Children brought up by them, sometimes, exhibit cruelty in their behaviour and they do not have any guilt feeling for what they do. Life under torture will be a life of torture later in life. What is required is a 'psychological discipline' which will ensure 'sentimental morality' later in life. This is the reason why parents and teachers are advised not to employ cruel punishment methods against erring children. If reported to police, legal action will be taken against such parents and teachers. There is something called "authoritarian morality" and the children who are brought up by parents in an atmosphere contaminated with very many rules and strict regimentation are likely to become victims of authoritarian morality. No moral training which is defective shall be imparted.

Provide opportunities (**pull factors**) for the developing child for thinking and judging his own acts in the light of the moral values and principles—permit him to act out of responsibility and conviction—correct him with a proper understanding when behavioural aberrations are seen in him—and above all love him as much as one can. All these positive stratagems will be helpful for the total moral/ethical development of the child in an upright way in the right direction. Children should be given **pull factors** (environments), under proper guidance with sufficient space and full scope for developing a healthy autonomy in moral matters.

Children want models for moral training. When they see exemplar models who practise morality and keep up moral principles and values, they are inspired. Naturally and necessarily, such models will generate in them high moral values. Parents and teachers are the best models for the children to follow. The biographies of really great men—especially of the sages, *sadhus* and saints are really inspiring to the growing children.

Integration, prudence and sincerity are very important in moral training. How? When animal instinct goes beyond a level, there should be a moral thinking and a judgment to pull down the intensity of the animality in man. When the moral ego is at work, there comes a moral obligation to act in accordance with such thinking and judgment. There should be an integration of one's moral thinking, feeling and acting and if the conscience is a mature conscience, there will be a harmony among the three functions, namely, thinking, feeling and acting. For example, when one is moved by the animal instinct (called *acquisitiveness*) to steal, his moral conscience tells him not to do so as it is a crime (a moral wrong). Feeling and thinking may not be enough. He should feel his strong moral obligation not to steal when moved by the animal instinct. If he still steals, his act should arouse in him guilt feelings. If he does not have the feeling of guilt, then it means that he does not possess a mature conscience in him. An integrated conscience needs a balanced and harmonious training pattern in morality.

Prudence means 'judicious or wisely conscious in practical affairs'. A mature conscious must be prudent because prudence helps a person to make a judicious and correct judgment about the proper course of action to be taken to control the animal instinct which works excessively. I spoke about ethics and its difference from morality. People have a tendency to say "my conscience is always right" when it is not. A Chief Justice of a High Court just now tells that he did everything according to his conscience. Though he says so, the people who saw his actions in the TV a few days ago openly and loudly said that he was not sincere in his statement. Commit a crime and then justify it by insincerity is not moral at all. Though ethics is individualistic, criminologists always say that one's conscience listens not only to his inner calls and persuasions, but also to others, the community, the society and especially the authority of elders around him. Control the instincts by morality and moral values—sincerely and prudently. If ethical principles are applied, let them be approved by the morality too. Certainly, it will control crimes and reduce criminality in society.

Note

1. I have a YouTube Channel intended to create awareness in police investigation literacy and it is 'Voice of Neethie' in You Tube—i.e., VoNTV.

4

Push-Pull-Ego Factor Theory of Crime Causation: Spirituality

Spirit has the following meanings and they are (i) the incorporeal part of man in general and of an individual, or an aspect of this, such as the mind or soul; (ii) this part, or such an aspect, with relation to the religious, intellectual, cultural or other concerns proper to it; (iii) a supernatural, incorporeal being, as a ghost; (iv) a fairy, sprite, or elf; (v) an angel or demon; (vi) the divine influence as an agency working in the heart of a man etc. (Webster's). Accordingly, spiritual means (i) of, pertaining to, or consisting of spirit; incorporeal. (ii) of or pertaining to the spirit or its concerns as distinguished from bodily or worldly existence or its concerns. (iii) of or pertaining to spirits or to spiritualists; supernatural or spiritualistic. (iv) characterized by or suggesting predominance of the spirit or things of the spirit. (v) of or pertaining to the spirit as the seat of the moral or religious nature. (vi) of or pertaining to sacred things or matters; religious etc. Out of the meanings given to **spirit** in Webster's Dictionary, *the divine influence as an agency working in the heart of a man* alone is important to control animal instinct to reduce crime and criminality. Again, spiritual means incorporeal here. Divine influence means the intervention of God/gods which detracts one from the commission of crimes. A true and sincere believer in God/gods or religion cannot involve himself in the commission of crimes. **Faith**—i.e., Trust that is not based on proof; **Belief**—i.e., confidence in the truth or existence of something not immediately susceptible to rigorous proof. A few examples are—

(1) Faith—

(i) God will punish the crime-doer, criminal, sinner.
(ii) There is the hell for those who commit mortal sins (felony) and purgatory [Catholics] for those who commit venial sins (misdemeanor)
(iii) God's commandments or direction given as a rule of action or conduct (Religion's Precepts) are there in all religions—Hinduism, Buddhism, Jainism, Christianity, Sikhism, Judaism etc. Some religions claim that they give revealed truths from God/gods and the violation of God's/gods' precepts entitle the crime-doers or sinners for eternal punishments—a concept difficult to understand for the ordinary mortal man.

(2) Belief—

(i) There is a cosmic law that the crime-doers have to suffer the consequence of the crimes they commit here on earth. **Belief** is different from **Faith** and therefore those who have only **Belief** need not necessarily be theists. Most of the people have both **faith** and **belief.** That is the reason why the number of the atheists, agnostics, rationalists and so on are not many.
(ii) Aristotle lived in 384-322 B.C. No one today sees him, but everyone believes that he was alive during that period.

How Does Spirituality Control and Reduce Crimes?

'Faith' relates to a 'spiritual being' said or believed to be objectively in existence. A **'Devil in theology is Satan**—the supreme spirit of evil. **Satan** is at enmity with God. God in theology is the Supreme Being, the creator and ruler of the universe. On the other hand, a 'god' means one of the several deities, especially, a male deity presiding over some portion of the worldly affairs. For some, **Sun** is a god; **Fire** is a god; **Water** is a god. Some adore **Snakes** as gods and thus the Nature's Forces are gods. Religion and faith in God/gods may be always brought to assert that God/gods can and they do control and reduce crimes and criminality. Almost the same view is expressed by those who worship **Satan** or so named 'Evil

Spirits'. There are **Satan** worshippers and believers in black magic and occult practices and they have recourse to them for control and reduction of crime and criminality.

Pre-scientific theories of criminology centred around demonology. Demonological theories said that the devils caused crimes. According to the demonologists, crime is caused by demonological instigation and man's innate deprivity. Adam and Eve violated God's command because of the temptation offered by Satan who appeared as a serpent. Exorcism was the often resorted method to expel the Satan and thus to control/reduce crimes and criminality. Some religions hold the view that the devils are at work to force people by temptations to commit crimes always and every time and the only escape or solution is God's intervention to protect the fragile man from the temptations of devil. They advocate prayer and penance to get themselves from the devil's temptations. For expelling the evil spirits/ghosts which have entered into man's body, some *poojarees* and 'prayer men', have recourse to severe whipping to the extent of the whipped becoming unconscious. Cases are registered now against such evil practices. Exorcism and whipping are not the methods of controlling crimes.

Demonology among the Ancients: Control and Reduction of Crimes

Researches conducted some time back in a Reformatory in Illinois showed that 99.5 per cent of the inmates were suffering from mental pathology. Researches conducted recently proved that 12 per cent of the inmates in Sing Sing prison were mentally diseased or deteriorated. 19 per cent were found to be 'psychopathic'. Still recent researches revealed that only 1.5 per cent as psychotic; 6.9 per cent as psychoneurotic; 6.9 per cent as psychopathic and 2.4 per cent as feeble minded. These observations related to a study conducted on 10,000 felons in United States. For Schilder, 83.8 per cent of the offenders were normal individuals. H. Warren Dunhan and M.H. Erickson too said the same things. Whatever that be, people in ancient times (Chinese, Egyptians, Hebrews and Greeks)—i.e., half million years ago believed that mental disorders were owing to demons and they conducted *'trephining'*—i.e., a surgery on the skull which caused the disease. 'Good and Evil' spirits were widely used to explain lightening, thunder, earthquakes, storms, fires, sickness and many other events which primitive men did not understand. God's anger and displeasure to the bad actions of men was expressed by them in many ways. By such punishments, God expelled the bad spirit which caused criminality in people. In the Old Testament, we can see many stories which exposed the possession by bad spirits. Whenever a person engaged in behaviour contrary to the teachings of the then priests and temple worshippers (their teachings were the laws at that time), then they were treated as people possessed by evil spirits. Expulsion of the evil spirits was the only way to control and reduce crimes—i.e., violation of the teachings of the priests and temple worshippers then. For example, Saul in the Old Testament presumably disobeyed God (disobeying God was a crime) and the result was that God's Spirit left him and the evil spirit thus allowed to enter him. Afterwards, we see the efforts taken to expel the evil spirit from him. Jesus Christ too did the same thing. He cured a man with an evil spirit (unclean spirit) by casting out the multitude of devils that plagued him into a herd swine who in turn became possessed and "ran violently down the steep place into the sea" (Mark: 5:1-13). Even today, some simple and pions religious people believe that the devils cause crime and criminality in people and society. Take any prayer (in Christian religion) recited and we see the people helplessly and hopefully praying to God to save them from the clutches of the evil spirit so that they do not violate any laws—divine or man-made.

Incantation, noise-making and the use of various horrible-tasting concoctions and gymmicks such as cutting the head of the cocks/hens, purgatives made from animal dung, speaking ununderstandable languages, ash-spreading, flame blowing were/are used to expel the evil spirit possessing a man. In extreme cases, flogging, starving etc. will be resorted as methods of exorcism. Sometimes, the *poojaries* will sexually exploit girls and young boys. Plato (429-347 B.C) studied criminal acts and he argued that people who were mentally disturbed were not responsible for the crimes they committed and therefore they ought to be exempted from punishment. Of course, they were to pay for the damages caused by them.

Coming to the middle ages, it is noted that demons were still found to be the cause of criminal acts. During the early medieval period, the demons were expelled by prayer, holy water, anointed oil, blessings of the priests, spittle of the 'holy men', kissing of relics, going to pilgrim centres, and disciplining etc. In order to control the crime and reduce criminality, there were no methods available for those who had faith in evil spirits/devils. On the other side of devils' instigation and the innate depravity of man, we see God as a supernatural power to help a man to control crimes and reduce criminality. How? No man can control crime and reduce criminality without God's blessings—this argument rules many men even today. Faith in God means blind faith in God and nothing more—nothing less. Nothing impossible for God and God can make a sinner to be a saint or a saint to be a sinner? Those who have ardent faith in God cannot and will not commit crimes. Christians have a number of biographies of Saints (for example, St. Augustine who was a sinner converted to a saint as a result of prayers by his mother) and in many of such biographies God intervened in their lives to make them saints.

Every religion has a supernatural being called God. Besides, the tribes have their tribal gods everywhere and in the **Exodus**, the departure of the Israelites from Egypt under Moses in the Old Testament (the second book of the Bible containing an account of the **Exodus**), the narration of the people adoring an idol with a human body and an animal head shows that the people in general wanted/want a god to pray and to feel peace at heart. During the **Exodus**, they committed many crimes and Moses is said to have gone to Mount Senai to pray to God until at last he got Ten Commandments from God. Theology is a vast field of study, thought and analysis that treats of God, His attributes and His relations to the universe. Faith in God and prayer to God to save the mankind from the sins is a topic in theology. Throughout the history of man, Faith in God/gods is seen to be a panacea for all sorts of crimes and criminal behaviour.

Development of Faith in God as a Panacea for Crimes and Criminal Behaviour

A child is often born into a religious faith—to a sect—to a denomination—to a caste—to a sub-caste. A philosopher said that man was born free, but chained everywhere. And the chaining by religious faith is really every strong. On the 28th day after birth, the Hindus have a religious function in which a thread is tied to the waist of the neonate. Muslims have their circumcision (i.e., removal of the prepuce of male, especially as religious rite). Jews, Sikhs, Prarsees, Jains and so on have their religious rites, practices, rituals etc. from the moment a child is born. Catholics among the Christians baptize their infants generally on the 7th day after birth. Buddhists have theirs and thus we see the infants born as the children of parents belonging to a particular religion are brought up in that **faith**. Every religion does implant fear of God in the infants and they cannot, as a rule, get out of it if they are brought up in a particular **faith**.

God has several attributes like: 'God is love, God is merciful, God is kind, God is...... is.........is' and all of the attributes are fine. Along with such attributes, the developing children are told and taught that God punishes the sinner. He does not tolerate sins and we have any number of narrations in the religious books about the punishment given to sinners by a punishing God. Punishing God is very harsh and He causes **fear** in developing children. Why does the God cause fear in children? The punishments given by the God cause deterrence and it is felt that the punishment will deter people from committing sins/crimes. I have seen many people at their death bed showing uncontrollable fear to die. Why? Many of them are afraid of the punishments they may get after death. Though many people are afraid of the punishments they may get after death, some are found to be suspicious of the reality of the existence of hell (and purgatory) after death. Though the theory of rebirth or salvation of the soul etc. are preached by the *Sadhus/Sannyasees*, many are really doubtful about the truth behind such teachings. Yet many people are inclined to believe in the life after death and the existence of soul etc. This is so, because such ideas are injected or inculcated to the minds of the developing child. Infants who are born with a '*tabula rasa*' do write indelibly these teachings and they cannot easily wipe them off. The foundation is so strong that most of the people cannot demolish it. My studies show the development of the spiritual personality in infants, children, juveniles, adults and so on with **faith in God** and **punishments after death** as under:

Stage	Period	Development of Personality with Faith in God
First stage	Up to 6-8 months from birth	Up to 6-8 months nothing much happens. The parents pray for the child and do many religious rituals and rubrics etc. at home. The child sees but does not understand anything much.
Second stage	From 8-18 months	The infant learns little or very little about the God and prayers to God, rituals and rubrics etc. As it grows older, it starts learning some little things about the rituals and rubrics. It may kiss an idol or statue or show respect and reverence to such statues, idols etc. The infant nearing 18 months sits with the parents when the morning/evening prayer is going on at home and thus starts internalizing the ways the prayers are recited. Sometimes, it may sing the prayer song in its mind. The child feels comforted. If the mother (parents and family) is able to provide a prayerful god-fearing atmosphere at home, a basic sense of **faith in God and fear of God** will be developed.
Third stage	18 months to 4 years	The infant develops further in his/her **faith in God and fear of God.** It realizes that he/she is a person belonging to a particular religion. She/he does not have any difficulty or problem to accept the God of his parents' religion. He/she adores the God of his religion, but does not

(*Contd.*)

Stage	Period	Development of Personality with Faith in God
		show such a worship to the God/gods in other religions. He/she realizes that there are other gods as well in the world. When the child goes to school, it sees children from other religions, sects, denomination etc. He/she adjusts with them and starts tolerating other children belonging to other religions too. The child goes to his/her temples, churches, mosques etc. and feels psychological satisfaction in praying to his/her God/gods. As the child grows still older and older, he/she participates actively in religious functions. He/she imitates his/her parents and joins with the children of his/her religion in group prayers and religious activities. The parents and other religious preachers inculcate in them many things including the punishment for law breakers and sinners. Lack of encouragement or support from the parents, teachers and so on has bad effects on the development of a religious personality in children.
Fourth stage	4 years to adolescence	The child acquires more and more information about his God, God's attributes etc. He develops a fear towards God as a punishment-giver for sins/crimes. The religious preachers purposefully create fear in growing children with ulterior motives. Some want business and

(Contd)

Stage	Period	Development of Personality with Faith in God
		for a profitable business, they make the God a benevolent being, merciful and loving as well as a tormentor and punishment giver for the guilty sinner. By the time a child becomes 13-14 years of age, the ground work is well prepared for further development of his/her personality.
Fifth stage	Adolescence to adulthood	The child develops a sense of identity. He/she knows his religion very well and thus he/she becomes 'religious proper'. He asks: 'Who am I'? 'What will be my role as a believer in God'? 'Will my God punish me for the wrong doings'? 'Will I be loved by my God'? I think that the child becomes very much worried about his life after death—about his salvation etc. Certainly, the children will have anxiety and fear. God becomes thus his/her anxiety and fear. Yes, the God is his real anxiety and fear.
Sixth stage	Adulthood and upwards	A sense of intimacy with God is seen. People participate very well with various religious activities. Some opt to take up work for God/gods. Girls go to convents (among Christians) and boys opt for priesthood. Youngsters opt to do temple, mosque, gurudwara works and some become spiritual men-entirely devoted to work for the God.

It may be remembered that many people who have **faith in God and fear of God** have developed their personality owing to the **Pull Factors** provided to them from birth. People hear stories of God/gods of punishing the wrong-doer/sinner and the right and wrong actions are decided by the powerful within a particular religion. The spiritual leaders enjoy a lot of power and authority. They frighten people and terrorize them in the name of God and they do so with ulterior motives and the motives being more position, more power, more authority and more money and fortunes. People learn more about the God/gods, divine laws, particular religion and they learn to control them. Interactions of the **pull** and **push factors** are very important and decisive for the development of **faith in God and fear of God**.

God and Deterrence

Punishing God/gods may always frighten people—especially the wrong-doers/sinners. Fear of God is an expression heard often amidst the people who claim to be religious. Fake astrologers and soothsayers bring gods and goddesses and their anger as the cause of many evil doings of man and they suggest special *poojas* and rituals to please the gods/goddesses and perform occult practices. The purpose may be to frighten people and make them to desist from the commission of bad things. They also perform special *poojas* to keep away the devils from instigating people to commit crimes. Superstitious beliefs are seen not only in people who are illiterate, uneducated, not civilized and so on but also among well educated modern men and women. Curse of God/deities is again an expression used against people who commit crimes/sins. Some people have compulsive desire to connect wrong doings/sins to God's curses. They suggest ardent prayers as an effective remedy—as the only remedy to save themselves from the curse of God or gods.

Belief as a Controlling Force of Crimes

Criminologists make a distinction between **faith** and **belief. Faith** is always related to God and religion whereas **belief** is not. **Belief** is a confidence in the truth or existence of something not immediately susceptible to rigorous proof. Atheists, rationalists and agnostics have no **faith** in God and the supernatural existence. They may not believe in the existence of a soul or in the existence of a force which may punish the soul after the death of a man/ woman. Nevertheless, they too will have **belief** in the invisible. They may speak about a **cosmic law** and may argue that man suffers the consequences of his acts—particularly, of the wrong doings/sins. The theory of *Karma* believed by some is an instance in point. *Karma* means in Hinduism, Budhism, an action, seen as bringing upon oneself inevitable results, good or bad either in this life or in a reincarnation. In **theosophy,** it is the cosmic principle of rewards and punishments for the acts performed in a previous incarnation. Theosophy means any of various forms of philosophical or religious thought claiming a mystical insight into the divine nature. There are people who are not religious but they have **belief** in the theory of *Karma.*

We take note of terrorism, fundamentalism, extremism, fanaticism, Maoism, Naxalism etc. and those who adhere to such thoughts have **beliefs** which they cannot subject to proof. The Maoists act on a belief that the success is through the barrels of a gun. This belief causes crimes of very many kinds. Take any philosophical thoughts and principles. They are not susceptible to rigorous proof empirically; yet people have beliefs in such thoughts and principles. The '*....isms, ...ologies, ...sophies*' which are based on crime and criminality are in existence and those who profess, promote and propagate such **beliefs** may involve in the commission of various kinds of crimes. Empiricism is a philosophy which adheres to the doctrine that all knowledge is derived from sense experience. What about rationalism? It is the doctrine that reason alone is a source of knowledge and is independent of experience. In theology, rationalism means the doctrine that human reason, unaided by divine revelation, is an adequate or the sole guide to all attainable religious truth. What is idealism? It is any system or theory maintaining that the real is of the nature of thought or that the object of external perception consists of ideas. In short, a man cannot live and survive on earth without **beliefs** in many things—real or unreal—which are invisible. Man lives in '**hopes** and **expectations**'. If he does not have 'hopes and expectations', he is dead. 'Hope against Hope' is an expression seen in St. Paul in his epistle to Romans (Ch. 4:18). Children are given hopes and expectations from their birth itself. The child who does not eat food is told by his/her mother that she will get hold of the moon in the sky for him/her and the hope given by the mother makes the child to eat food. People live on hopes, survive on hopes, behave on hopes, withdraw from an act on hopes—and the hopes and expectations are the part and parcel of human life on earth.

The objectives of punishment is built on hopes and expectations. The deterrent theory of punishment is built on a hope that punishment deters people—criminal or potential criminals from committing crimes/offences. Of course, my studies and observations give me ample proof to assert that the hope is not altogether baseless or meaningless. Give enough **Pull Factors** to growing children about imprisonment to crime-doers and so on. Certainly, it will deter the children from committing crimes. This is what parents and teachers do. There is a saying: "Spare the rod and spoil the child" and it means that the theory of deterrence has its effect in the control and reduction of crimes. As long as a man has the impulse of fear and anxiety, deterrence will be effective in controlling criminality in society. The light hearted learn their fate from the punishments awarded to the crime doers.

The hopes and expectations of the Classical School of Criminology, it is seen, were not without effects. Accordingly, penalties were given according to the seriousness of the offences committed. The hope was that the penalty deters people and it should never be more harsh than necessary to put down the offender's impulse under Bentham-Beccaria's hedonistic calculus. On the basis of this belief, punishments are given to drug offenders, rapists, terrorists and so on even today.

The belief is that punishment deters not only individuals who are prone to commit crimes, but also it gives a general deterrence to society. I used to tell in my classes (Penology) that the punishment is given not because a man has committed an offence, but in order that others may not commit a similar offence. Yes, I notice that the hope may not deter those involved in organized criminality, *Mafia* crimes, terrorists, insurgents, suicide-squads, political criminals and so on. Nevertheless, it does deter people who commit less serious crimes. Hardened criminals are not seriously affected by this hope. In my researches, I notice that this belief does not often work with offenders in whom **animality**—i.e., intense instincts and accompanying emotions are the ingredients—is at work in an intense way. Further, the belief does not have much value in circumstantial crimes resulting from the pressures of unusual animal instincts and in accidental crimes where intent is lacking. Nevertheless, the developing children ought to be told about the impact of crimes and the punishments awarded to criminals to control and reduce criminality (animality) in them.

There was a **belief** in ancient times that retribution—i.e., requital according to merits or otherwise, especially for evil acts—would be an effective method to control crimes, delinquency and criminal activities. Such an approach was seen during the time of Hammurabi (18th Century B.C. or earlier), the King of Babylonia. The **belief** in retribution—i.e., in *lex talions* made the King to have recourse to the principle known as 'ən eye for an eye or a tooth for a tooth'. The retributive rationale was based on the **animality** of the man. Moses and his Pentateuch containing his dispensations, or system of rules and ordinances gave retributory punishments based on the principle—'an eye for an eye; a tooth for a tooth'. St. Thomas Aquinas spoke of free will and full consent to explain the causes of sin which man committed. Sin is the transgression of the divine law. In other words, a sin was, according to him, a transgression or willful violation of some religious or moral principle. As far as criminology is concerned, the Classical School supported the above Thomist explanation of *free will*—i.e., man as a free moral animal deliberately chooses to do right or wrong and that in the nature of things where he selects to do the evil, he deserves to be punished. When we study the history and development of retributive justice, we notice that it created many physically handicapped people in society. The number of one-eyed, one-legged, one-handed, penisless, tongueless men got multiplied into many thousands every day. It created more liability to society. Of course, the **belief** in retributive justice created fear among the people and it could reduce crimes and regulate criminality to certain extent. Nevertheless, it was found that the cure was worse than the disease. Even today, some countries in the world resort to such retributive approaches. The approach is cruel and wild so much so that the civilized community does not favour such inhuman methods. It is nothing but animality expressed in another form and precisely therefore, it has no scope in the present world of correction, reformation and personality development.

Never train a child following the principles of retributive justice. Children brought up in an atmosphere of retributive justice are likely to develop pervert personality and mental disorders. Seeing the meaninglessness of the retributive justice, Jesus Christ spoke of the doctrine of love and concern. The New Testament (Bible) is full of such love and mercy. Following the doctrine, the Catholic Church in 1704 switched over to imprisonment as an alternative to corporal punishments. Thus, the First Prison called the Papal Prison was constructed in Rome to house the convicts. No doubt, the effect of uncontrollable animal instincts and irresistible impulses, psychopathic personality and other extenuating circumstances did mitigate the full rigours of retributive justice. Never have recourse to the retributive justice for reducing crimes and controlling criminality.

Incapacitation—particularly death—is certainly a punishment to prevent crimes permanently. Yes, it will be effective when crime is considered from the point of view of 'man centered'. He is finished by death. But, the crime is never prevented when it is considered from the point of view of 'act centered'. Remember that murder or manslaughter will be in existence so long as man has animal instincts. Transportation of criminals is not in existence today. Temporary incapacitation is seen in imprisonment and a permanent incapacitation is seen in life-imprisonment till death.

The protection of the society is assured, to some measure, by close confinement in prisons. The convicts are confined and are prohibited to have contacts with people outside the prison. But, majority of the imprisoned come out and we notice recidivists. It means that imprisonment gives no promise of real protection to the people. The prisons do not have adequate number of trained correctional staff and the custodial staff cannot meaningfully do the correctional role. Whatever that be, it is not good to punish children by confinement and therefore, there are people who suggest punishments to the parents for the wrongs committed by their little children. Confinement is not found to be a good way to educate children and elders the ways to control their instinctual forces. The individuals who are confined are likely to repress their anger to such negative actions and precisely, they may rebel against such crude and cruel methods. Ultimately, the result will be counter-productive.

No infants, children, juveniles, adults or the old men can control their animal instincts permanently or 24 x 7 days a week. They will express their animal instincts and it depends upon the intensity of the influence exerted by the **pull factors** or environment. Nevertheless, the punishments given will certainly make them to think seriously about their doings and misdoings. If they feel that they commit wrong, then some of them are likely to feel remourseful for the guilt. They may take penance and expiate for the wrong they committed. There are people who, instead of expiation and atonement become antagonistic to many in society and around them.

No doubt, the children and the adults (the old as well) should learn to control their animal instincts and they need training and education. A better approach is to take deterrent-corrective-reformative stratagems to reduce crime and criminality in society. The deterrent-reformative-corrective attitude and approaches have preventive and curative effects. How? It deters children and at the same time, it corrects their misbehaviour and reforms them. For example, counselling has good effects on children to modify their behaviour to be desirable and acceptable. Instructions in morality and religion are found to be good or effective methods to correct the erring children. The instructions, education, training and punishment etc. are only means to an end, the end being the control of animal instincts.

Beside the **belief** in the effectiveness of punishment as a means of controlling animal instincts, there are many other **beliefs** which are helpful to control man's instinctual energy. In other words, man's animal instincts must be controlled if one wants to reduce crimes in society. There is no option but to have recourse to such instinct-control mechanisms. Such **beliefs** are—

(i) a **belief** in the blessings of the departed elders—i.e., the parents and the elders who are dead are above us and they will shower their blessings if good behaviour is shown by controlling one's animal instincts.

(ii) A **belief** in the horoscope, soothsaying, astrological predictions etc. which compel them to be cautious of their behaviour—never, ever become emotional for a period of time. They divide the life-span of the people to several segments and caution them to behave in a particular way during a particular period.

(iii) A **belief** in fatalism—i.e., all events are predetermined or subject to fate. There are people who believe that they may go to jail if they do not control themselves. Controlling themselves means control their animal instincts.

(iv) A **belief** in their progress in life if they behave well in society. The school authorities give **Character and Conduct** certificates to convince people that the concerned individual is well educated and trained to behave controlling the animal instincts in them.

Spirituality means **faith** and **beliefs** and, as said earlier, they have an effective role to play to form the **ego** of a person. The **ego** of a person can be '**Spirituality dominated, animality dominated, morality dominated** and **intelligence dominated**', and the domination will be owing to the **Pull Factors** or environment. Everyone has a life retrospect.

Life Retrospect

Retrospect simply means a survey of the past time, events etc., contemplation of the past. Retrospect means looking back on past events. Every person has a unique retrospect. I used to think and say: "My life retrospect is my unique retrospect and no one else's. No one can claim for my retrospect". As far as one's spiritual retrospect is concerned, it is just very difficult, if not impossible, to change the spiritual retrospect—the **Faith or Belief or Both** experiences. One's spiritual experiences are his unique experiences and no one on earth can have his unique experiences. A man controls his animal instincts, accompanying emotions and thus reduces crimes or criminal activities by his **faith or belief or both** which is fully and totally based on his **Life Retrospect**. How?

(i) Our brain functions as a high-fidelity recorder.

(ii) The feelings which were linked to our past experiences (Life Retrospect) too are recorded in our brain.

(iii) Whenever we have committed a wrong act (crime) as the result of an animal instinct, the experiences we had (e.g., scolding by parents, counselling by elders, spiritual exhortations, God's punishments etc.) and the guilt feelings or unsettling of our mind owing to our wrong acts/ omissions are available for reply now vividly in our mind. We recollect them and the feelings forbid us to commit the wrong acts again. Life retrospect helps us to control our acts in the wrong way.

Faith in God is a powerful energy and force to stop people from committing crimes. **Belief** in many universal principles too are a powerful energy and force stopping people to involve in the commission of crimes. As vast majority of people are believers in God and at the same believers in many universal principles (real or false), most of the people desist from committing crimes or control their animal instincts. They do not want to suffer the evil consequences of the crimes they commit. They have fear and the **belief** and **faith** frighten them a lot.

Earlier, I said about **Spirituality Dominated Ego.** What do I mean by it? It is as under—

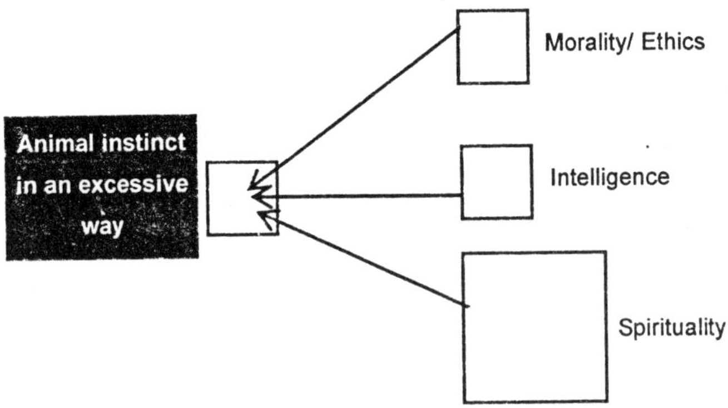

Fig. 4.1: Spirituality Dominated Ego.

Here, against the animal instinct in an excessive way, **Morality** and **Intelligence** and **Spirituality fight.** As the **spirituality**—or the **faith, belief**—is more here, it overpowers the **Animality** or animal instincts in an excessive way and thus stops the instinct to overpower **morality/ethics and intelligence.** Resultingly, criminality is stopped.

Similarly, **Morality/Ethics** and **Intelligence** can dominate. How? Their dominance needs not necessarily control crimes and reduce criminality. Morality and moral principles, I repeat, are absolute and universal. But, ethics and ethical principles are purely individualistic. Each individual in his particular and specific situations makes his own principles. I repeat that ethical principles which a person has are purely subjective. Thus, we take note of Naxalite ethics, Maoist ethics, police ethics, lawyer's ethics, priests' ethics, doctor's ethics, judge's ethics etc. Therefore, if ego of a person is dominated by Naxalite ethics or Maoist ethics, then crimes and criminality may be promoted. They have the ethical principle that the 'end justifies the means'. This approach is not acceptable to the morality-principles which are absolute and universal. One's **Ethical Ego** should be formed uprightly in the right direction.

Again, the **Intelligence dominated ego** too needs not necessarily control the animal instincts and thereby reduce crime and criminality. Intelligence consists of critical analysis and the critical analysis may not be always on the basis of **Morality** principles. Take, for example, the terrorists, fundamentalists, fanatics, insurgents and so on. Their intelligence is in favour of extremism which contains murder, mass murder, genocide, looting, abduction, rapes etc. No control of animal instincts will be seen there.

In the above context, it becomes necessary to clarify **faith** or **belief** or **both** dominating in crime control and reduction. There are people who believe in a god who becomes pleased in human sacrifice. In India we see such, '**Faiths**' and in the Old Testament, Abraham takes his only son for human sacrifice. There are people who have 'Beliefs' which promote animal instincts and such 'Beliefs' are coming from pervert thinking, pervert intelligence and pervert ethics. Here I wish to emphasize that the Morality/Ethics, Spirituality and its Faith or Belief or both, Intelligence will control excessive animal instinct if and only if they are formed uprightly in the right direction. The **Pull Factors** are very important for the formation in an upright way in the right direction. The **Life Retrospect** will show how the **Pull Factors** are and therefore, criminologists look into the Life Retrospect by introspection to see how did the **Pull Factors** influenced the formation of **Ego** in an individual.

Remember that all people are structurally alike in that everyone has **Animality, Morality/Ethics, Spirituality** and **Intelligence**. People differ only in the quantum of the content of Animality, Morality/Ethics, Spirituality and Intelligence. I do not say that they remain separated in people. In all people, they overlap and resultingly, we cannot say that the animal instincts are controlled only by one of the forces (Spirituality, Morality/Ethics and Intelligence) operating. All forces work together, but one of them dominates. When **Spirituality** dominates, then morality/ ethics and intelligence too are at work. Similarly, when morality/ ethics dominates, Spirituality and Intelligence too are at work. Likewise, when intelligence dominates, then spirituality and morality/ethics too are at work. Take a mixture containing four ingredients—i.e., A, M/E, S, I [Animality, Morality/Ethics, Spirituality, Intelligence]—then the mixture will have the qualities of all of them. If the ingredient 'S' is more, then the mixture will have the qualities of that ingredient more in that mixture. This is what is called **Domination**. If the **Dominating Ingredient** is uprightly formed in the right direction, certainly it affects the commission of crimes/control of crimes. In other words, if **Animality** dominates, then crimes will be the aftereffect. On the other hand, if **Spirituality** dominates it will control the **Animality** provided the **Spirituality** is uprightly formed in the right direction. One notices in human history that gods have murdered thousands of people just because the believers in such gods were suffering from a spirituality which was not formed uprightly in the right direction by the **Pull Factors**. Pull Factors play a decisive role in the shaping of one's personality. A tree grows well depending upon the environments and likewise the personality develops in the right direction depending upon the **Pull Factors**. Religion is a powerful energy and a 'religious' does not mean that his spirituality functions always in the right way. Religious fundamentalists and fanatics commit crimes after crimes owing to their pervert personality or a personality that is not uprightly formed in the right direction.

Since the **Pull Factors** vary from person to person, every individual develops an **Ego** basing or depending upon the **Pull Factors**. People born and brought up in the low castes in India develop an **Ego** depending upon the treatment they receive from the society, culture etc. The black will develop an **Ego** basing on the treatment they receive from the white community. The poor, the physically handicapped, the illiterate, the socially privileged, the affluent, the manual labourers, the white collar professionals, the blue collar employees, the powerful and the influential and so on develop an **Ego** according to the **Pull Factors**. What is food to one will be poison to another. We live in the same society, but what a variety of thoughts! They influence us! The intelligence thinks depending upon the pull factors; the morality is shaped according to the pull factors; the ethics is developed on the basis of the pull factors. Hence, the **Life Retrospect** will explain well the activating forces to control animal instincts which operate powerfully in us.

Can crime and criminality be controlled by spirituality? Yes, spirituality can and will control the animal instincts to a certain level and thus the crime and criminality may be controlled. The role of intelligence is discussed in the chapter that follows.

5

Push-Pull-Ego Factor Theory of Crime Causation

Intelligence

Goddard said that crime was committed by people having a low I.Q. Cesare Lombroso spoke about atavism and morphological features as the causes of crimes and criminality. Atavism postulated, as pointed out earlier, a revision to the primitive or sub-human type of man. In other words, atavism is the reappearance in man (crime-doer) of the characteristics of apes (a remote ancestor in the process of Darwin's evolution) and his view that a criminal was atavistic meant a reversion to the characteristics of a remote ancestor or a primitive or earlier type—here, it is **Ape**. Lombrosian concepts were not fully accepted by criminologists like Charles Goring (1870-1919) and so on. Goring could not find any differentiating physical characteristics between criminals and non-criminals. However, he found that 'weak mindedness' was probably the most important single factor in criminality. Gabriel Tarde (1843-1904) too said that atavism and physical anomalies were common among criminals and non-criminals. Hooton supported partly Lombrosian view and Raffaele Garofale (c. 1852) too partly supported the atavistic explanation of crimes and criminality. Goddard too seemed to have taken a view that the criminals suffered from low intelligence and had the characteristics of the animal during the evolutionary process. We are not at all interested in the arguments and counter-arguments about the role of intelligence in the causation of crimes and criminality. We are keen only about the influence of intelligence in the control of animal instincts and reduction of crimes in society.

Can *Intelligence* control animal instincts and thus control and reduce crimes? Yes, certainly it can and it does. How? Binet (1909) thought of intelligence as comprising of such capabilities as (i) comprehension, (ii) inventiveness, (iii) persistence, (iv) memory and critical analysis. Criminologists are concerned with the *critical analysis* functions of intelligence. Analysis here is the process of studying the criminal nature of something or of determining its essential features and their relations with crimes and criminal behaviour. The critical analysis is also done on the basis of the morality/ethics, spirituality—i.e., faith or belief and the intelligence decides whether or not one can find a justification for the act/ omission he does. If there is an intelligent justification, then there is no crime even if it is not accepted by a large section of the people in society. How does one make an intelligent analysis?

1. Life Retrospect Analysis

Life experience is really a unique experience and no one on earth can know everything or many things of another's life experiences. A man has four areas in his mind and they are (i) **Aware to self and Aware to others;** (ii) **Aware to self and Unaware to others;** (iii) **Unaware to self and Aware to others and finally,** (iv) **Unaware to self and Unaware to others.** A person who makes a life-retrospect analyses and evaluates everything—the pros and cons—of acting in a particular way basing on his life experiences. Life has taught him a lot and his life experiences make him to take a sober decision even when he is excessively pressured or compelled by his animal instincts. We have heard many people saying: "I would have shown him my real colour; but I controlled because I learned a lesson from my past experiences". This is his life retrospect analysis.

2. Life Script Analysis

The pull factors write many things in a man's mind during his developing stage. By the help of his memory (memory is a function of intelligence), he recalls what is written in his mind. There is a proverb: "The cat that has fallen into the boiling water will be very much afraid of even cool water". Why? The script in its mind is so frightening or terrifying that it withdraws from the situation.

One may have uncontrollable animal instincts when he faces a live situation. But, he exerts very great counter forces to counterattack his instinctual temptations.

The biographies and the life experiences of many write a script in many people to follow their footsteps when they face pressuring situations. The life of every great man is a script which can be written in everyone's mind so that the instinctual (or animality) temptations can be controlled by adopting the methods the great men had followed or resorted to in their lives.

3. Subjective Scale Analysis

Everyone has his own subjective thoughts about him. 'I am so and so'; 'I have power and authority', 'I am O.K; you are not O.K', 'I am a spiritual man—god man', 'I am a woman', 'I am an old man' and these thoughts pressure him to resort to a special or particular strategy in a given situation. One's thoughts about him may not the best ones to control his animal instincts. A criminal may have the thought that criminality is not bad. He thinks that "it is the right of the poor man to misbehave" and this sort of subjective analysis may not be accepted by the moral intelligence of a sober man. The intellectual analysis of one's thoughts which are pervert ones may lead to crime and criminality. The intelligence will as well teach him to become calm and collected during a situation of tension caused by animality.

4. Normative Scale Analysis

Forget about the subjective analysis of one's behaviour in a situation of tension. People say: "I behaved emotionally and I feel sorry about it". Why? He compares his subjective analysis of his behaviour to the objective or normative principles which are in existence in his mind. The normative principles may be (i) "Don't get provoked when you are provoked by others"; "Don't get angry when you are hurt by others". These and similar rules/principles/ advice can and will control a person to abstain from instinctual or emotional behaviour. The intelligence will evaluate the merits and demerits of such principles from the Life Retrospect or Life Script as the case may be.

5. Social Scale Analysis

Social scale comes into being out of a social consensus. People get annoyed-angry-aggressive when they see waste materials including human and animal waste deposited on road, in the open market or in public places. From the social intelligence (Group Intelligence), people make agitations to compel the Governments to take appropriate steps for waste management. During the agitation, people may have recourse to mob behaviour including violent behaviour. How to control the violent behaviour of the agitating mob? Police and other law enforcement officials resort to various methods and stratagems to calm down the emotions of the mob. Social scales are the result of society's intelligence and the people are expected to abide by such social norms. If the people do not control their emotions against the social evils, then there will be chaos leading to law and order problems

6. Cultural Scale Analysis

Culture is the ways of behaviour built up in a society by a group of human beings and transmitted from one generation to another. There is the wisdom and intelligence of many generations and people behind the culture. Thus, we have the Bhahmin culture, Anglo-Indian culture, tribal culture, Christian/Muslim culture etc. They may conflict one another resulting in fights, disputes and conflicts. Criminology tells of cultural conflicts theory and cultural lag theory to explain the causes of crime. Cultural lag means the "slowness in development of one part of a culture in respect to another part". An intellectual analysis will tell us to have cultural tolerance if one wants to control crimes. In many situations, the cultural tolerance is found to be lacking. As a consequence, there will be many kinds of crimes which include mass murders, genocide, lootings, arson, rapes and molestation of women. Intelligence is overpowered by the animal instincts and negative emotions. It can be subsided only if the negative emotions are well controlled.

7. Majority Scale Analysis

The intelligence of the majority of people in the society enacts several rules and regulations to control the animality in man. This is what is supposed to take place in a democracy. The Legislators are said to be the representatives of the general public and what is enacted by them in unison or in consensus are considered to be the majority view. There is a village saying: "do an act which will please three people out of four and it means that majority in a given situation is right". The criticism against this approach is that there are situations in which the majority has gone wrong. The counter argument is that the majority is right in majority of situations. If the majority goes wrong, then it will be agitated against at least by a minority of people. There will be instinctual reactions culminating in criminality and crimes. *Sati* in India is a classical example and the *anti-sati* laws were enacted to educate the people about the ill-effects and meaninglessness of *sati*.

8. Generation Scale Analysis

Generation means the entire body of individuals born and living at about the same time. The term of years accepted is the average period between the birth of parents and the birth of their offspring. Generation gap means the lack of communication between young people and their parents or between one generation and another, brought about by differences of tastes, values and outlooks etc. A generation consists of a group of individuals—most of whom are of the same approximate age having similar ideas, problems, attitudes etc.

As far as the generation gap is a reality, there will be frustrations and conflicts between two generations. If not intelligently tackled, the conflicts and frustrations may result in crimes and criminality. The parents train their children with their social, cultural, religious etc. values which may not be acceptable for the younger generation. However, studies conducted on the relationship between generation gap and criminality prove that emotional control is the best option to compromise the two generations.

9. Custom Based Analysis

Custom means the habitual practice—i.e., a practice so long established that it has the force of law. In sociology, it means a group pattern of habitual activity usually transmitted from one generation to another. The customs prevailing in society are likely to cause crimes if not intelligently handled. For example, the patriarchal system prevailing in some societies or the matriarchal system seen in some societies create a lot of problems and conflicts. The women are treated like an inferior gender [sex] and the custom in patriarchal system is to rule over the women-folk. This indeed is not acceptable for a person who makes an intelligent analysis. The women liberation movement throughout the world and the arguments for sex-equality and gender justice are the after-effects of patriarchal customs. What about the transgender community?—about hermaphrodites? What is required is an intelligent approach and an emotional control to solve the issues.

10. Tradition Based Analysis

Tradition means the handling down of statements, beliefs, legends, customs etc. from generation to generation, especially by words of mouth or by practice. Among the Jews, tradition means an unwritten body of laws and doctrines or any one of them, held to have been received from Moses and handed down orally from generation to generation. For Christians, it is a body of teachings, or any one of them, held to have been delivered by Jesus Christ and His apostles and not committed to writing. Thus, every religion has such traditions. Some of the traditions are meaningless, yet, the 'so called' intelligent approach is to live with them rather than fight against them. Have control over emotions.

11. Morality Based Analysis

Morality and moral principles are to guide people to control their animal instincts and accompanying emotions. No one knows when did the moral laws come into being. In Hinduism and Buddhism, *Dharma* means the essential quality or nature. *Dharma* in Indian concepts speaks of *Sadharanadharma* and *Sivadharma*. If one wants to live and lead a life of a man of morality—irrespective of his age, status and occupation/profession—he must follow *Sadharanadharma*—i.e., the general code of conduct. The Puranas (i.e., any of the large number of traditional collections of epics, myths, popular lore etc. embodying the principles of popular

Hindu religion and ethics) give a list of 10 general moral principles. They are: *Ahimsa* (non-injury), *Ksama* (forbearance), *Indriyanigraha* (self-control), *Daya* (compassion), *Dana* (charity), *Sauca* (purity), *Satya* (truth), *Tapas* (penance), *Asteya* (non-stealing) and *Jnana* (wisdom). All of them are intended for man to control his animal instincts and thereby to reduce criminality.

Manu enumerates nine rules and they are (i) forbearance, (ii) forgiveness, (iii) control over mind and heart, (iv) non-stealing, (v) purity, (vi) control over senses and intellect (vii) knowledge, (viii) truth and (ix) freedom from anger. According to the *Arthashastra* of Kautilya, the list of moral rules include (i) non-injury, (ii) truth, (iii) purity, (iv) good will, (v) forgiveness and (vi) patience. I must add, justice equity, good conscience, justice related to sex, gender, age, weakness and human rights to them. "Mahabharata gives a comprehensive law:" "What is harmful to oneself, one should not do to others". This is the quintessence of morality or *dharma* and it speaks loudly about how should one control his animal instincts. The intellect of everyman endorses the same.

12. Ethics Based Analysis

Sadharanadharma gives the rules which are universal, absolute and eternal. They are to be applied to specific situations. The rules coming under *Sivadharma* which refers to specific responsibilities incumbent upon an individual person according to his stage of life and his social status are individualistic. In other words, *Sivadharma* means *ethics* which is subjective or individualistic. The intelligence of a man interprets the general rules of moral behaviour and he adopts a particular mode of behaviour as the best in a given situation. Such a behavoiur, if done, should not cause guilt feelings in him. In other words, any ethical behaviour which is not surcharged by undesirable animal instincts and unacceptable emotions is approved by the intelligence.

13. Rationalism Based Analysis

Rationalism—i.e., the principle or habit of accepting reason as the supreme authority in matters of opinion, belief or conduct. In criminology, principles of rationalism can be accepted only if they are in tune with the principles of justice, equity and good conscience. Reason and reasoning power need not necessarily be from a conscience which is uprightly formed in the right direction. The reason and the intellect may give instructions to behave in an instinctual way which may not be acceptable by the law of justice. Instinctual behaviour beyond a permissible limit is a crime and the intellect which thinks rightly will not accept it.

14. Empiricism Based Analysis

Empiricism in philosophy says that all knowledge is derived from sense experience. Sense experience means the experience derived from animal instincts. Experience derived from animal instincts beyond the permitted level is a crime. Sex is an instinct and the experience derived from the sexual instinct should be below the permitted level. According to Rationalists, any behaviour not justified by good reason and legal intelligence is a crime. Empiricism without intelligence and intellectual analysis is not accepted by criminologists as it will not control man and his behaviour to reduce crime and criminality.

15. Penological Analysis

Punishment—punishment everywhere—but no punishment eradicates or wipes off criminality. Winston Churchill once said that 'the mood and temper of the public with regard to the treatment of criminals have always been an unfailing test of civilization in any country' Why? The punishment must be awarded not by emotions, but by intelligence. Today, emotional punishments are avoided and intellectual punishments are awarded. Resultingly, the objective of punishments has come to be the 'development of right personality'—and that alone will reduce crime and criminality.

16. Correction Based Analysis

From retributive approach to crime-doers, control of crime has come to the correction of the offenders. It means that the approach has come from an utter unconcern to a person and his personality to his positive and intellectual ways of correcting the error. An intelligent analysis of the principle of *'an eye for an eye; a tooth for a tooth'* proved that the theory of *lex talionis* created more harm than good to the individuals and society. The correction of the crime-doer helps him to control his instincts and negative emotions to reformation, resocialization and reintegration to the society back as a law abiding citizen. Correction oriented intelligence always inculcates the ways and methods to control one's animal instincts to reduce crime and criminality.

17. Reformation Based Analysis

Reform means the improvement or amendment of what is wrong, corrupt or unsatisfactory etc. Reformation include an amendment of one's conduct. For the reformation or amendment of one's conduct, it is very essential to control one's animal instincts, and accompanying emotions.

18. Hedonism Based Analysis

Hedonism which says that pleasure or happiness is the highest good may not be acceptable to the intelligence. Pleasure up to what level? Any pleasure beyond a level becomes displeasure to others. Hence, devotion to pleasure as a way of life will cause crimes and criminality. The intelligence realizes this truth and therefore it puts many restrictions and controls over the pleasures of the earthly life. Precisely therefore the Classical School of Criminology insisted to award punishments (pain) proportionate to the pleasure one enjoyed and that was called the imposition of punishment basing on a hedonistic calculus. This approach was adopted when the penal codes were drafted in many countries and it helped to some extent for the people to control their pleasure giving instincts.

19. Epicureanism Based Analysis

Epicurean thoughts tell us that luxurious tastes or habits, especially in eating and drinking is everything in life. The approach encourages animal instincts and makes people to behave like animals. Animal-like behaviour dangerous in social life is or ought to be controlled by morality/ethics, intelligence and spirituality. Eating and drinking is very important, but is not everything in life. In studies, it was proved that maternal instinct (mother's instinct to her children) is the strongest instinct in man and it means that the instinct of food-seeking is less powerful than the maternal instinct. Certainly, it can be controlled and there are people who commit suicide or starve until death to achieve a noble aim.

20. Demonological Analysis

Devils do only wrong things and demonological approach says that the devils instigate people to commit crimes. This prescientific approach has its roots in explanations which were not scientific. Demon, devil, satan and so on exist only in one's imagination or phatasy. It has no support of the intelligence of man. Demonology does not accept animal instincts and accompanying negative emotions as causes of crimes. There is a fight between demonology and rationalism, empiricism, idealism etc. Demons are invisible and therefore, they cannot be punished. If the crime-doer is possessed by demons/devils, then no criminal liability can be fixed on the crime-doers. Intelligence throws away demonological analysis of crime and delinquency.

21. Psychotherapeutic Analysis

Manias are punished. Phobias are not. Some of the mental disorders can be cured and in such cases, intellectual explanation will be: '*treat the crime-doer psychologically*' rather than by any other inhuman methods. Some people have excessive animal instincts and they become negatively emotional. Some people have an inadequate formation of their superego. In both cases, what is required is not punishments for their wrong doings; rather they should be psychologically and intelligently treated. Intellectual evaluation of the wrong doings of those who suffer from psychological disorders will make them criminally not liable for their otherwise criminal acts. For, they do not know the nature of the act or what they are doing is contrary to law. Of course, intelligence is a powerful energy to control the animal instincts in man, but becomes helpless when crimes are committed by people who suffer from some type of mental disorders.

22. Internet Based Analysis

Internet has become a cause of criminality and crimes. People who are addicted to internet use misuse the facility, sometimes, to commit crimes. The criminal morphing, sexual pervertions, black mailing, vulgar talks and scenes, blue sex and many such immoral and irreligious activities are seen in the social media. Facebook, Twitter, Blogs, You Tube etc. are misused by some people to commit immoral or illegal acts.

The animal instincts in some make them to make use of internet facility to commit a lot of economic crimes, bank frauds, cheating, sexual exploitation, fake advertisement, *Mafia* activities, organized crimes etc. The law is helpless to initiate legal action against many internet crimes as the criminals operate their crimes from countries which cannot be reached easily by the investigating team. Intelligence alone can save the people from internet crimes.

23. Theology Based Analysis

Theology is the field of study, thought and analysis that treats of God, His attributes, and His relations to the universe. Theopathy is the religious emotion excited by the contemplation of God and many who claim to be the god-men exploit people with ulterior motives originated from their animal instincts. Such people are not god-men, rather are animal-men who make use of or misuse their religious status to commit crimes. Addiction to prayer is a psychological problem and they can be subjected to various kind of exploitation by those who wear religious garb. Intelligence or intellectual analysis may work against them and if successful, then crimes can be reduced. The 'god-men' speak out a lot of lies and falsehood-theophany, i.e., manifestation or appearance of God or of a god to man—to psychologically and intelligently impress upon those addicted to prayer to acts which are believed to be pleasing to God/gods. It is virtually impossible for the intelligence to win over the animal instincts found operative in god-men and as such difficult to control crime and criminality.

24. Superstition Based Analysis

Superstition has many meanings and they are (i) an irrational belief in or notion of the ominous significance of a particular thing, circumstance, or the like; (ii) a system or collection of such beliefs, (iii) a custom or act based on such a belief, (iv) irrational fear of what is unknown, especially, in connection with religion, (iv) any blindly accepted belief or notion. My studies on those who suffer from superstition give me enough proof to assert that any amount of rational arguments or intellectual discussions will not make them to desist from the commission/omission of the acts they do. The **pull factors** during their infancy and childhood are so strong that they are not susceptible to any kind of intellectual discourses. They continue to commit crimes and cases are reported in plenty to show the crimes committed by people who suffer from superstition. Even internet facilities are misused for this purpose and people commit murder, suicide, human sacrifice, looting, sexuals exploitation etc. as a result of their superstition. No morality, no spirituality, no intelligence generally will be capable of or powerful enough to control the animal instincts of those who act upon superstition.

25. *'...ology-...sophy-...ism'*

There are a lot of '....ologies', '....sophies 'and '.....isms' which are powerfully operating in the present day society. The animal instincts seen behind Maoism, Terrorism, Fundamentalism, Fanatism etc. are causes of many types of crimes including bank robbery, genocide, abduction etc. The animal instincts found behind the philosophies which promote crimes and criminality are many. There is a new word coined by me and, as said earier, I call it **'Theosophism'** which means *theology, sociology and philosophy* which cause crime and criminality. **Theosophy** is any of the various forms of philosophy or religious thought claiming a mystical insight into the divine nature. I have seen such 'divinities' who mint a lot of money and the structures and wealth they have may be beyond human imagination. Those who are addicted to religious fundamentalism fight one another in the name of gods. They have battle with gods and the battle among the gods (theomachy) cause a lot of crimes. I find that any kind or amount of intellectual discussions or intelligent arguments will not force them to abstain from the expression of their animal instinct to commit crimes and criminality.

26. Heredity Based Analysis

Heredity is the transmission of genetic characters from parents to offspring, dependent upon the segregation and recombination of genes during meiosis and fertilization. Heredity gives potency for development and the development of the potentialities depends heavily upon the **pull factors** (environments). If the **pull factors** are very powerful for the development of a particular animal instinct, then certainly, it will develop accordingly. Provide the pull factors for developing cruelty, then it will be developed. Hence, if one wants to see that the criminality is not developed, provide sufficient pull factors to develop moral values, spiritual values (positive) and intellectual exposition for desirable personality traits. Reading of books containing values of terrorism, fundamentalism, religious bigotry etc. will cause problems and issues. Viewing of crime movies and enjoying discussions on the commission of crimes and criminality will have, normally, bad effects and impacts on developing children. Therefore, it is suggested that the **pull factors** should be praiseworthy so that moral, spiritual and intellectual values are inculcated to children if one wants to control animal instincts and thereby to reduce crime and criminality.

27. Witchcraft Based Analysis

To quote James C. Coleman—"During the latter part of the nineteenth century, beliefs concerning demonical possessions took a horrible turn for the worse... possessions in which the individual was actually in league with the devil. The latter persons were supposed to have made a pact with devil, consummated by signing in blood a book presented to them by Satan which gave them certain supernatural powers. They could cause pestilence, storms, floods, sexual impotence, injuries to their enemies, and ruination of crops, and could rise through the air, cause milk to sour, and turn themselves to animals. In short, they were witches". The history of witchcrafts in crime causation is horrible and painful and the days of persecution are unthinkable now. Intelligence could do nothing to solve the problems connected with witchcraft. The witch mania is still found in some people and no intellectual arguments can convince them of the foolery of witchcraft torture. The animal instinct seems to be very powerful.

28. Socio-Cultural Factors Based Analysis

Society, out of its intellectual analysis, makes rules and laws to regulate the activities *hic et nunc*. The social law is that there should be religious, communal, political harmony in society. But what do we see today?

The society has a culture and there are cultural laws. 'Respect the elders and Teachers' is a cultural law. That is a social law too. So far so good! Ours is a society which has a caste system. There are high castes and low castes. There was a time when untouchability was in existence. Today we do not see (?) untouchability between the high castes and low castes in many places in India. Yet, the cultural laws do not allow the high castes and low castes to come closer—beyond a line. The reluctantly accepted social law is that they must come closer to the extent of marrying without caste considerations. Among the low castes, there exist cultural conflicts. The society has many groups on the basis of politics and one sees conflicts between political parties and religious groups. An intellectual analysis will convince anybody that communal conflicts and religious bigotry, caste discrimination etc. are the expressions of animal instincts and undesirable emotions. What to do? How to go about, if the people are not prepared to abide by the emerging social laws?

29. Endocrinology: Chromosomes Based Analysis

Endocrinology is the science dealing with the endocrine glands and their secretions, especially, in relation to their process or functions. Endocrine malfunctioning was considered to be a cause of crime. The explanation is rejected by criminologists owing to the dearth of sufficient scientific evidence to prove the same. If endocrine malfunctioning is the cause of crime and criminality, treat the disease medically. Intelligence has nothing much to do.

XYY chromosomal pattern is brought to explain criminal behaviour. XXY or Kline Filter Syndrome has been linked with antisocial behaviour, especially alcoholism and homosexuality. XXYY males exhibit generally the same physical features of XXY males. XYY males are of special interest to criminologists. However, the explanation given by those who connect chromosomal abnormality to criminal behaviour lack clarity and enough scientific evidence. It is found to be only a modern version of demonism. Here too intelligence has nothing much to do. They need medical treatment.

30. Victimology Based Analysis

Victimology is essentially a study of crime from the point of view of the victims. A victim is a person who, owing to an unlawful act, has sustained moral, spiritual, material, physical or intellectual damage. In some cases, the victims are found to be the cause of crimes. They may provoke the crime-doers. The attitude of the victims of crime may be of 'submitting, conniving, passively submitting, co-operating, contributory, provocative, instigative and/or soliciting. In plain words, we take note of the fact that in certain cases, the crime-doers and the victims are activated by the same animal instincts or by different animal instincts. As a result, the crime has occurred. The intelligence may have the power to control the instincts in the victims and the victims of crime become so because he/she neglects the intellect's imperatives—i.e., do not go close or closer to the crime doer. There are different kinds of victims and some are innocent victims. If the crime doers are not controlled by the moral or spiritual imperatives, then the victim/s ought to listen to their intellect's imperatives.

31. Personality Based Analysis

Personality, as a rule, refers to the total behaviour (including criminal behaviour) of a person or individual. Personality consists of the values which determine the characteristic ways in which a person behaves on crucial issues—i.e., the *character* and the basic emotional patterns—characteristics of an individual—i.e., *temperament*. Emotions accompany animal instincts. The **pull factors** have a great role to play for the formation of one's personality. All social values are good if they are morally acceptable. Again all spiritual values are good if they are reasonable, rational and sensible to human intellect. The intelligence decides the acceptability of the values and shapes the personality. That is the reason why Gordon W. Allport said "Personality system is a complex product of biological endowment, cultural shaping, *cognitive style* and spiritual groping". Crimes and criminality can be controlled only if the personality is shaped by an upright intelligence in an upright way.

32. Geography and Topography Based Analysis

In early nineteenth century, geographers said that the climate was the cause of crime (Thermal theory). According to them, crimes against human body were committed owing to hotter climate and the same against property were owing to colder climate. They did not say anything much about crimes other than the crimes against human body and the same against property. There were many other crimes [e.g., cyber crimes] which intelligence designed and executed. By 1830, statisticians interpreted crimes on the basis of socio-economic conditions which prevailed in society and they asserted that socio-economic conditions were the cause of crime. Topography spoke about high altitude, coastal area etc. as causes of crime. Apparently the geographers, statisticians and topographers seemed to be right, but actually, they failed to appreciate the role of intelligence in causing and controlling of crimes and criminality. Intelligence with the right moral and spiritual values can and will control animal instincts and thereby reduce crimes and criminality. This can happen anywhere and everywhere whatever may be the geography, climate or topography. There are countries where the climate changes are not very visible (e.g., Kerala); there are countries where the geography and topography are the same, but the crimes committed in different countries having the same climate change very considerably. Hence, it is argued that morality and spirituality with an upright intelligence is the best to control animal instincts and thereby crimes and criminality.

33. Family Based Analysis

A family is a community of people emotionally connected. Criminologists believe that everyone should feel at home in his family. Home is built by emotions and not by bricks. The emotional relationship within the home (family) must be marked by *mutuality*.

Mutuality needs togetherness not only in bodily or physical matters, but also at the emotional, moral, intellectual and spiritual aspects. The members in a family live together in mutual understanding.

A problem family is said to be a cause for crimes and criminality. Why? There is no emotional sharing in such families. 'How to share the emotions' must be the main concern in any family, but the animal instincts in the individual do not permit the sharing of pleasant emotions. The intellect says that the companionship is not only an individual's birth right, but also a natural human need. There should be an emotional (positive) relationship between man and woman. That is not seen. The relationship seems to be instinctual (negative) and that is the reason why divorce, separation, desertion are seen in an incredible way in the modern families. The ancient love-poems from Egypt, Mesopotamia and Sumeria show the rich tradition of positive emotions in ancient families there. The films, print media, sermons in churches, poems, literature show the need for emotional (positive) families and the intelligence supports such families to reduce crimes.

34. Mass Media Based Analysis

Mass media without moral values may be dangerous and without spiritual values (rational and reasonable) may be very dangerous. For example, some governments stop the publication of communal riots, religious bigotry, racial conflicts etc. in the print and visual media. They do so because the publicity will create an epidemic in commission of crimes. The media teach and the people learn by suggestion, imitation and identification etc. Intelligent media containing moral and spiritual (reasonable and rational) values may be the best to control animal instincts (negative) in human beings. Sex pervertions, crimes, cruelty, smuggling, value distortions, *Mafia*, crime syndicates etc. are projected as noble in the mass media and the weak minded people are attracted to such immoral and criminal acts. The benumbing of the intelligence makes the people to become sterile to such criminality in society. Parents, teachers, religious preachers, moralists, civic minded citizens, the governments, universities, therapy centres, family building organizations must come forward with intelligent instructions to bring down crimes and criminality.

35. Stress and Frustration Based Analysis

Stress and frustrations are closely related to conflicts. Stress means 'any stimulus, as fear or pain, that disturbs or interferes with the normal physiological equilibrium of an organism'. Animals and men have them. As far as human beings are concerned, it is the physical, psychological, moral/ethical, intellectual, spiritual or emotional strain or tension. Frustration means making a plan or effort etc. worthless or of no avail. It is a barrier thwarting a person from reaching a goal. As far as a crime-doer is concerned, he is in a state of frustration or mental conflicts at least just before the commission of a crime. Any moral advice or spiritual exhortation may not be successful. If they are given in an intelligent way—convincingly—then it may work wonders. The psychological counsellors and therapists do so and in prisons, the correctional staff always make attempts to inculcate moral and spiritual values (reasonable and rational) into the convicts. There are reformed convicts who are resocialized and reintegrated to the society after their incarceration.

36. Poverty Based Analysis

During 1940s, criminologists in the West conducted a number of studies to know the correlation between poverty and crime. Some of them found that there was a positive correlation between the two. My studies on poverty and crimes show to me that the poor people usually commit poor crimes (value of the property stolen is not that high) and the affluent people generally commit affluent crimes (value of property will be unimaginably very high). Poverty stricken people commit crimes which have more of a nuisance value and the ordinary policemen handle such criminals in iron hands. The affluent people commit shark crimes of affluence to which even higher-ups in law enforcement and politics keep their eyes shut. No action is generally taken against them. Moral values, spiritual values and sober advice from the intelligence do not work well and effectively with poor people. Even the released convicts become recidivists and most of them are poor people who are pick-pockets, burglars, dacoits and so on. If poverty is eradicated by intelligent methods, then a solution can be sought out. Financially, poor people commit crimes out of their animal instincts and intelligence alone cannot solve the problems.

37. Unemployment Based Analysis

Unemployment and underemployment have been the sociological factors for many to involve in the commission of crimes which include even drug trafficking, smuggling, gang crimes, *Mafia* crimes etc. Some of the unemployed tell me that moral advice and values will not provide jobs for the unemployed. They say further that spiritual preachings and values cannot offer employment to the unemployed. What is required is an intelligent management of the financial resources so that maximum employment opportunities are created. Unemployment is a powerful **pull factor** leading to crimes and criminality. Class conflicts want to make unemployment as an industry so that maximum number of youth turn into anti-government activities in the form of protests which will include damages to public property etc. The animal instincts in the unemployed are exploited for the political advantages. Nothing may stop them from violent agitations until employment is provided.

38. Bureaucracy Based Analysis

Bureaucracy means the government characterized by a rigid hierarchy of bureaus, administrators, and petty officials. Interestingly enough, a bureaucrat means an official who works by fixed routine without exercising intelligent judgment. In many countries one may see a corrupt bureaucracy and in democratic countries, the bureaucracy may be controlled by the political parties in power. The fortune seeking bureaucrats may do anything if they are humoured and thus the bureaucratic crimes are plenty. The unholy nexus among the political leaders, bureaucrats, businessmen, middle men, *goondas* and so on are very notorious and together they mint money, exploit the general public, loot the masses, consume the tax payers' hard earned money by various nefarious methods. Morality/ethics, spirituality (rational and reasonable) and intelligence (positive) may not work with them. As a result, the animal instincts become uncontrollable forces and energy to violate the laws for their advantages. Punishments and disciplinary actions have little effects in preventing bureaucratic criminals.

39. Organized Crime (Syndicate) Based Analysis

Organized crime has an Oyster Bay definition and accordingly the objective of the syndicate is to wring exorbitant profits from the society through the commission of crimes. The oldest form of such a crime is **prostitution.** The **criminal fence** is another form practiced from ancient times. **Smuggling** into and out of the country, **the drug traffic, hooch production, storage and sale,** gambling, **the numbers, policy, bolita, lookie, illegal lottery, horse race gambling, racketeering, loan sharking,** and thus we take note of organized crimes committed in very many ways—starting form Advertisement and going through Boxing.... Football..... News Services.... Real Estate..... Transportation... to Zooplasty. Extortion, protection rackets, counterfeiting of nationally famous products, production of blue films and other preserve forms of sexual diversions, manufacture of spurious medicines and contraband articles etc. are indicative of the new patterns of organized criminality and its penetration into legal business enterprises. As the animal instincts have surcharged energy to involve in the commission of crimes, intelligence, morality and spirituality have no importance to control them.

40. Affluence Based Analysis

Affluence means abundance of money, property etc. wealth and presently we take note of very wealthy people absconding from India after committing crimes. They cheat the banks and today (3-5-2018), there is the news of a businessman who absconded from India after cheating a bank (the amount is 25,000 crores of Indian rupees). The corporate crimes are increasing incredibly in India and they become richer and richer by their criminality. They have unholy nexus with the politicians of the ruling government and they include 'honourable' Ministers and highly positioned/ respected bureaucrats. They commit crimes with the connivance of the police, income tax, enforcement directorate, advocates and some unscrupulous judicial officers. Who will bell the cat? And the corporate flourish well with full immunity. The ball is passed by one official authority to another and that authority passes the ball and the play is going on in cheer and joy. The crimes they commit make the nation pauper and the people suffer the consequences. They purchase the media and they support the corporates. Every nexus partner in corporate crimes jump—and theirs is the frog jump and the satellite thus goes even to the space. People do not and cannot see it by their naked eyes. Morality, spirituality and intelligence cannot overpower them and the criminality flourishes.

41. 'Political' Based Analysis

What are the political crimes? They are not defined in the penal codes, because politicians do not want a definition for political crimes. Nevertheless, sedition, spying, assassination of political power or overthrowing a government etc. may be enumerated under political crimes. Kittrie enumerates the following offences under political crimes. They are (i) Treason, (ii) Sedition, (iii) Espionage, (iv) Acts endangering the external security of a State, (v) Rebellion and (vi) Incitement to civil war. They are, according to him, offences exclusively against the sovereign authority of a country and precisely therefore he calls such crimes as purely political offence.

There is a common saying that the politics has no morality. Everything is justified in politics (?). Politicians say that 'lambs alone may not save our world; nor will lions take us to any length'. Political crimes are natural, necessary and inevitable in a society so that people will get better administration and governments. If that is the view, where is the place for morality, spirituality and intelligence?

42. Unholy Nexus Based Analysis

Holy nexus seems to be a *tamasha* and unholy nexus is a reality. Many people have noble aims including spiritual objectives when they begin a holy nexus and often it is proved that the holy nexus is not really holy. It is something established only in the pretext of nexus. On the other hand, there are any number of unholy nexuses, the purpose or objective is to make exhorbitant money or to serve purely the parochial interest of the nexus partners. Thus we have local nexuses, regional nexuses, state-wide nexuses, national nexuses and international nexuses. The nexus can be between two individuals, among a group of people, among many enterprises including institutions established under the Constitution of a country. The JEL crimes are examples in point to show the unholy nexus established among the institutions under the Constitution of a country. JEL crimes, as stated elsewhere, mean the crimes committed by Judiciary, Executive and Legislature being or becoming nexus partners. Sometimes, the media too join with the JEL partners. As the partners are highly influential and affluent, no one can fight against them forcefully. The result is that the crimes flourish in society. Morality, Spirituality and Intelligence helplessly look at the partnership as they are helpless to react. The animal instincts overpower the MESI (Morality, Ethics, Spirituality and Intelligence).

43. Law Enforcement Based Analysis

Law enforcement means a lot in a democracy. I made a study and I could unearth nearly 600 types of enforcement crimes committed by law enforcement officials [Police] during the course of their profession. If we take the officials dealing with crime and criminality, the enforcement crimes start with registration of false cases and proceeds via illegal arrests, unauthorized detention, violation of human rights, employment of torture, misuse of authority, abuse of power, concoction of evidence, production of false witnesses... to exercise of pseudo-authority and corruption and malpractices to extort money and fortunes. Do they have guilt feelings when they do so? Do they have the fear of punishments when they do so? The law enforcers become the law violators and 'all is well that ends well'. They are rewarded for the excellent work done during enforcement. Their outstanding performance is eulogized by 'everyone'. However, their law of conscience alone may have a different view for the work done by them.

Morality/Ethics fails; Spirituality fails; Intelligence ceases to express its capabilities and analytical powers. Animality alone overpowers and result is a multitude of enforcement crimes!

44. Judiciary Based Analysis

Judiciary is said to be the last hope in a democracy and that is what the lawyers and the vested interests propagate. But some judges of the Supreme Court (including a Chief Justice of India) and High Courts are having a different opinion. According to some judges, a section of the judicial officers are corrupt and susceptible to temptations. How sad it is to see such judges who are, sometimes, accused of crimes against women. The judges are criticized by the media so much so that the public trust on judiciary is at best suspicious or ridiculous.

The judicial officers are blamed to show partiality and forgive me, Oh God, a vast majority of those convicted for death penalty come from low castes. Out of 386 persons convicted for capital punishment in India [2013-2015], ¾ were members of the minority communities and *Dalits*. 75 per cent were economically very poor. There was a time the blacks were punished for capital punishment by the white judges in the West. The judiciary consisting of the Bench and the Bar are accused of administering less justice, wounded justice, no justice and injustice. Some judicial officers lack education and training and they administer justice in their own way. The morality, spirituality and intelligence do not have much importance in reducing the crimes in judiciary or control criminality among the judicial functionaries.

45. Gender and Sex Based Analysis

The distinction between sex justice and gender justice is not clear to many. Academicians may say that sex is biological and gender is socio-cultural. No doubt, there is miscarriage of justice in this area; but more injustice is seen to the justice (?) administered to the members of the transgender community and hermaphrodites. They are abused sexually and not treated always as people with dignity. Girl children are sexually abused by the near and dear to them (including the father, step-father, brother, uncles and so on) and rape cases reported go up at an alarming rate. The convictions for such cases are around 20 per cent. The discrimination shown to women is very visible in the case of wages and no special care is given to the special needs of women at working place. There is sexual harassment at work places and the flesh trade is in full swing not only in urban areas, but also in rural areas.

The animal instinct—sex—and the accompanying emotion called lust are not controlled by morality, spirituality and intelligence properly. As a result, sex crimes and gender injustice seen in society is beyond human imagination.

46. Human Rights Based Analysis

Human rights?—What are they and why they are? Even some of the senior level police functionaries and judicial officers seem to be ignorant about them. Resultingly, they tolerate human rights violations; ignore them and at times, encourage them. Human rights violations are seen in all Government departments, but action is taken, mostly, against police functionaries. Complaints against police are flowing to Human Rights Commissions in hundreds. The Human Rights Commissions in India, as the allegation goes, are Commissions without teeth and nail. The Protection of Human Rights Act does not confer powers to the Commission so much so that the decisions of the Commission are at times ignored and at other times reluctantly implemented. Today, one sees human rights violations in all fields and the governments are partly deaf and blind. Government officials continue to commit human rights violations in many ways and remedy to such violations seldom comes within a reasonable time. This is injustice which no morality or spirituality or intelligence can tolerate or approve of. The animal instincts of the government officials find expression in violating human rights laws—relating to life, equality, freedom and dignity.

47. Equal Justice Based Analysis

Justice to the crime-doer, to the victim of crime/abuse of power or misuse of authority, to the society and tax-payers, to the judicial system itself in an equal way is what is called **Equal Justice**. Criminal justice is different from victim justice. Both are different from just justice claimed to be administered by the judicial system. The system must conduct a self-examination and say whether or not it administers justice to the justice system itself in an enviable way. Yes, justice must be administered and it should appear to all that justice has been administered. This is not seen in these days, because the tax-payers who maintain the system do not have a feeling that justice is done to them. The distributive system of justice gives full satisfaction to all. How? The system honours morality and moral principles, spirituality and its principles, intelligence and its analysis. Justice system gets applause from the general public if only and only if it is transparent and accountable to the public. Justice should be awarded in time. Any undue delay caused to administer justice is a miscarriage of justice and in such instances, every verdict of acquittal is a miscarriage of justice. Let everyone get justice-equal justice in time.

48. *a priori* Based Analysis

a priori means 'from a general law to a particular instance'. Immanuel Kant (1724-1804), a German philosopher is associated with this concept. There are principles in jurisprudence and the principle which is general is applied to particular instance. Many of the principles applied in criminal cases are taken from ancient Roman Law and it seems that some of them need amendment in the changed socio-cultural-politico-economic situations. They are not done and precisely therefore the justice administered on the basis of the 'general law' in the ancient times becomes today injustice or less justice, no justice or miscarriage of justice. For example, the most applauded principle in Roman Jurisprudence is 'let one hundred criminals go unpunished, no innocent person must be punished'. No. The present principle is or should be: 'one hundred criminals should not go unpunished and no innocent person should be punished'. Why? Hundred criminals going unpunished is a grave crime and injustice and it should not be allowed. The Roman Jurisprudence will not, in some cases, help to control crime and reduce criminality. The analysis of the intelligence goes wrong in the applications of the Roman Jurisprudence. Again, the acquisitorial system and the inquisitorial system—the principles behind both systems will ensure miscarriage of justice. Precisely therefore it will not be helpful to control crime and reduce criminality. Noquisitorial system[1] of justice is now favoured.

49. Social Justice Based Analysis

Constitution of India speaks about social justice and what does it mean? The rich become richer and the poor become 'more and more' poor. There may the pulpit preachings, parliament discussions, platform addresses, election promises, street corner meetings, debates, workshops, classes and university courses about social justice. As no social justice is seen, the animal instincts in the socially handicapped people burn and they result in the commission of crimes including Naxal attacks, Maoist activities, political agitations etc. Social activists tell me—"No one listens to the social injustice when it is exposed. 20 per cent do not care to listen and 80 per cent forget it if at all heard". The affluent, the corporate, the powerful, the political leaders and 'religious men' are glad that there exists social injustice. For, they can cash on it if there is social injustice. They survive on social injustice!

Intelligence speaks about the morality of social injustice and suggests many ways and methods by which crimes to establish social justice are controlled or reduced. Land reforms, minimum wages for work, labour legislations, sex-equality regulations etc. are the result of the role played by the intelligence against social injustice—less justice—wounded justice and miscarriage of justice.

50. Noquisitorial System Based Analysis

What is the 'Noquisitorial System' of Justice administration? Experience hitherto teach that neither the acquisitorial (adversary) system of justice administration nor the inquisitorial system of justice administration proves to be good to administer *just justice*. Hence, the intelligence finds out an alternative and that is 'Noquisitorial System' of justice administration. In such a system, neither the prosecution nor the defence is favoured by the justice system. The justice system is built on the premise—that is, a basis stated or assumed—on which reasoning proceeds. In this system, the accused is neither presumed guilty nor innocent. The principle followed is that he 'may or may not be' guilty or 'may or may not be' innocent. The burden of proof lies on the prosecution or defence who wants to establish its stand.

The instincts in the officers of prosecution are found to be the cause of many crimes during investigation and prosecution. They abuse their power and misuse their authority in the accusatorial system of justice. The defence behaves instinctively to prove their innocence by concocting evidence and manipulating records in the inquisitorial system of justice administration. Instincts more than intelligence, morality, spirituality play their role in both systems of justice administration. Intelligence coupled with morality finds a solution by the 'Noquisitorial System' of justice administration. No presumption either in favour or against any one is seen so much so that justice is ensured better in Noquisitorial System of justice administration.

Control of Crime and Criminality by Intelligence

Intelligence tests conducted on the convicts in prisons and on people outside the jails have shown that there was no marked difference between the two population. There will not be any marked differences between the two population. Why? I am of the firm view that many real criminals live outside the prisons. People escape conviction from court of law by various methods and the prison population consists of individuals who are from low economic strata of the society. They could not employ expensive lawyers who extract huge amount of money. How many political leaders, highly placed bureaucrats, white collar professionals, veteran lawyers, efficient law enforcement officials, 'pious and religious' men who are corrupt committing crimes are seen in the prisons? Seldom they are convicted or if at all convicted, they get out of the prisons from the appeal court. Today, god men, *Avathars*, leaders of social welfare organizations, NGOs, voluntary agencies, religious heads and pious men and divinities are accused of many crimes including sex-scandals and looting people.

Crime-doers are intelligent people and it can be proved by administering intelligence tests. What I find among them is that they are not able to apply their intelligence with morality and spirituality (values) to overpower the animality (animal instincts) in them. In other words, animality overpowers their morality, spirituality and intelligence.

Kerala is a small State in Southern India having a population of less than 3½ crores and the prisons accommodate less than 4000 convicts at a time. What does it mean? It means that the intelligence tests carried out to measure the I.Q. of the convicts in prisons is meaningless and ridiculous. Take the intelligence test to the Income-tax officers, to doctors in multi-speciality hospitals, to administers in the corporates, to highly placed businessmen, to the top level government administers, to the leaders of political parties, to those who stay in the suites in seven star hotels, to the members of higher judiciary, to the owners of the factories and companies, to the managers of the self-financing educational institutions, to administrators of the charity centres, to the reputed NGOs, to the 'religious' and 'pious' institutions, to the organized syndicates, to the banks and other financial institutions, to the so-called Divinities etc. When the intelligence test is administered to the personalities in such places, one may get high and very high I.Q. without Morality and Spirituality. Moral and spiritual (rational and reasonable) spheres will be alien to those people who are highly intelligent.

Intelligence tests to measure the I.Q, of the crime-doers has never been the research areas of psychologists so far although the first practical use of such tests was seen in France at the beginning of 20th century. A psychologist named Binet developed an objective test to select the less capable school children who must be admitted in special schools. The American version of this test by Terman called Stanford-Binet test is internationally accepted and used now. Other tests for both children and adults were developed later. However, I am not aware of any tests developed so far to measure the I.Q. or the intelligence with or without *Morality and spirituality* of crime-doers anywhere. Crime and criminality were not at all a special area of interest for Intelligence test psychologists in India or abroad.

In order to assist in the classification of service personnel during World War I, psychologists developed the Army Alpha and Army Beta group tests of intelligence. Similar group tests were utilized by educators and criminologists. Criminologists went to prisons to find out the criminals and the objective of such tests on the convicted was to find out the I.Q. and compare it with the general public. It was wrong to do so. The armed services, schools and industries in the West used the I.Q. tests for the benefit of the institution, rather than that of the individuals. In other words, the purpose was to choose/select individuals for specific purposes. The I.Q. tests conducted on the convicts were of no use as the results got out of conducting such tests were of no use either in the correction of the inmates or in their reformation, resocialization and reintegration to the society back. People violate not only State-made laws (seen in Penal Codes), but also violate social, cultural, institutional, moral, ethical, religious laws. They are not seen in prisons as convicted inmates. They live outside the jails.

The definition of intelligence itself has been a difficult problem. Then what is the definition of '*criminal intelligence*'. About *intelligence,* most psychologists have no difficulty to agree that individuals who do well on tasks involving judgment, attention, memory, vocabulary etc. are intelligent. Such information are of little use for criminologists and penologists. There is something called 'social intelligence' which means the 'ability to deal with people'. People having 'social intelligence' may commit crimes against property, forgery, organized crimes, white collar criminality etc. Push-Pull-Ego Factor theory of crime causation is not at all concerned with the I.Q. level in mechanical intelligence, conceptual intelligence, pious and religious intelligence, moral intelligence etc.

Push-Pull-Ego Factor theory of crime causation raises the question: 'Whether heredity or environment is a more important determinant of intelligence?' Psychological studies of identical twins and fraternal twins suggested that intellectual ability is determined partly through heredity. The environment factors are also extremely important in influencing intellectual development. The **Push-Pull-Ego-Factor** theory puts the same question differently—i.e., whether or not **Pull factors** or **Push factors** more important as a determinant of criminal intelligence. By criminal intelligence we mean an intellectual analysis which favour the commission of crimes or criminality. Such an intelligence will have morality-spirituality interpreted in such a way that criminality will be the result. **Push factors** interact with **pull factors** and the result is an **Ego Factor** which favours criminality. The animal instincts come under **Push Factors** and the environment comes under **Pull Factors.** Heredity consists of the animal instincts too. My observations and studies show that the **pull factors** (criminal or crime producing environments) lead to the formation of a personality favouring the commission of crimes and the same (non-criminal environments) lead to a personality development which does not favour crime and criminality. The I.Q. of the individual develops accordingly through the interaction between the **Push** and **Pull factors.**

Intelligence has creativity or intuitiveness; Some crime-doers are 'more creative' and some are 'less creative'. This depends upon the **pull factors.** Intelligence has comprehension, expansion, reasoning and analysis, memory, intuitiveness as its qualities. All these are developed owing to the **Pull Factors** provided to each one.

How Does the Ego Factor Differ in People?

All individuals are structurally alike in that they all have an **Animality,** a **Morality/Ethics,** a **Spirituality** with **Faith** or **Belief,** and an **Intelligence**. It may be pointed out at the outset that the Animality, Morality/Ethics, Spirituality and Intelligence will be unique in every individual in content. They also will be unique in the working or functioning of the Animality, Morality/Ethics, Spirituality and Intelligence.

I studied 306 murderers who were convicted for life imprisonment and I could unearth the background of each one of them. I could learn that the **pull factors** for them were not very conducive to develop their **intelligence** in an upright way in the right direction. This was contaminated. Ideally, the AM/E SI (Animality, Morality/Ethics. Spirituality, Intelligence) Squares are separate. In many people, the squares overlap. I call this overlap in the squares as **contamination**.

Fig. 5.1: The Ideal Squares in an Individual.

Fig. 5.2: The Contaminated Squares in an Individual.

The contamination of the Intelligence can be not only with Spirituality as shown in Fig. 5.2, but also with Morality/Ethics as shown in Fig. 5.3

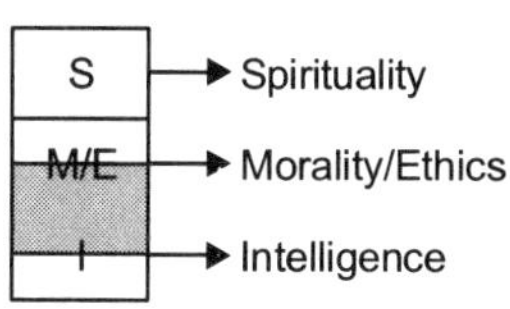

Fig. 5.3: Contamination of morality/ethics with intelligence.

In my view, the morality principles are universal, eternal and absolute. But it can be applied to a particular way—subjectively. When individualistic interpretation is given, individuals will take up an approach of committing crimes. The intelligence accepts it and thus the intelligence is contaminated with an individualistic morality. For example:

1. The Morality principle is: 'Don't become corrupt and make money'. The individualistic interpretation is: 'There is nothing wrong in becoming a corrupt person if one's salary is very poor'. In other words, the poor man can become corrupt to make money. The *Intelligence* accepts this subjective interpretation and does not overpower the *Animal Instinct* which expresses a sort of greed to make money. Crime is the result.
2. The Spirituality principle is: 'God punishes the corrupt man'. The individualistic interpretation is that God who is omniscient knows the financial problems and will forgive the wrong-doer. The *intelligence* accepts this subjective interpretation and does not overpower the Animal Instinct to make money by corrupt practices.

In other words, the *Contaminated Intelligence* makes an individual to involve in the commission of crimes and criminality. Again, the *Intelligence* can be contaminated by Morality/Ethics and Spirituality. For example:

1. The Morality principle is: 'Never, ever cheat a person'. The subjective interpretation is that cheating a person means a dishonest action without integrity of character. *Intelligence* accepts it as a noble advice and overpowers the *Animal Instincts* which are then subdued.
2. The Spirituality principle is that 'God will reward those who look after their old parents when they are sick'. The individualistic interpretation is 'Yes, it is' and the old parents are not ignored. Here, the *Intelligence* overpowers the *Animal Instincts* and thus no crime is committed.

The *Morality/Ethics* and *Spirituality* with Faith or Belief give correct or wrong advice to the intelligence to take a decision or make a judgment.

Blocking of Morality/Ethics

There are situations in which the Morality/Ethics will be blocked as under:

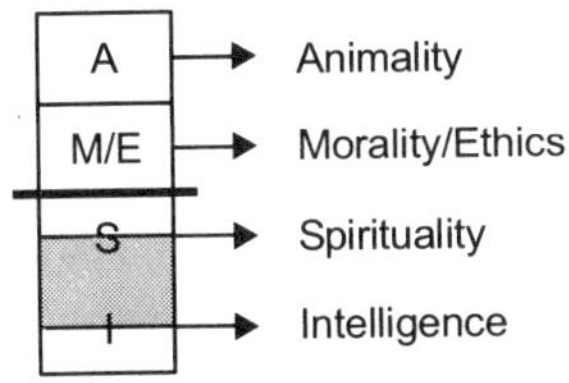

Fig. 5.4: Blocked Morality/Ethics.

In the above case, the *Intelligence* is contaminated by *Spirituality* alone. *Morality/Ethics* is blocked. For example, a person has a belief in human sacrifice—i.e., sacrificing a child for the pleasure of god. Here, the Morality/Ethics is against it. It is an offence to do so under the penal law. Yet, being contaminated by the *Spirituality*, his intelligence accepts it and promotes the *Animal Instincts* to have recourse to human sacrifice which is a crime.

Conversely enough, a person has a faith in a god who does not allow young women to come near to him for worship. But the morality/ethics tells that men and women are alike and equal before god. The *Intelligence* contaminated by *Spirituality* blocks the Morality/Ethics and does not allow the entry of young women to the holy of holies to worship him.

We notice communal conflicts and religious bigotry on the basis of the blocking of Morality/Ethics. Likewise, the *Spirituality* can be blocked as under:

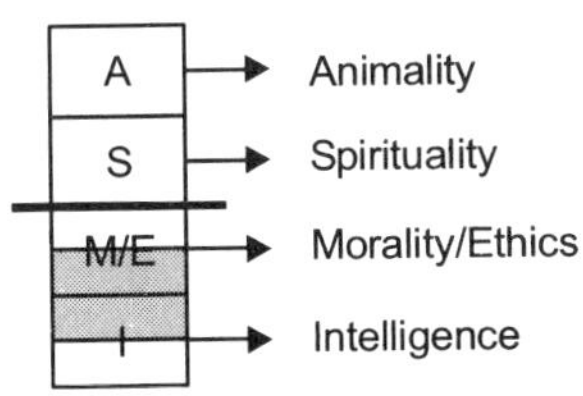

Fig. 5.5: Blocked Spirituality.

The Morality/Ethics is that euthanasia is morally right as it is an act of putting to death painlessly a person suffering from an incurable and painful disease or condition—i.e., mercy killing. But *Spirituality* or God does not allow it. Man should be allowed to die a natural death. As spirituality is blocked, the intelligence accepts the *Morality/Ethics* and permits mercy killing.

On the other hand, Spirituality says that those who love god should convert people to accept their religion by becoming a member. Morality does not permit compulsory or forceful conversion. Freedom of religion is a Constitutional right. If Morality/Ethics is blocked, the contaminated Intelligence will favour conversion under pressure. Terrorism, extremism, fundamentalism and fanaticism may be the result. The result is mass murder and genocide etc.

Push-Pull-Ego Factor theory here says and teaches that an upright Ego formed in the right direction is the only way to control the *Animal Instincts* and thereby reduce crime and criminality.

Blocking of Intelligence

There may be people whose *Intelligence* is blocked completely as shown in Fig. 5.6.

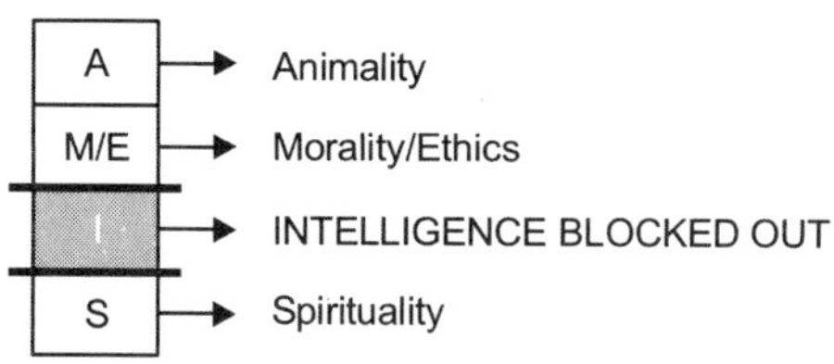

Fig. 5.6: A Person with the Blocked-out Intelligence.

A person with a blocked out Intelligence (see Fig. 5.6) is a psychotic individual. He cannot commit crimes as he is a person of unsound mind-crimes as he is a person who is suffering from mental retardation—is one who has a blocked intelligence. He too cannot commit crimes. Hence, the argument of Goddard that criminals are people of low intelligence is not true. A person can commit a crime if he has at least an average intelligence. He should be able, to evaluate the *pros and cons* of an action.

Conflicts Between Spirituality and Morality/Ethics

There may be situations in which the Spirituality conflicts with Morality/Ethics as shown in Fig. 5.7.

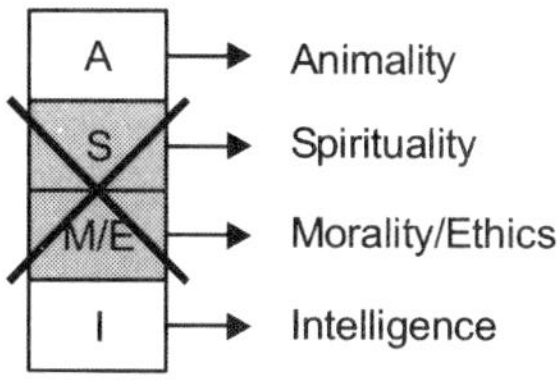

Fig: 5.7: Conflicts Between Spirituality and Morality/Ethics.

Here, *Spirituality*-principles go against *Morality/Ethics*—principles. In other words, they conflict each other. The *Spirituality* is not blocked; likewise the *Morality/Ethics* is not blocked. What can the Intelligence do in such situations? The intelligence will be stuck at this situation and may take a decision either favouring *Spirituality* and disfavouring *Morality/Ethics* principles or disfavouring *Spirituality* and favouring *Morality/Ethics* principles. A third option too is available—i.e., behave in any one of the various ways a person does in a conflicting situation. Such a behaviour may be criminal as well. If it is criminal then *Animal Instincts* play an important role and such a behaviour will not control crime or reduce criminality.

Principles in Morality/Ethics Conflicts with One another

The *Morality/Ethics* consists of the social, cultural, customary, traditional, moral/ethical, institutional, religious, State-made laws, regulations, rules etc. One kind of law may be complimentary to another/others or contradictory to another/others. If they are contradictory, then they may conflict with one another.

In such situations, the Ego will have to probe into the *Life Introspect* or *Life Script*. He looks into what he has experienced in the past or what is written in his mind by the interaction between hereditary potentials and the environment. In other words, the **Pull-Push Factors** assume a lot of importance. If the State made laws are in the Life Script, then a decision is taken accordingly to control or activate the animal instinct.

If the principle in Spirituality—**Faith** or **Belief** or both—conflicts each other, there too the Life Retrospect or Life Script assumes importance. Theist, Atheist, Rationalist, Empiricist, Idealist, Agnostic thoughts may come to play and the decision will be accordingly taken for the animal instincts to proceed further.

Animal Instincts, Emotions and Intelligence

Every animal instinct gives pleasure and pleasure is happiness. Behind the commission of any and every crime, doubtlessly there is pleasure. That is the reason why the Classical School of Criminology emphatically stated that hedonism was the cause of crime. For example, one feels: "If I had some money, I would feel better" and he makes money. Further he thinks: "I had more and more money I would feel better and better" and thus, the instinct called acquisitiveness (accompanying emotion is the feeling of ownership) becomes greed. Greed is different from need and anybody who has become exhorbitantly rich has become so only by commission of crime. My observation convinces me that no one can become exhorbitantly rich by observing all the laws in letter and spirit. He can live and continue to live without much difficulties.

We usually try to bring ourselves ease, pleasure, relaxation, happiness and mental peace etc. by satisfying our instincts. How long one can get pleasure and mental peace? Eating makes a man happy; sex gives him pleasure, laughter offers relaxation and the question is how long?. Any instinct and emotion beyond a limit must be controlled and thus there are many laws—social, cultural, moral, religious, State-made etc.—for the same. If one wants to satisfy his animal instincts excessively he has no option, but to violate the laws. Violation of the law is a crime and therefore his *Intelligence* along with Morality/Ethics or Spirituality with faith/ belief or with both interfere to control the excessice satisfaction of the instincts. If one cannot control his instincts and emotions, then crimes will be the result. Self-control is the best control for not committing crimes. This is otherwise called **'Self' governing** in criminology.

Emile Durkheim (1858-1917) said long ago that "Crime is normal in the society's framework". Yes, it is true because people have *animal instincts* and so long as they are in the man, they are sure to be expressed by all people at some time or other. Every time, man cannot express his animal instincts within the permitted limit. He may go beyond the limit and then it will be against the law—social, cultural, religious, moral or State-made etc. Resultingly, he commits a crime. Durkheim said again that "crime is not pathological, rather it is normal and inevitable". Inevitable means unable to be avoided—or—that is unavoidable. I do not agree with him as my studies show that some crimes are not inevitable. It means that only some crimes—not all crimes—are inevitable and as such cannot be avoided. If they are unavoidable, it means that the animal instincts in people cannot tolerate them any longer. For example, religious law of human sacrifice to gods cannot be tolerated and the animal instincts in people will resist it. Durkheim said further that crime was desirable for the simple reason that it does a lot of social functioning. I disagree with him as I find that some crimes are responsible and very much needed for social disfunctioning. For example, the crime of racial discrimination is a social menace and is not desirable. At the same time, some crimes are desirable especially the crimes committed by people for sex-equality and gender justice etc. Commission of certain crimes becomes necessary for the social transformation and development of society. Crimes are normal—but some crimes are useful—some other crimes are inevitable and all types of crimes are natural. For, I repeat that crimes are human acts, and very much a social fact. Man has intelligence and every human act guided by spirituality, morality/ethics (uprightly formed in the right direction) cannot be treated as a crime whatever may be the law in existence.

In my studied view, a crime or criminality can be controlled only by intelligence genuinely and properly guided by morality/ ethics or spirituality or both together only if and if only they are uprightly formed in the right direction. The crimes seen today are—

(1) Violent Personal Crimes, (2) Occasional Property Crimes, (3) Occupational Crimes, (4) Political Crimes, (5) Public Order Crimes, (6) Conventional Crimes, (7) Organised Crimes and (8) Professional Crimes etc. Marshall Clinard and Richard Quinney have distinguished eight types of crimes thus based upon the criminal career of the crime-doer, the extent to which the criminal behaviour has group support, the correspondence between the crime-doer and the legitimate behaviour and the society's reaction to the offender. Such crimes, in my view, are activated by animal instincts. To the list given above, I put the following crimes too. They are: (1) Bureaucratic Crimes, (2) *Mafia* and syndicates, (3) Terrorist Crimes, (4) Religious (fundamentalist) Crimes, (5) 'Holy' Crimes, (6) *Theosophism* Crimes, (7) '.......ology Crimes,

(8) Shark Crimes, (9) Meat-eater crimes, (10) Slum Crimes (11) Traditional Crimes, (12) Democracy Crimes, (13) Charity Crimes, (14) Corporate Crimes, (15) Cyber Crimes, (16) Political Crimes, (17) Criminal Politics, (18) Economic Crimes, (19) Cognate Crimes, (20) Grass Eater Crimes, (21) Definance Crimes, (22) Human Rights Violations, (23) Crimes Against Just Justice, (24) Judicial Crimes, (25) Media Crimes, (26) Gender and Sex Crimes, (27) Victimological Crimes, (28) Social Crimes, (29) Internet Crimes, (30) Social Media Crimes, (31) Self-destruction Crimes, (32) Domestic Crimes, (33) Institutional Crimes, (34) Crimes against Crimes and thus the litany is very long. In my opinion, none of the above crimes can be controlled or reduced by the intelligence of the person committing crimes—with morality, spirituality or both uprightly formed. This is otherwise called the **Self Governing** to control crime and reduce criminality. I have seen many people who have turned out to be law abiding citizens by **Self Governing.** A litany of crimes seen today in India by me (The tip of the Iceberg) is given in Appendix. Next Chapter is about control and reduction of crime dealt with and discussed in the light of Push-Pull-Factor theory of crimes causation.

Note

1. The term 'noquisitorial' was coined by me removing 'Accusa...' from Accusatorial system and 'Inquisito' from Inquisitorial system. Instead, I prefixed 'No' to 'quisitional' to coin 'Noquisitorial' system of justice.

6

Push-Pull-Ego Factor Theory and Control

Reduction of Crime and Criminality

Can crimes and criminality be prevented? This is a question raised by everyone in any society. The emphatic answer to the question is an emphatic **no.** Why? The simplest reason is that crime and criminality—both are in the blood of every human being. A man cannot live without violating laws—social, cultural, moral, religious, ethical, State-made, institutional, local, regional, special.... laws, rules, customs, traditions. **Dos** and **Don'ts** are there in every society. Some are oral, some are written, some are personal, some are social, some are cultural, some are religious, some are traditional, some are institutional, some are unwritten etc. How can a man live without violating some of them during 24 x 7 days a week? 24 x 365 ¼ days an year? From birth to death? As said repeatedly earlier, Yes, crime is a human act and very much a social fact. Man alone can commit crimes and no animals can commit them.

The police and law enforcement agencies cannot and do not prevent crimes permanently. At the most, they may control crimes to an extent for some time and thus reduce criminality. While doing so, they themselves involve in the commission of several crimes and they are called **Enforcement Crimes** which are nothing but the crimes committed by the law enforcement officials during the course of their job or profession to control crimes and criminality or otherwise.

The mother, parents and family cannot prevent crimes and criminality among the children. What they generally do are (i) give advice, (ii) give admonition, (iii) give psychological punishments,

(iv) give physical punishment, (v) give counselling etc. Domestic crimes are plenty and one observes conflicts between the parents, among the children, between the parents and children etc. so much so that there exists no normal family anywhere—always. Every family has many problems and the problems include violation of many laws as well. Yet, they can control domestic crimes and reduce criminality to a limited extent.

The neighbourhood of every family may have crimes and criminal activities. Some people hate their neighbours and they fight one another. The children in neighbourhood are many and they possess different characters. Children may be born in slums where a slum culture exists. Slum culture may consist of a variety of crimes including a gang culture.

The community based on religions, denominations within the religions, sects, economic status, professional/occupational positioning, political affiliation, business and trade, regionalism, sex etc., may have specialities. Crime and delinquency have been and are currently being explained (by criminologists) by the bad influence of the community. Every community has a sub-culture of its own and the sub-culture may have crimes as well. For example, the community of the businessmen will have business crimes which include (i) tax violations (ii) anti-trust violations, (iii) commercial bribery, (iv) false weights and measures by retailers, (v) submission of publication of false financial statements to obtain credit etc. to quote a few.

Schools, teachers, fellow-friends in educational institutions, school atmosphere inculcate values to children. But the reality is that the schools and educational institutions are contaminated with many kind of criminal behaviour. Even little children studying in primary schools become susceptible to exploitation by political parties, drug abusers, strikes, boycotting of classes, gheraoing of teachers etc. The closure of colleges and universities, postponement of examinations, destruction of public properties etc. have become quite common in these days. Violence in the campus is no news today and it includes gun powder politics, bombs, murdering of fellow associates, cruel ragging etc. Yes, the youth in the universities are at stake and there is unrest in all educational institutions. It is expressed in very many ways and at times, we notice the teachers and the students embrace extremism, terrorism, insurgency and other violent activities.

What about the society? We notice crimes and criminals everywhere. Just look at the crackpot theories and popular explanations of the causation of crime. From demonology and innate depravity, the quest for identifying the causes of crimes has come to the **ego** of man. Anyway, every man is born into crime and criminality. No one can escape from it. Yes, the Hell is empty because all devils are on earth now tempting everyone to commit sins, vices, illegal acts, crimes, offences, anti-social activities, immorality and evil things. The devils are most industrious and they involve in their work very ardently and actively. The devils are to me the **animal instincts** in man. Therefore, I am convinced that we can control crimes and reduce criminality only by controlling the animal instincts in man.

Push-Pull-Ego Factor Theory of Crimes Causation

When we think of a criminal behaviour, we go to the earliest writings of man—Chinese, Egyptian, Hebrew, Greek and Indian—and they provide striking examples of crimes committed by people. Coming to India, what do we see in *Ramayana*? It is an epic concerned with the life and adventures of Ramachandra and his wife Sita. No one, it seems to me, has studied *Ramayana* from a criminologist's point of view. One sees many episodes of law violations, immoralities and evil doings. What do we read in the Old Testament. It starts with the creation of man and subsequent commission of crime (sin—i.e., violation of God's commands) by Eve and Adam. The Old Testament contains a number of crimes, immoralities and evil doings. What happened to the great Athenian Philosopher Socrates (469? – 399 B.C)? He was poisoned to death. Christ, Jesus of Nazareth was crucified by Pontius Pilate (the Roman Procurator of Judea, A.D. 26-36?); He was the final authority concerned in the condemnation and execution of Jesus Christ.

What is seen in ancient literature? Long before the development of modern criminology, the writers of the novels, epics and the drama have written very brilliant and interesting characterizations of criminal behaviour. The ancient authors developed such characterizations not through any systematic sociological, psychological, criminological, socio-cultural or legal studies but by their sensitive and keen observation of human behaviour. In my view, they themselves had such criminal energy in them and they put it in writing. Many crime-authors today tell me that their writings reflected truly their own experiences in life. The reality was not, probably, otherwise with the ancient authors as well. I do not think that they had any intention to develop criminological literature. They had an emotional force that science did not reveal to them at that time. Read Shakespeare (1590-1610) and all his writings contain all sorts of crimes. They are seen in *Hamlet, Othello, King Lear* etc. Father killed and mother seduced in *Hamlet*, all the perfumes of Arabia would not sweeten this little hand in *Othello* and the daughters' neglect of the father at his old age in *King Lear* etc. showed the crimes and immoralities. They are seen today as well.

What is seen in Greek poems and dramas? In his play *Media*, Euripides (480-460 B.C) described and analysed the emotions of jealousy and revenge as displayed by the mother who murdered her children. The jealousy and revenge were nothing but the manifestations of animal instincts in man. I do not think that Euripides had any scientific knowledge about instincts, drives, motivations, ego etc. when he wrote the play. He had an intuision and experience of jealousy and revenge in his life. Coming to Sophocles (495-406 B.C.), what do we notice? In *Oedipus Complex* and *Electra Complex*, he spoke about incest, an offence under the penal laws. Severe feelings of remorse and guilt were expressed in Orestes.

Criminal Behaviour Today

Today, I read a metropolitan newspaper and I could find 70 per cent of the space was devoted to crime news. I took another English newspaper and I found 62 per cent having crime news. The crimes were murder, sexual offences, sexual abuse of children, corruption, torture by police, custodial death, people's protests, political crimes, suicides, family murder-suicide, bureaucratic crimes and a variety of other immoral activities. I have been collecting crime news in the daily news papers for the last 25 or more years. My wife used to help me to cut the paper news and put them in files. Thus, I have a news paper crime-news bank at my disposal. During 1990s, the space occupied by crimes news in some national news papers was 60 per cent [+ or –]. Gradually, crime news occupied more space in the news papers and now it is 70 per cent, a little more or a little less. There is a gradual development.

What about the T.V news? The news channels—more than 6 in the vernacular—give 24 hours news, discussions, talk shows etc. and nearly 90 per cent of such programmes center around crime and criminality. What about the movies? Most of the commercial films are crime thrillers and they are in great demand. They show animal instincts in very many ways and intensities. The film songs are full of instincts and emotions. Recently, I got a Malayalam book authored and the contents of the book were Malayalam Films and their effect and impact [positive and negative] on crimes and criminality. Comparing to T.V. news paper and films, crime stimulating programmes are less in Government owned Radio (All India Radio). Now the F.M. Radio owned by the private companies broadcast crimes, criminality and crime thrillers every time. Many of the cultural programmes like mimicry, dramas, *Kathaprasangam* etc. have crimes as the central themes. The discussions in the train compartments, in passenger omnibuses, restaurants are about crimes and to cut short many people talk about crimes at home—even at the dining table. Crimes, crime investigation, crime trials in courts etc. become indispensable in the present day society. They have become the most demanded commodity in the market. A crime-centric life is the culture today. It is there in politics, in administration, in religion and where not?

Take any crime in the news paper, television, radio, drama etc. and see the causes cited. They are (i) cruelty, (ii) escape, (iii) enmity, (iv) sex, (v) laughter, (vi) repulsion... and thus the cause of the crime at its roots is found to be instincts and emotions with or without intelligence. No criminal is found to control his thoughts, rather everyone expresses his instincts and emotions beyond the level permitted. Since crime is natural and is an expression of instincts/emotions, some explain crimes under Labelling Theory. A crime is nothing but a label attached to a particular human act.

Crimes and Criminality as the Criminologist Sees...

Any human behaviour up to a limit is no problem for anybody. A criminologist looking at any human behaviour with a scientific mind appreciates it to decide whether or not it is *abnormal. Ab* means away from and abnormal means *away from the normal*. What is then normal? Any behaviour up to a certain limit is normal. What is that limit? The limit is decided by the society, by the culture, by the State, by the morality, by the ethics, by the institution, by the religion, denomination, caste, sub-caste, race, etc. To be honest and open, the problem of defining a behaviour to be abnormal and that abnormal behaviour is criminal is indeed the most difficult one. The society, the State, the culture, the institutions etc. make the laws and they fix the limit. Some laws are written and many are unwritten. The unwritten laws work, sometimes, more powerfully than the written laws. If someone goes beyond the limit there will be resistance from many quarters. I wrote a book in Malayalam, **Vultures amidst Criminals** and got it published. It discusses the limits crossed by some people (vultures) who fly above the law. Their behaviour is not treated as crimes because the laws cannot do anything much against them. It means that the abnormal behaviour for many is just normal behaviour for a few—they are vultures who fly over the clouds and precisely, they are not affected by rain on earth. In spite of their flying over the clouds, there will be resistance—open or hidden—and it will be enough to fix the limit. Hence, a crime is defined as a violation of a law—whatever may be the nature of the law.

Push-Pull-Ego Factor Theory of the Causation of Crime

A criminologist is concerned with the **Push Factors**. Psychologists are concerned with the personality of individuals. Criminologists do not speak of criminals' personality as they do not see people with criminal personality. They see criminals and they do not say that all criminals possess a criminal personality. Psychologists speak of the influence of heredity and environment—and the interaction between heredity and environments when they speak of personality development. Criminologists do not speak of a criminal personality development as they do not see criminal personality in any so named criminals. Heredity provides the potentialities for development. Heredity is an important source of individual differences. At conception, every individual receives a genetic endowment from his/her parents. It is this genetic endowment which provides for physical equipments such as his/her sense organs, muscles, glands, nerves etc. They are very necessary for his/her development into an adult human being. The special and specific characteristics of these equipments, certainly, vary widely from one person to another.

No doubt, heredity influences the determination of some traits more than others. The influence is seen very visibly in physical features and in many constitutional factors such as sensitivity, vigor, vulnerability to disease and intelligence. Psychologists have noticed that the infants differ in their 'generalized sensitivity' during the first few weeks after their birth. What do we observe in infants? They take note of (i) some infants startle at even slight sounds or cry if sunlight hits their faces. Some seem to be insensitive to such stimulations. (ii) Difference in physical vigor predisposes some baby infants to energetic activity and self-assertion; others are more passive and are inclined to fantasy pursuits. (iii) Some babies react to sudden changes in routine by developing a fever; others have digestive disorder, a skin irritation, or a sleeping disturbance. Thus, one may see many (more and more) symptoms if the overall functioning of the organism is disturbed.

Man has superior brain which he has inherited from his parents. Human brain is found to consist of more than ten billion nerve cells—*neurons*—with numerous interconnecting fibers and very generous connections with other parts of the body. They produce incredibly great communication network with extraordinarily excellent overall functioning of the human organism, for interpreting and storing new-newer experiences, and for reasoning, rationalizing, memorizing, imagining, imaging and problem solving. Individuals differ vary widely in their intellectual level.

There exist constitutional difference in individuals. Heredity, no doubt is an important factor in providing basic equipments for developments. It determines how an individual reacts to his/her environments **(Pull Factors)** and how it influences his/her development. Criminologists are more concerned with instincts in man. Instinct is an inborn (hereditary) pattern of activity or tendency to action common to a given biological species. It is natural and impulsive and is animated by some inner force. It is a powerful energy which activates a person to do things in a particular way. Psychologists have identified many instincts and I want to add more to those so far identified—about which no much researches have seen done so far. My studies on 306 life convicts in prisons showed that most of them committed crimes as they were activated by instincts with accompanying emotions. Emotions, to quote Webster's, is an affective state of consciousness in which joy, sorrow, fear, hate or the like, is experienced, as distinguished from cognitive and volitional states of consciousness: usually accompanied by certain physiological changes, as increased heart beat, respiration, or the like, and often overt manifestation, as crying, shaking or laughing. When I studied 306 life convicts (in murder cases) in prisons, I wanted to know the effect of emotions, on their commission of crimes. I could learn that they were subjected to or affected by emotions which accompanied some instincts in them. In criminology, I find that emotions play a greater role than reason to commit crimes. Yes, when passion comes, reason flies away.

By **Push Factors**, I mean animal instincts in man. In other words, the factors which urge some action or course. In my studies on various kinds of criminals, crime-doers, offenders, sinners, immoral people, anti-social individuals and so on, I noticed that animal instincts pushed them to violate the law. Push Factors—i.e., the animal instincts may be (i) Push Factors at the source, (ii) Push Factors at the surface. In many cases, push factors at the surface can be easily identified. In other cases, one will have to probe into push factors at the source. Criminologists will be able to unearth such push factors at the source if they try for them. Police investigating criminal cases always try to locate both source and surface push factors. A court of law may not be interested to find out the source—Push Factors to convict offenders, but criminologists are interested in the WHY of crime causation and in the How of crime control and reduction of criminality. They always search for both types of Push Factors.

Earlier, abnormal behaviour was classified as (1) Psychosis, (2) Psychoneurosis, (3) Criminal behaviour and (4) Mental retardation. Psychosis is a 'severe personality disorder involving loss of contact with reality and usually characterized by delusions and hallucinations' (Coleman). It means that his intelligence is at stake. It does not work. Brain ceases to function. The animal instincts dominates the intelligence. Neurosis (psychoneurosis) is a mild functional personality disorder. In psychosis, personality disorganization is seen with respect to persons, place, time and situations whereas in psychoneurosis, it is observed in any one or more of them. In both cases, the intelligence does not overpower the animal instincts in the special area/s. In mental retardation, one observes low intelligence which renders the person to some degree ineffective in handling his affairs. In all the above three cases, one sees **Animal Instincts** and **emotions** overpowering the intelligence. Morality, moral principles, values, laws, spirituality, spiritual principles, values do not work. What about in crimes and criminality? Here too, intelligence does not function properly. It can be, as Goddard said, due to low intelligence (mental retardation) or owing to the failure or refusal of the intelligence to overpower the **Animal Instincts.** There may be very intelligent people who commit crimes in a very intelligent way. I am not concerned with the mechanics or execution of the crime. It may be with intelligent planning and thoughts. Nevertheless, at the bottom or root of the crime, we can observe some **Animal Instinct/s** overpowering the intelligence. My interviews with the convicts for life imprisonment proved that their intelligent planning and execution of the crimes were dominated by **Animal Instinct/s.** In Diagnostic and Statistical Manual of Mental Disorders (DSM), what is stated above can be seen/studied with more clarity and specificity. It is of little importance in our text.

Demonology and crimes among the ancients were discussed earlier (Adam and Eve violating God's command). About half a million years ago, for the Stone Age Cave men, 'good' and 'bad' spirits meant demons. They had no idea about 'Animal Instincts' and therefore, it was easier for them to attribute man's evil doings to evil spirits. Forget about the Stone Age Cave men. Coming to Moses in the Old Testament (1300-1200 B.C?), we see God's protection being withdrawn from those who committed evil things and subsequently, such people became the slaves of evil spirits. For instance, Saul disobeyed God (violation of God's Law) and resultingly, God left him (abandoned) and an evil spirit was allowed to enter into him. Jesus Christ-unclean spirit-casting out the devils-Swine-Sea story is known to all who have read the New Testament. Of course, *exorcism* was employed to banish the devils. At the same time, Moses had recourse to retributive justice (An eye for an eye; a tooth for a tooth) which Babylonian King, Hammurabi followed (*Lex talionis* about 18th century B.C. or earlier). It was then observed that *exorcism* with retributive punishment had no much effect in the prevention of crime and criminality. They continued to increase and thus, the methods were avoided by many people. How can the **Animal Instincts** in men be whipped off by **exorcism**? Foolishness indeed! Hippocrites (460-357 B.C), the Father of Modern Medicine knew the importance of heredity and predisposition etc., but was little aware of Animal Instincts and their influence on human behaviour. In my view, the demonology was the ancient term for 'Instinctology'—i.e., study of instincts on human and criminal behaviour. Prisons were in existence from time immemorial—first as *Detention Centers* and later (1704) as Detention cum *Punishment Centers*. We do not see any instinctological treatment to control crimes and reduce criminality. Prisons were never considered as a center for instinctological treatment—rather were meant for retribution or deterrence—and even today, the conditions inside the prisons in many countries are punitive in nature inflicting greater pain and suffering and imposing severe restrictions on inmates. They never help them to have the capacity to control their instincts, rather they promote more and more instinctual reactions. They may turn out to be recidivists at last. The Standard Minimum Rules for the Treatment of Prisoners adopted by the United Nations in 1957 too did not consider *animal instincts* in man as a cause of crime. My revision of the same Rules may be helpful to adopt new approaches to the inmates in prisons (Centre for Personality Development).

Instinctology and Treatment in Prisons

The medieval period in the history of American Prisons witnessed barbarism, torture and brutality. The incarceration was really painful and it resulted in public agitation against the barbarity—passing of Penn's Charter of 1862. It did give importance to instinctological treatment and humanitarian approaches. Earlier, the Quaker's Movement in 1775 led to the remodeling of Philadelphian prison on the basis of humanitarian treatment. However, the approach got deterioration towards the end of 18th century. In spite of the deterioration of instinctological treatment, the Americans were fully aware of the need for human treatment based on instinctology. It gave birth to the Pennsylvania system (1790) and Auburn System (1818-19). In Pennsylvania, one sees emphasis given to spirituality to control their instinctual energy.

The inmates were subjected to prayers and appropriate discourses so that they behaved themselves with greatest propriety and decorum (Negley K. Teeters).

The Pennsylvania System in prison management enforced severe solitary confinement and resultingly most of them committed suicide or suffered from mental disorders. Consequently, many prisoners were pardoned and released in 1823 and thus came into existence the Auburn System which insisted solitary confinement in complete isolation. The prisoners were to spend their time in penance and repentance for their crimes. Stupidity indeed! Whipping the prisoners was a usual punishment given to those who broke the rule of silence. It was called a 'system of discipline by repression and labour under fear' (Sellin). It was a brutal system which never recognized the role and importance of *Animal Instincts* in the causation of crime.

The Elmira Reformatory (During 30 years from 1870) superseded the Pennsylvania (Separate System) and Auburn (Silent System) System and thus came into existence reforms accepting instinctual energy in the causation of crimes and criminality. The prisons no longer remained as the dump-houses for the inmates. By 1930, individualization of the inmates became the object of punishment. Thus started treatment methods accepting individual needs and chances of rehabilitation. For that, it was necessary to accept the instinctual energy and the emotions of the inmates. Till then, the emotions of the inmates had no importance in rehabilitating the inmates. In my view and considered opinion, any correctional method without taking into account the instinctual impact and energy will be a useless exercise—a futile mission.

What do we see in the British Prison System? Did it accept instincts? The prisons in England were aweful. They contained brutality and inhuman treatments (John Howard). No consideration to instincts and emotions was given. In 1778, the British passed an Act which marked the beginning of prison reforms. Nevertheless, it is in 1833, they permitted the inmates of prisons to meet their friends and relatives more frequently at fixed intervals. In 1894, Gladstone Committee recommended some measures which recognized instinctual impacts in commission of crimes and criminality. In 1898, the Prison Act was passed. The British administration established penal colonies in America and Australia and transported offenders with twin objectives and they were (i) reduce overcrowding in British Prisons, (ii) meet labour problems in English colonies. Evidently, it was not for correcting the prisoners taking into account their instincts and emotions. For example, the penal colonies in Australia had only male offenders transported. As a result, the British settlement in Australia virtually remained womanless which created sexual problems. Finally, the system was abolished. The prison reforms from 1925 to 1960 helped the social workers to render their services to prisoners who needed emotional treatment. Open prisons were constructed and there were 3 open prisons for women. More and more Borstals were established for boys and girls. In 1953, 'Hostel System' was introduced for long term inmates. The Hostel System which respected the instincts and emotions was appreciated by the Prison Commission in 1962. The British Prison System accepted classification of prisoners, group therapy, counselling, vocational training, training for moral upliftment, community services, after-care services, parole etc. In short, a system which honours the human rights, instincts and emotions has come into existence there.

The Russian Prison system provides facilities for education, recreation and religious discourses. A system of self-government is seen there. No doubt, the Russians accept instincts and emotions of the inmates. United Nations Organisation (UNO) is very keen in prison reforms. Many countries modify their prison rules with a view to mitigating the rigours of prison life—recognizing instincts and human emotions. The Canadian prisoners are allowed to visit their ailing relatives and friends. British prisoners are permitted to be at the bed side of their dying relatives. Japanese prisons considers parole as the most important treatment method. Indian prisons have introduced many methods to correct, reform, resocialize, rehabilitate and reintegrate the prisoners back to society. The prisons everywhere give a lot of importance for instincts and emotions of the inmates for correction.

Animality as the Push Factor in the Casuation of Crimes

Coming back to our main theme—i.e., Animality as a **Push Factor** in crimes and criminality, we may conclude that any effort to control crimes and reduce criminality must contain means and methods to control the *Animal Instincts* and accompanying emotions in man. How? In order to understand the working of the human mind, it is essential to study the working of the **Pull Factors** for the formation of the **Ego Factor.**

Pull Factors in the Formation of the Ego Factor

The Animal Instincts and emotions **[Push Factors]** are constantly shaped by many forces and pressures in our environment. These forces and pressures are called the **Pull Factors.** It has been proved in psychological researches that different physical environments foster somewhat different characteristics, even among individuals with similar inheritance/heredity. It has been observed in its constellation of favourable and unfavourable conditions and in the special demands it makes on organisms living within it. (James C. Coleman).

Every person is born into a socio-cultural environment. No doubt it influences his psychological development very dramatically. Through his contacts with the socio-cultural environment, he learns the values—moral as well as spiritual—he believes in. He learns the language—fair or foul—and the customs—good or bad and the competencies necessary for dealing with life problems.

Socio-cultural environment means (i) economic, (ii) educational, (iii) religious, (iv) caste, sub-caste, (v) racial, (vi) colour, (vii) sexual including transgender, hermaphrodites, (viii) regional, national, (ix) familial, (x) political, (xi) sect, denominational, (xii) linguistic and thus one can see favourable and unfavourable conditions/climates surrounding a person's hereditary potencies/potentialities. For example,

(i) A low caste individual has a unique personality different from a person of the high caste.
(ii) A male different from a female—both different from a person belonging to the transgender community.

Doubtlessly, no man is an island. Everyone belongs to a group and each group of people fosters its own cultural pattern by the systematic teaching of the younger members of the group. For example—

(i) A child born into Catholic faith usually becomes a Catholic in due course. His spiritual values will be of a Catholic.
(ii) A son of a butcher and reared among butchers is likely to become a butcher with butcher's values and outlooks.

The more uniform and thorough education of the younger members of the group, the more alike they will become. The developing child becomes a member of several subgroups—enumerated above on the basis of sex, caste, belief, faith, class etc. and these subgroups foster their own values (moral and spiritual). Everyone has a status and a role in a society. One and the same person is a member in various subgroups and precisely therefore, he is subjected to various role expectations.

Everyone has interpersonnel relationship. Relationship with the mother, parents, family members is the first. Then it extends gradually to the neighbourhood, community, peer group, teachers and many other important people around him. His personality development depends much upon his experience with those people who matter. For example, a child who is neglected or mistreated by his parents is likely to develop a personality different from another child who is accepted and loved at home. Broken homes, family disorganization, divorced or deserted homes, unemployed and overcrowded families, orphanhood—all of them are found to have their influence in developing children. In one study, it was found that the delinquent children did not get the warmth and affection from their parents. Their parents were more lax and used erratic discipline on their children (Sheldom and Eleanor Glueck).

The values (moral and spiritual) and behavioural patterns children learn depend mostly and heavily on whether their parents are impulsive or mature. Impulsive parents cannot and do not help children to acquire the capacity to control their instincts and emotions. Cruel, selfish, intolerant parents are found to develop cruelty, selfishness and intolerance among the developing children. Whether or not a developing child should have spiritual or material values is decided to a great extent by his parents, teachers and so on. They inculcate the values in the growing children. To quote James C. Coleman again: "Since each individual belongs to somewhat unique pattern of subgroups and experiences a unique pattern of interpersonal relationships, he participates in the socio-cultural environment in an individual way. As a consequence of such 'differential participation', no two of us live in quite the same world. Thus, the socio-cultural environment is the source of differences as well as commonalities in personality development".

What do the criminologists say about the impact and after-effect of the interaction between hereditary potentialities **(Push Factors)** and environment **(Pull Factors)**? The genetic endowment or heredity provides the essential basis and sets the limits for both physical and psychological (criminal too) development. The shaping or the formation of the potentialities into realities (actualities) depends mostly and heaving on our physical and socio-cultural environment. My studies on 306 life convicts in the prison revealed that their personality development during the early infancy was far away from being satisfactory. The socio-cultural environments **(Pull Factors)** were such that they exerted a lot of influence in their later life. Bad neighbourhood, slum life, heterogeneity of background and moral standards of people, physical deterioration of the areas, low income, delinquent sub-culture, delinquent underprivileged environment, social and occupational failures etc. affected adversely their development.

Now we have identified the Push and Pull Factors and in Criminology, I put **Animal Instincts** along with other hereditary potentialities in the **Push Factors**. In the **Pull Factors,** I put the socio-cultural environments. They interact to form the **Ego Factor** in people. The information given below [up to 14 years of my grand children included] is taken from my research observations.

(1) During the infancy and early childhood (0-6 years), the child learns to relate himself emotionally to parents, siblings and other people. I have six grand children (Aged now 3 years to 15 years), and I observe in them how do they relate themselves emotionally to their parents and siblings. They use 'I' and 'We' and they mean the members of their 'own' family and parents. They form an identification with their own sex. Certainly, they learn to distinguish right from wrong and respect values, rules and authority. The child of 5 years of age tells another child of 3 years of old the rules of behaviour and the values in life—particularly, in religious matters. They pray together following the same rules and rituals. They eat together, play together, view T.V. together... together... together.

(2) During middle childhood (6-12 years), how do they learn the values? They learn appropriate masculine or feminine social role with sex values. They learn to appropriate masculine or feminine social role with sex values. They develop a conscience (Superego), morality and a scale of values. They learn spiritual and religious values. They learn to control their animal instincts. They learn to give and take. They adjust with age mates and social groups. They learn to share the responsibility. An intelligence based on moral and spiritual values gets developed. They experience guilt when they violate the social, moral and spiritual laws. They pray to God (in many cases) and ask pardon if they violate the rules and laws. They learn to control their emotions and instincts **(Push Factors)**.

(3) **Adolescence (12-18 years):** They achieve a clear sense of identity and accept the body changes. Accordingly, they acquire more masculine or feminine social role. [There was a time, children were married at the age—13-14-15 etc. or even earlier.]. They achieve emotional independence from parents and adults. They feel the need to love people of the complimentary sex and thus they develop a concern beyond oneself (themselves). They achieve social responsibility and more moral and spiritual values. They feel the need for family life. They build a conscious value system in harmony with what is expected from them.

(4) **Early Adulthood (18-35 years):** They complete their formal education to a great extent. Education means formation of character with upright values. Starting a job, occupation or profession with moral values, getting married and starting to have a family life preferably in domestic areas—in a religious atmosphere; bringing up children born in the wedlock; developing an acceptable philosophy of life.

(5) **Middle Age (35-60 years):** Accepting values for greater civic and social life; helping teen age children to become responsible with values acceptable; adjusting to aging parents.

(6) **Later Age (60+ ...):** Adjusting to decreasing physical strength and accommodating with physical ailments (if any); adjusting to the death of spouse/friends/relatives/kith and kin; preparing mentally to die; becoming more religious and spiritual.

(7) **Tasks at all periods:** Developing and making use of one's physical, psychological, moral, social, spiritual and emotional competencies; accepting oneself and developing basic confidence to control one's animal instincts **[Push Factors]** not to go beyond the level recognized by the society; accepting and building enviable attitudes and values; participating creatively and responsibly in family and other groups; living as responsible citizen respecting laws.[2]

These, the values which one can and must develop at different life periods can be summarized under two major heads—namely **Moral** and **Spiritual.**

Moral Values	*Spiritual Values*
Social laws	Religious laws
Cultural laws	Theistic laws
Institutional laws	Atheistic laws
Customary laws	Agnostic laws
State-made laws	Rationalist laws
(relating to specific subjects)	Empiricist laws
Interpersonal laws	Idealist laws
Sexual laws etc., etc.	Existentialist laws
Hedonistic laws	Superstitious laws
Epicurean laws etc., etc.	Satanic laws etc., etc.

In all the fields stated above, there exist an object or a quality desirable as a means or as an end in itself. Value means an ideal-worth-merit implying intrinsic excellence or desirability. Value is the quality of any behaviour that renders it desirable or acceptable to others. Value means the spiritual qualities of mind and character or moral excellence.

The Ego Factor and Crimes

An infant grows. He/she (including transgender) grows as a person different from others. A child is born to a community, caste, sub-caste, religions, denomination, sect, cult, culture, wealth, family status, nation, sex including transgender and hermaphrodites, colour, race etc. and accordingly, the child gradually becomes a particular 'me', 'I', **'Ego'** or 'Self'. This 'I' ness is what is called **Ego.** It is formed by the interaction of the Push and Pull Factors. In other words, the **Ego** is the **Knead** which comes out of the interaction between the **Push** and the **Pull** Factors. The **Knead** has the qualities (good and bad) of the **Push** and **Pull Factors.**

Some criminologists in the West speak of **Self-Concept** to mean **Ego,** while some social scientists say **Self-Structure** to mean **'Ego'**. The term **'Self'** or **'Self Concept'** is often used in reference to the way the individual views himself and the term **Self Structure** is more likely to be used when others view the individual. I do not agree with both views. For, the **'Ego'** cannot be used to mean in either way stated above. It is the **Knead** formed out of the interaction between the **Push** and **Pull Factors.** It has nothing to do with how an individual views himself or observers view the individual. Therefore, the **Ego** is not to be confused with **Self-Structure** or **Self-Concept.**

In Criminology, W.C. Reckless and Simon Dinitz spoke of *Self-Concept* and *Containment* Theory. They raised a question: "Given the alterative of law abiding and law violating behaviour, why some people turn to one or the other?" According to them the answer is simple. They said—

"We live in a society of alternatives where the **Self** has more and more opportunities for acceptance or rejection of available confrontations". Hence, they introduced the idea of '*Self Concept*' as the key factor to explain this phenomenon. Their theory holds the view that if an individual possesses a *favourable self-concept,* then he is directed toward law abiding behaviour, otherwise—i.e., an *unfavourable self concept,* he is directed toward delinquent behaviour. Reckless and Dinitz empirically tested their theory on juvenile delinquents. They studied the **self concept** of 125 good boys and 101 bad boys. They found that a favourable concept of **self** would act as an inner buffer or inner containment against deviance, destruction, lure and pressure. As this book cannot devote more space for the criticism of Reckless and Dinitz, I do not go for it. I say that I cannot and do not subscribe to the views expressed in *Self-Concept* and *Containment Theory.* Already there were criticisms about their measure of **Self-Concept,** inadequacy of the control group in the empirical study, the selection criteria and the conclusions arrived at. I do not want to elaborate them further. I may say that the **Ego** of the **Push-Pull Theory** has nothing much to do with the *Self-Concept* or *Self-Structure*. Why? The Push-Pull theory considers the *Ego* of an individual consists of four important areas. They are as under:

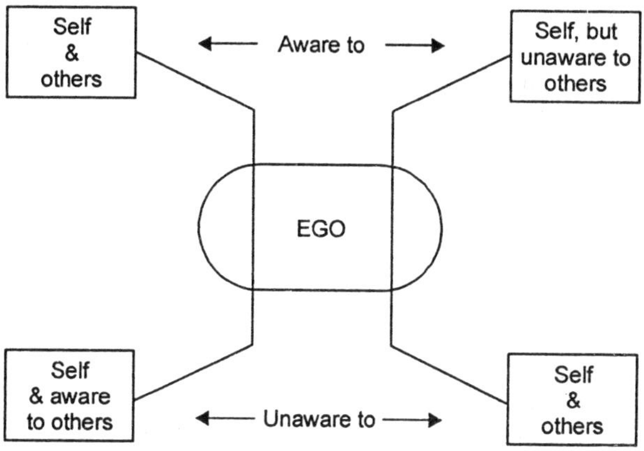

Fig. 6.1: Areas in the EGO.

In simple terms, the **Ego** consists of contents unaware to the Self. Therefore **Self Concept** theory has no scope. The **Ego** consists of contents *unaware* to *others*. Hence, Self-Structure theory has no relevance. The **Ego** which is a **Knead** formed by the **Push** and **Pull Factors,** consists of both **aware and unaware contents**. My interviews with the life convicts proved that some of them could not say anything about why did they commit crimes. They had the instincts—**Push Factors** which forced them to commit the offence. One person killed another by stabing and on post-mortem, it was revealed that there were more than 42 injuries on his body. Such cruelties are seen and the reasons for the expression of such cruelties cannot be answered by the killer. **Push-Pull Ego Factor** theory assumes:

(1) An individual cannot understand him fully, whatever may be his qualifications, merit, efficiency and intelligence. Self-Concept is an impossibility.
(2) Other individuals cannot understand fully another individuals whatever may be their qualifications, merit, efficiency and intelligence. One hundred people will have several hundreds of evaluation about a fellow member.

(3) No one can predict the way he may behave if the **Pull Factors** change. The **Ego** of a person is susceptible to change depending on the **Pull Factors**. The pressures of the **Pull Factors** and the weakness of the social order will change the **Ego** of any person.

(4) The **Ego** has a conscious part which knows the **Morality/ Ethics, Spirituality with** *faith* **or with** *belief* **or with** *both*. The moral values and the spiritual values—with **Intelligence**—will and can overpower the **Animal instincts [Push Factors]** which in turn will make the **Ego** to control the instincts and thereby control crime and criminality. *Examples*—

1. I have heard little children saying 'Excuse me' for the wrong they have committed.
2. I have heard people praying to God: 'Oh, god, pardon me for the sins I have committed knowingly or unknowingly'.
3. I have seen people taking penance and going to pilgrim centers to get absolution for the sins (crimes) and at the Confessional of the Catholic church, the faithful confess their sins.
4. I have seen people compensating the victims of their crimes by cash or kind. They suffer from an unsettling of their mind till they make the compensation. My father used to settle others' issues by fixing victimological compensation.
5. I have seen people donating huge amount of money to temples, mosques, churches and *gurudwaras* as a compensation to the wrongs they have committed.

Yes, people violate the laws not because they want to violate the laws and thus commit a crime, but because they are pressured to do so. They have no option, but to commit crimes. This is the reason why victimologists argue that the victims of crime can become the cause of crimes.

Fundamental to an individual's **Ego** is the **Value Assumptions**—i.e., his view about the right and wrong, good and bad, moral and immoral, desirable and undesirable, having values and having no values etc. As said earlier, the moral values are universal, absolute and eternal. Everybody behaves according to the moral/ethical and spiritual values—they are *the frame of reference* for one to decide whether or not he committed an offence.

The moral/spiritual (both) values which a person has give him a self identity, self ideal etc. People have intelligence which is either controlled by moral values or by spiritual values or by both. They become the **inner controls** of his behaviour. For example, an **Ego** which has moral or an upright spiritual or both values will not commit rape. For, he thinks it to be a moral evil or a spiritual sin. An **Ego** which has moral or an upright spiritual value is referred to as his **Conscience** by criminologists or **Superego** by psychoanalysts. An **Ego** with an intelligence controlled by moral or an upright spiritual values will control his Animality (Animal Instincts) and thus he can control crimes and criminality.

Ego: The Knead at 13-14 Years of Age

Push-Pull Factors interact each other and the fundamental or basic structure of the **Ego** or the **Knead** is made by the time a child reaches 13-14 years of age. One can build a super structure on this foundation.

The moral and spiritual values uprightly formed in the right direction are at the source. Suppose, water is added to it, then it will become loose and if water is added more and more it will become more and more loose and if water is added more and more it will become more and more watery. Still, the basic values of the **Ego (Knead)** will be there. One cannot get out of it. As the infant grows up—and up, there can be some changes in the **Ego (Knead)** and the values. There will not be a total or substantial change in the fundamental values formed during infancy/childhood. I have seen hardened criminals crying over their past wrong doings. I have heard terrorists repenting over their evil doings. There are people who accept a different faith (religiously) for marriage once at the time of marriage going back to their original faith afterwards. No, as a rule, never a new man with a substantial change in the original values can be found. In my studies, I have specially noticed the fact that the floor of the prison cells contains the tears of the inmates there. That is the reason why atonement has been accepted as an objective of imprisonment. Yes, the intense guilt reaction of Lady Macbeth, after planning and taking part in the cruel murder of Duncan, is depicted well by Shakespeare in her uneasy sleepwalking and symbolic hand washing etc. It is, in my view, certainly a conflict of her values with the wrong act she committed. What about Judas after his betrayal of Jesus Christ?

"It is an accustomed action with her, to seem thus washing her hands: I have known her continue in this a quarter of an hour" (Macbeth, Act V, Scene I). She had the feelings of uncleanliness and of uneasiness of mind. My experience and association with the clinical work of Dr. Gregory Peechatt, a psychotherapist in Rochester, State of New York, U.S.A. too give me enough proof to show that the conflict between one's values and evil behaviour expresses itself in guilt feelings. It is like this—

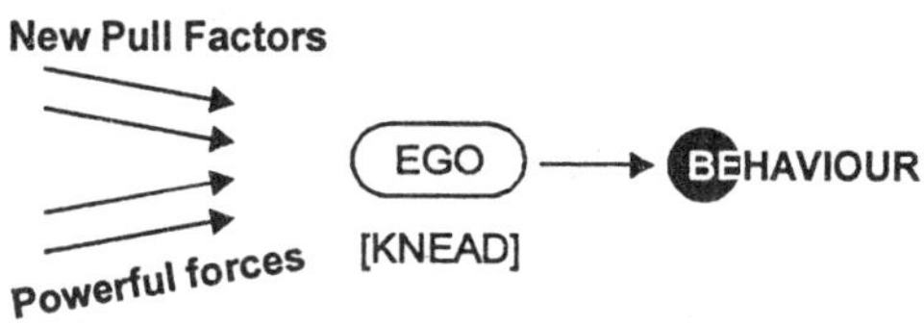

Fig. 6.2: Pull Factors of Powerful Forces on Ego (KNEAD).

In the above picture, we see very powerful **Pull Factors** pressuring on the **Ego (Knead)** of an individual at any age. The ego reacts to the pressures of the **Pull Factors.** If the **Ego** is dominated by the intelligence containing moral or/and spiritual values uprightly formed, then the **Knead (Ego)** gets more strength and power to subdue the pressure of **Pull Factors.** The reinforcement of the moral and/or spiritual values uprightly formed in the right direction becomes essential—necessary to overpower the **Pull Factors.** If not, the **Pull Factors** will put down the **Ego (Knead)** and the result will be a violation of law. In the above picture, the behaviour after the **Ego (Knead)** fighting with the pressures of the **Pull Factors** can be either a violation of law or observance of the law. It depends upon the overpowering effect of the **Ego (Knead)** on the pull factors.

When the reinforcement of the moral and/or spiritual factors uprightly formed are sufficient to overpower the **Pull Factors,** then no crime is resulted. If not sufficient, a crime is resulted. If the values are not formed uprightly in the right direction, then too, crimes will be the result. The parents, family, neighbourhood, community, group, society, religion etc. do their best to see that the social and spiritual values are uprightly formed and developed. Without it, a law abiding living will be impossible.

The **Knead (Ego)** is subject to continued modification but the values which are fundamentally in the **Knead (Ego)** remain as they are in spite of the modification. Hence, if the modification is consistent with the values fundamentally seen in the **Ego,** there arises no problem. If not, problems can come into being sharply divergent or contradictory values are not usually put into the **Knead (Ego)** as the discrepancies make people uncomfortable. People protect themselves from dangers of inculcating unacceptable values.

Push-Pull-Ego Factor Theory and Control of Crimes and Reduction of Criminality

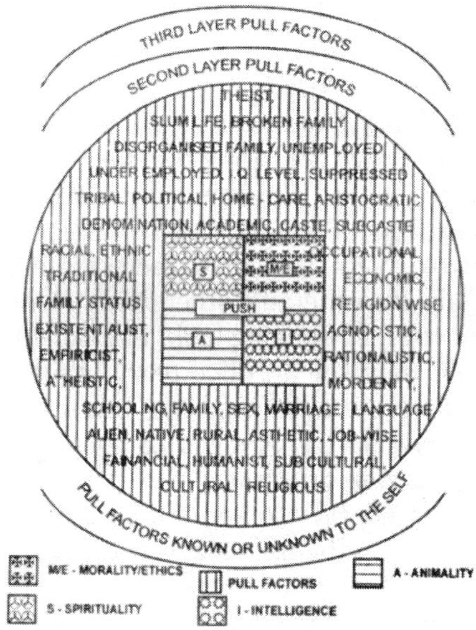

Fig. 6.3: Individual Mind (Pull Factors Around) [Pull and Push Factors shaping the Ego and the Ego factor of an Individual.

The **Ego (Knead)** of a person is as given above.[3] It is this **Knead (Ego)** which interacts with **the Pull Factors** at a given time in a man's life. How do we control crimes and reduce criminality is the area of discussion now.

Every person defines or describes him. But, I think that very-very few people may say: "I am a criminal". Every one violates laws and everyone is well aware of it. People often ask to themselves and at times to others: "Who am I?" When a person introspects, he may understand that he is a violator of laws. Nevertheless, many people do not generally ask the question: "Why do I behave the way I do?". A pick pocket, a gambler, a dacoit, a rapist, a *Mafia* chief, a bureaucratic crime-doer and so on generally do not ask such a question. Some may at times do so and then the next question is: "How do I control my acts or reduce my violation of laws and criminality in me?" No doubt, it is a method of analyzing an individual's thoughts, feelings, acts, behaviour etc.

Push-Pull-Ego Factor theory has its own explanation as under: Imagine two women quarrelling and they shout at the other in abusive language and filthy expressions. Their arms are tense and held high in the air. Suddenly and surprisingly, they see their old teacher whom both of them respected. The women's body posture, tone of voice, language and expressions began to change. Their arms fell quietly down and they together smiled at the most respectful teacher. How? Why? Of course, they controlled their **Animal Instinct [Push Factor]** to combat.

Imagine two drivers. They drive their cars in over speed. One wants to overtake the other; the other does not allow overtaking. One sees traffic rage. Everything looks like causing an accident at any time. Soon, they see a police party involved in checking vehicles. They asked two drivers: "Are you driving the cars in a harsh way—in over speed? Are you competing each other? Are you driving the cars in a rash way?" Hearing everything which the police party asked, they smiled at them and said that we were driving cars observing the traffic laws and rules. No doubt, both drivers have a feeling that they drove the vehicles without observing the road rules and traffic laws. Anyway, the intervention of the police party made them to control their **Animal Instinct** called **'Self Assertion'**.

Let us start from the **Ego [Knead]** which has four areas say, **Animality, Morality/Ethics, Spirituality** uprightly formed with **Faith** or with **Belief** [or both]. In other words—

1. Everyone has **Animal Instincts** (Animality) in him.
2. Everyone has **Intelligence + Morality/Ethics.**

3. Everyone has **Intelligence + Spirituality uprightly formed with Faith or Belief** (or both).
4. Everybody has **Intelligence + Morality/Ethics + Spirituality.**[4]

An analysis of the first case (2 women quarrelling), we see the **Animal Instinct** (Animality) is overpowered by Morality/Ethics when they saw their one-time teacher whom they respected. It means that one area can be overpowered by another area. In the second case, the **Animal Instinct** of *Self Assertion* was overpowered by Morality/Ethics when the two drivers saw the police team. No doubt, the Morality/Ethics, Spirituality principles and values are stored in one's mind. The memory in intelligence can and does recall the stored values whenever necessary.

Coming to crime and criminal behaviour, the **Ego (Knead)** has four areas which may be called

(i) **Animality Ego State**
(ii) **Morality/Ethics Ego State.**
(iii) **Spirituality Ego State**
(iv) **Intelligence Ego State**

The Animality contains the **Animal Instincts** which may activate a man to commit a crime. Man is an evolution from animals and therefore everything which activates an animal is seen in man too. But, beyond an extent/level permitted by the society, it becomes a crime or criminal behaviour. No doubt, crimes and criminal behaviour are to be controlled for human coexistence. They can never be prevented as animal instincts are natural, necessary and inevitable for activating animals and men.

For controlling the **Animal Instincts,** there is the Morality/Ethics Ego State which contains the moral/ethical principles and values inculcated to the human mind by the mother, parents, home, neighbourhood, community, teachers, society etc.

The *Spirituality Ego State* contains spiritual values uprightly formed in the right direction based on Faith or/Belief. They can also be wrongly formed in the wrong direction.

The *Intelligence Ego State* contains the memory, expansion, comprehension, analysis and intuitiveness etc. which a man employs with moral/ethical and/or spiritual values.

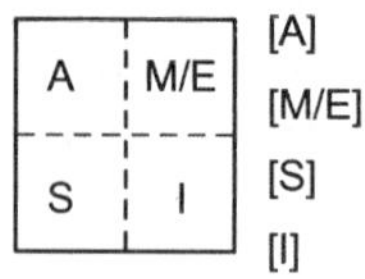

Where [A] represents Animality
[M/E] represents Morality/Ethics
[S] represents Spirituality
[I] represents Intelligence of the Ego (Knead).

Fig. 6.4: Animality, Morality/Ethics, Spirituality and Intelligence represented as [A], [M/E], [S], [I] for Further Discussion.

Further discussion will be based on the representation **[A], [M/E], [S]** and **[I]** as shown above.

When a man overpowers his animal instincts by moral/ethical principles/values, we may say that he is behaving from **[M/E] of his Ego (Knead)**. Similarly, when a man overpowers his *animal instincts* by spirituality principles/values, we may say that he is behaving from **[S]** of his **Ego (Knead)**.

Intelligence plays an important and vital role whenever one behaves from **M/E** of his **Ego (Knead)** or from S of his **Ego (Knead)** or from **M/E** and **S** of his **Ego (Knead)**. Intelligence gathers information and makes an analysis in every situation. It can be:

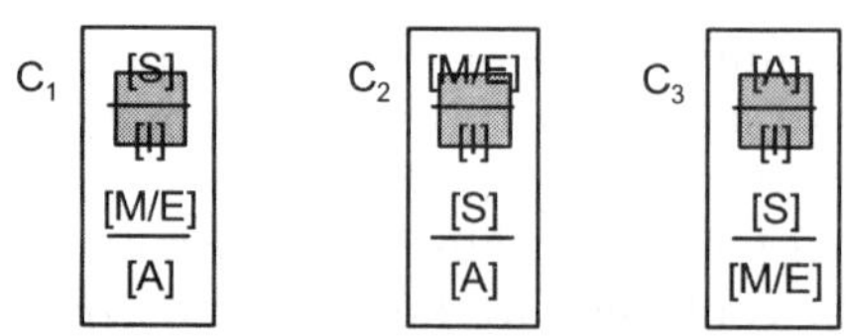

C_1- Intelligence analysing the situation **(Pull Factors)** by applying **[S]** values.

C_2- Intelligence analysing the situation. **(Pull Factors)** by applying **[M/E]** values.

C_3- Intelligence analysing the situation **(Pull Factors)** by applying **[A]** values.

Fig. 6.5: Intelligence analysing a situation by **[S], [M/E], [A]** values.

Case Illustrations

(1) A girl named P, a believer in Hindu Faith fell in love with a boy named Q, a believer in Christian Faith. P and Q decided to marry legally without following the religious

formalities in a church or temple. They made an application before the civil authorities under Special Marriage Act.

The father of P became angry. Being moved by the **Animal Instinct**, viz., **Pugnacity** (Combat) he decided to kill Q. He made plans to kill the boy. He knew that what he was going to do was an offence under State's Penal Law, was a sin under the religious law etc. His *Intelligence* analysed the situation by applying **[S]** values uprightly formed in the right direction. In other words, his **[S]** values overpowered his **[A]** and thus decided not to kill the boy.

In the above case, if he has **[S]** values wrongly formed in the wrong direction, his intelligence would have supported his decision to kill the boy. This is a real case now appearing in the media in Kerala State.

(2) A NGO collected huge amount of money from the public in the name of treating cancer patients. People liberally donated a lot of money for the noble purpose. The Chief Administrator of the NGO wanted to misappropriate a few lacs of Indian rupees for his personal needs. He knew that the misappropriation of money is an offence under the State-enacted penal laws as well as a moral evil under the laws of morality. His *Intelligence* analysed the situation by applying **[M/E]** values and his **[M/E]** values overpowered his **[A]** and thus decided not to misappropriate the fund collected for the treatment of cancer patients. The **[A]** was *Acquisitiveness* with an accompanying emotion of *feeling of Superiority*.

(3) X and Y were brothers and they were enemies. Y had four daughters aged 30, 32, 35, 37. Y had a lot of mental tensions as he found all his daughters remained unmarried. He could learn that his brother X was behind this situation. He propagated bad and immoral stories about the daughters. As a result, all the marriage proposals could not be proceeded. Y decided to put an end to the evil doings of his brother. He wanted to wipe off his brother. His *Intelligence* analysed the situation by applying **[A]** values and he found **[S]** and **[M/E]** justifications for the decision he took. He had victimological arguments too—i.e., the victim of crime

might become a cause of the crime. Well, he killed him knowing fully well that he did an offence under the Penal Laws of the State and a sin under the religious laws and a vice under the moral laws. Here one sees **[A]** overpowering **[S]** and **[M/E]**.

Control of Crime and Criminality by Self Analysis or Introspection

I have found in my experience that **Self** control is the best control to reduce crime and criminality.

Look at the diagrams below and see how an individual can control himself/herself from involving in the commission of crimes. Activation is always from the **Animal Instinct/s** in man.

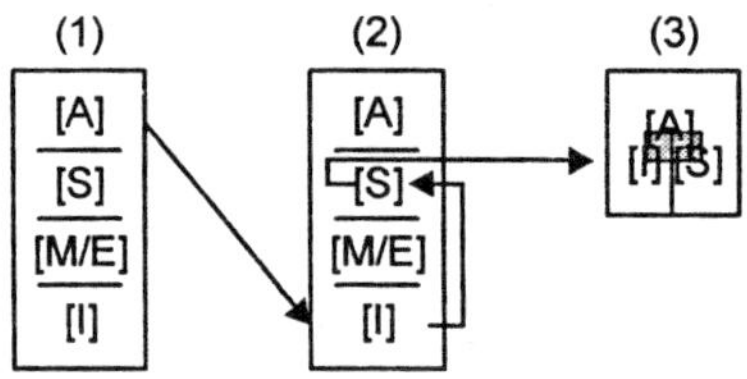

Fig. 6.6: Introspection-1.

(i) A person wants to forge a document and thereby he wants to amass wealth. In (1), the activation comes from his Animal **Instinct (Animality)**, say—*Acquisitiveness* (emotion is feeling of ownership) and on *Self Analysis*, it is sent to his **[I]**—i.e., Intelligence—which makes an analysis via **[S]** as shown in (2). **[I]** and **[S]** together make the self analysis and from the **[S]**, it is sent to the **[A]** as shown in (3). There in (3), the [A] is overpowered by **[I & S]**—the result is that he does not commit a forgery. Self Analysis made him to arrive at such a decision.

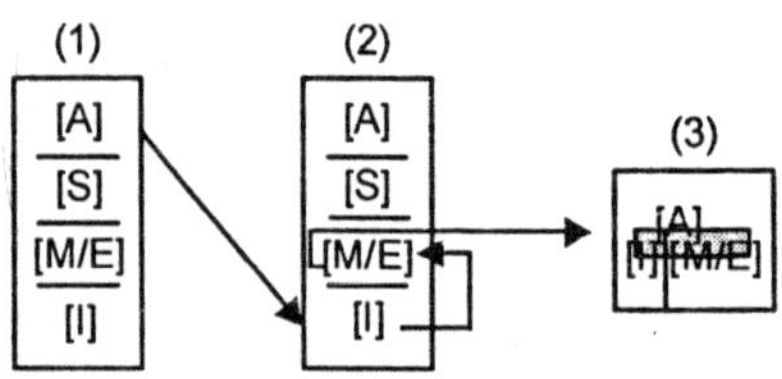

Fig. 6.7: Introspection—2.

An individual desires to molest a tribal girl and thereby he wants to satisfy his **Animal Instinct—Sex**, accompanying emotion is lust—and on Self Analysis, it was sent to his **[I]** which analyses it through **[M/E]** as shown in (2). From **[M/E]**, it is sent to **[A]** as shown in (3). In (3), the **[A]** is overpowered by **[I]** and **[M/E]**. Consequently he does not molest a poor girl from the tribe.

What happens if **[I]** does not send to the **[S]** or **[M/E]**? Necessarily the **[I]** goes back to **[A]** and a crime may be the result. Again, if the **[S]** or **[M/E]** are not uprightly formed in the right direction, then also crime will be the result. Thus we may see the terrorists, fundamentalists, fanatics and so on.

The **Ego (Knead)** which is overpowered by **[I]** & **[S]** or **[I]** & **[M/E]** or by both. **[I]** & **[S]** & **[M/E]** interact with the **Pull Factors** (environment) exerting pressures and finally win over it. If it cannot win over the pull factors, then also a crime may be result. **Push-Pull-Ego Factor** theory is all about the fight between the **Push** and **Pull Factors** and the ultimate winning in the fight.

Self Analysis is done by groups as well. A group of people can become a crowd. A crowd can become a mob and the mob can commit violent crimes as under.

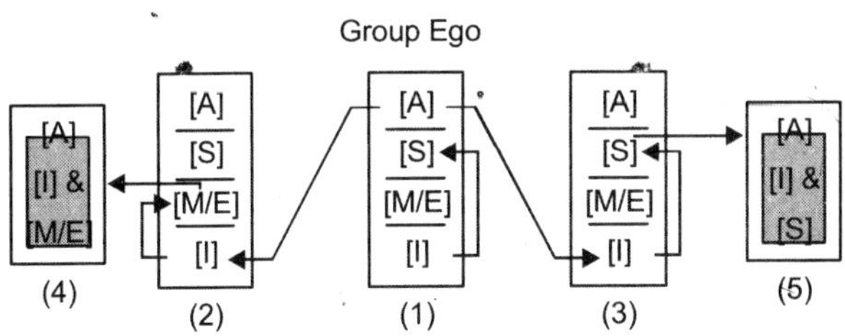

Fig. 6.8: Self Analysis by a Group.

A politically sponsored students' union in a College Campus decides to declare a strike. It is a group of students and there is a **Group Ego** for such groups. Birds of the same feather flock together is what is seen then. The group Ego sends **[A]**—i.e., *Self Assertion* with *Feeling of Superiority* as the accompanying emotion—to **[I]** of the group (see the diagrams (2) and (3). From the **[I]** of (2), it is sent to **[M/E]**. The **[I]** & **[M/E]** overpower **[A]** and thus the group crime or criminality is controlled.

Again, the **Group Ego** sends **[A]** to the **[I]** as shown in diagram (1) and (3). From the **[I]** of (3), it is sent to **[S]**. The **[I]** & **[S]** overpower **[A]** and thus the crime or criminality is controlled.

Simultaneously, **[A]** can be sent to **[S]** as well as to **[M/E]** from the **[I]** and certainly the **[I]** along with **[M/E]** and **[S]** can overpower the **[A]** and thus, the crime or criminality is controlled.

If **[S]** and/or **[M/E]** do not effectively overpower the **[A]** of the group, then the politically sponsored strike may turn to violence. The members of the students' union may boycott classes; may attack the fellow students; may throw country made bombs etc. Such group behaviour—a crowd behaviour, a mob behaviour is seen in many parts of the country. The terrorists and fundamentalists do the same throughout the world.

Analysis by Others

'Others' here means the parents, teachers, moralists, spiritual men, social workers, concerned citizens, police and other law enforcement officials, educators, courts, media etc. They can educate and inculcate **[M/E]**, **[S]** values to individuals and groups. This is what is seen in classes imparting moral instructions in schools and educational institutions, in religious discourses, retreats, exhortations etc. The value oriented articles in the media and the editorials in the news papers do the same. The police and other law enforcement officials perform the same thing. They may punish the offenders through a court of law. The **[M/E]** and **[S]** values are inculcated to the developing children at their family and thus the entire society makes attempts to inculcate **[M/E]** and **[S]** in the people. They make several plans and schemes so that the power of the **Pull Factors** is reduced. Punishments by the parents, teachers, courts etc. will help a lot. The criminogenic factors are put under control by police surveillance and patrolling. The sociological factors which may cause crimes are eradicated. The poverty eradication schemes, the employment creation activities etc. are intended for the same purpose. The strengthening of the **[M/E]** and **[S]** values by any methods or means is a positive stratagem to reduce crime and criminality in society. By these different and various methods, the individuals will be able to control their behaviour. See the transactions between [X] and [Y] in the next page.

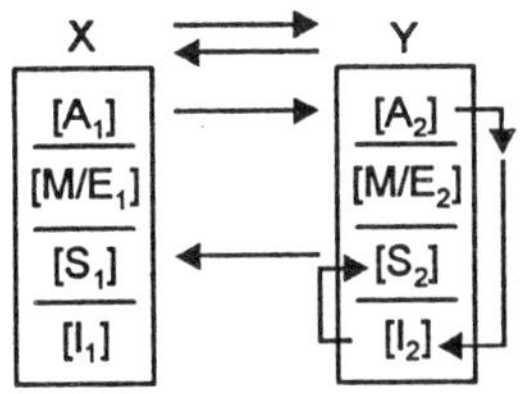

Fig. 6.9: Transaction resulting no crime.

Transaction likely to result in crime/criminality between X and Y, two individuals. In (Fig. 6.9), the transaction (i.e., to beat Y) is activated from the $[A_1]$ of X. Y receives it at $[A_2]$ and his $[A_2]$ does not respond from his $[A_2]$ to X. Instead, he sends the response to $[I_2]$ and from there to $[S_2]$. From his $[S_2]$ the response goes to $[S_1]$. The result is 'no crime'. For example, X wants to beat Y and with that in mind, he calls epithets and shouts at Y in filthy language. Y instead of calling bad names and speak vulgar language. (i.e., reaction from his $[A_2]$, he sends his reaction from $[S_2]$ via intelligence. In other words, he tolerates it or he withdraws from the situation.

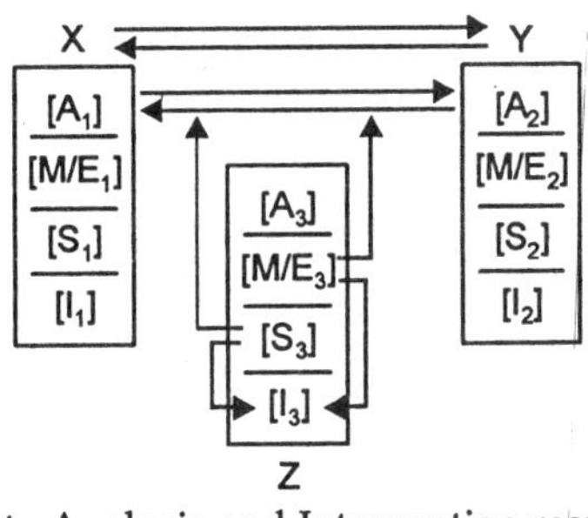

Fig. 6.10: Third Party Analysis and Intervention resulting in no crime.

X and Y have transactions. But, one sees that the transaction is initiated from the $[A_1]$ of X and it is received by $[A_2]$ of Y. Here Y responds from his $[A_2]$ and it is likely to result in crime/criminality. In such cases, the analysis is done by a third person Z and he intervenes in the issue. His response is from $[M/E_3]$ or $[S_3]$ or from both via $[I_3]$. If it works well, there will not take place a crime. It means that a third person/party can also make the analysis. This is what is happening in heated discussions. In psychology of crime, we use to advice third party intervention for setling issues.

In my book *Advanced Criminology or the WHY of crimes* (ISBN: 13: 978-93-5125-265-8), I have given many illustrations to reduce all sorts of crimes. To conclude, I may insist that *'Morality/Ethics, Spirituality with Faith, Belief or both*—uprightly formed in the right direction is a powerful energy which can and will control and reduce criminality. Animals have no morality/ethics; no spirituality based on faith, belief or both Philosophers in the past said that 'man is a rational animal'. Today, that concept of the ancient philosophers is not accepted. Today's description of man is that *'man is an intelligent, moral/ethical, spiritual animal.* Basically, he is an animal and the *specific difference (s.d)* between man and animal is *'Morality/Ethics, Spirituality and Intelligence'*.

Footnotes

1. Instinctology—this term is coined by me for my Push-Pull-Ego Factor theory of crime-causation.
2. Adapted in part from Erikson, Kagan and Mass, Wilmer and Katinsky and James C. Coleman.
3. For more information and detailed discussion, read *Advanced Criminology Or The Why of Crimes*, (ISBN:13:978-93-5125-265-8) by James Vadackumchery, Concept Publishing Company (P) ltd., New Delhi, 2017.
4. Spirituality may or may not be uprightly formed in the right direction. It can also be wrongly formed in a negative (evil) way.

Appendix

Crimes and Criminality: Seen and Unseen

'... sophies' crimes
'...isms' crimes
'...ologies' crimes
'Above Grammar' criminality
'*Acha Din*' criminality
'Conviction' crimes
'Court-made injustice' crimes
'Eating Tax-payers' money crimes
'Fourth Estate' crimes
'Goonda service' criminality
'Government Bureaus' criminality
'Honourale Men' crimes
'Lesser Mortals' criminality
'Marginal Justice' crimes
'Mind Power' crimes
'Money Power' crimes
'Muscle Power' crimes
'No guilt feeling' crimes
'No Justice' crimes
'Offers and Off' crimes
'Parrots in the cage' crimes
'Partisan' criminality
'Perverted Justice' crimes
'Prejudiced Justice' crimes
'Roman kings' criminality
'Satan quoting Bible' criminality
'Self-employed goonda' crimes
'Simulated goonda' crimes
'Star' crimes
'Status' crimes
'Strict action' game by Government
'Vertue' crimes
'Waste Justice' criminality
'Yellow Journalism' crimes
7 Star Hotel crimes
Abetment to suicide
Abuse of power criminality
Adulterated preachers
Adulteration Syndicate
Advertisement Rackets
Affinity crimes
Affluence criminality
Agrarian clashes
Alcoholism
Amusement crimes
Anchovy crimes
Animals on roads
Anti-trust violations
Astrology crimes
ATM crimes
Attimary crimes
Avathar crimes
Bandh crimes
Black and White law enforcement crimes
Black market crimes
Black money nexus
Black-mailing
Blade Interest crimes
Blue film crimes
Bomb throwing
Booty sharing
Boycotting of classes
Bribery Fixing criminality
Broken home crimes
Bureaucratic crimes
Bureaucratic Terrorism criminality
Business crimes
Campus violence
Casino crimes
Caste and sub-caste criminality
Charity crimes
Cheese-cake girl crimes
Cheese-cake girls' criminality
Child prostitution
Chitty frauds
Cinema and TV Serial crimes
Clandestine crimes at workplaces

Clearance sale offences
Comfort zone crimes
Commercial bribery
Communal politics
Compulsory Contribution Crimes
Consensus crimes
Container Money crimes
Contribution crimes
Con-tricks
Corruption
Corruption in Judiciary
Corruption money splitting criminality
Court adjournments crimes
Credit frauds
Crimes against the old and aged
Crimes of communalization
Crimes of public lying
Crimes of the 'Haves and Have nots'
Crime-trade practices
Criminal politics
Criminalization of police
Cruel ragging
Cure miracles crimes
Custodial rapes
Custody torture crimes
Daughter-in-law crimes
Delay in disposal of criminal cases
Demonetisation crimes
Demonological crimes
Denomination crimes
Desertion crimes
Dharna criminality
Divinity criminality
Divorce criminality
Domestic Harassment
Domestic violence
Donation *Mafia*
Door to Door sale cheating
Dowry crimes
Drug addiction
Drug trafficking
Duplicate production companies
Easy money making
Economic offences
Economic Terrorism criminality
Election Manifesto crimes
Election promises and cheating
Employed goonda crimes
Employment crimes
Employment rackets
Enforcement crimes
Euthanasia
Exploitation crimes
Extremism
Fake Lottery Kings
Fake marriage
False Employment Bureaus
False weights and measures
Family Suicide
Fanaticism
Filth crimes
Flat construction *Mafia*
Flesh trade
Foot-path labourers' crimes
Foot-path markets criminality
Foreign Bank Accounts
Fortune seeking administration
Frightening '... ologies' criminality
Fundamentalism
Gang crimes
Garbage culture crimes
Gender equality fights
Gender justice crimes
Gheraoing
Giant Oaks crimes
Gold jewellery cheating
Goon Squad crimes
Goonda net-work
Gooney Bird crimes
Grass eater crimes
Group dance/song justice administration
Gun powder politics
Half-naked crimes
Hallelua crimes and pocket-picking
Hartal crimes
Hawala crimes

Hermaphrodites sex relation criminality
Hired *Jadha* workers' criminality
Hoarding of files in Government
Holy lies
Home-sale rackets
Homely Frauds
Homosexuality
Hooch *Mafia*
Hoodlum criminality
Hot and Cold law enforcement crimes
Human god criminality
Human waste-throw crimes
Icing the Justice Criminality
Ill Justice Criminality
Incarcerating the aged and infirm: an offence?
Industry crimes
Instant justice miscarriage crimes
Insurance frauds
Insurgency crimes
Inter-caste rivalry crimes
Inter-denominational fights and crimes
Internet crimes
Investment fraud
Jadhas and public order crimes
Jadtha crimes
JEL crimes
Judge made injustice and crime
Judicial crimes
Justice: Just-Ice criminality
Kick-back crimes
Kidnapping children for begging crimes
Kuri frauds
Labour disputes crimes
Lavatory crimes
Law abuse crimes
Legislature crimes
Lesbianism criminality
Less Justice Criminality
Lipstick tarring nexus crimes
Living together crimes
Lust criminality
Magical remedy crimes
Meat Eater Crimes
Media crimes
Media-Trial crimes
Medical guinea pig crimes
Medical Laboratory frauds
Mercy killing crimes
Miracle commodities
Miracle crimes
Miscarriage of justice criminality
Misuse of authority criminality
Mobile prostitution crimes
Modeling and Advertisement crimes
Modeling and Fashion Show crimes
Money chain and multi-marketing
Money laundering
Morphying crimes
Mosquito crimes
Mother-in-law crimes
MRI Scans Robbery
Murder-Suicide
Naxalism
Nexus crimes
No sign roads criminality
NOC Racket
Nokkukooli crimes
Non-use of authority/power criminality
Organ Transplantation Rackets
Parliament offences
Pest crimes
Pilgrim rackets
Pious plundering
Pipe money business
Police petition enquiry crimes
Police torture crimes
Political communalism
Political crimes
Political Terrorism criminality
Politicization of criminals
Prayer Addiction criminality
Prayer sellers
Problem families

Production of concocted evidence criminality
Pseudo-authority exercise criminality
Public property destruction
Public wastes crimes
Punishment for punishment sake: an offence?
Quotation goonda crimes
Real Estate criminality
Regionalism crimes
Registration of false cases criminality
Relay rapes
Religious bigotry
Religious fests and miracle drama crimes
Religious lies criminality
Religious looting
Religious *Mafia*
Religious processions on road criminality
Religious unaccountability crimes
Remote control crimes
Rent-a-girl sex work
Resort crimes
Road agitations and pious processions criminality
Road block crimes
Road rage crimes
Robbing customers
Rogue crimes
Rough use and misuse of mics
Sale of contraband articles
Self-assertion crimes
Sex justice crimes
Sex rackets
Sex work
Sex-industry crimes
Sexual harassment at home
Sexual recreation
Sit-in-strikes
Slogan criminality
Slum Crimes
Small Acorns crimes
SMS
Smuggling
Social media crimes
Song Album syndicates
Sons-of-soil crimes
Sound pollution on roads criminality
Spectrum crimes
Spiritual Euphoria crimes
Spurious prayer criminality
Street corner meetings criminality
Suite crimes
Sweet and Sour law enforcement crimes
Sweet-heart victimization
T.V. Addiction crimes
T.V. Confusion crimes
Tax evasion criminality
Terror causing '...isms' criminality
Terrorism
Thrill-seekers on roads crimes
Trade union crimes
Trafficking of women
Transgender sex relation criminality
Trespass crimes
Truancy crimes
Tutored witness crimes
Unemployment crimes
Unisex criminality
Unseen crimes in family
Unwed motherhood criminality
Vagrancy crimes
Vehicle drive by adjustments crimes
Verbal Diarrhea
Victim participation crimes
Victim precipitation crimes
Violence on road criminality
Visa Synidcates
Way-side sellers' crimes
White Collar Crimes
Wounded justice crimes
Wounded Justice criminality

Bibliography

Authoritative and authentic books authored by Dr. James Vadackumchery

Acquittals in Administration of Justice, Ph.D. Thesis, Kerala University, (mimeo), Thiruvananthapuram, 1983.

Activism, Accountability and Justice (*ISBN: 81-7341-4324-X*), Indian Publishers' Distributors, Delhi, 2004.

Advanced Criminology or The Why of Crimes, (*ISBN: 13: 978-93-5125-265-8*), Concept Publishing Company, Delhi, 2017.

Bankers' Safety: Methods and Techniques, (*ISBN: 81-7022-937-5*), (Second edition), Concept Publishing Company, Delhi, 2002.

Child Labour (Malayalam), State Literacy Mission, Thiruvananthapuram, 2000.

Contemporary Indian Criminology (*ISBN: 978-93-5125-100-2*), Concept Publishing Company (Pvt.) Ltd., New Delhi, 2015.

Crime and Society: Current Issues and Trends, (*ISBN: 81-7648-024-X*), A.P.H. Publishing Corporation, Delhi, 1999.

Crime, Law and Police Science, (*ISBN: 81-7022-995-2*), (Second edition), Concept Publishing Company, Delhi, 2003.

Crime, Police and Correction, (*ISBN: 81-7024-939-2*), A.P.H. Publishing Corporation, Delhi, 1998.

Criminology and Penology, Kairali Books International, Trivandrum, 1983.

Departmental Inquiries and Injustice, (*ISBN: 81-7024-899-X*), A.P.H. Publishing Corporation, Delhi, 1997.

Goodbye, Police: Memoirs of a Criminologist, (*ISBN: 81-7341-390-8*), Indian Publishers' Distributors, Delhi, 2005.

Human Behaviour and Law Enforcement, (*ISBN: 81-7024-688-1*), Ashish Publishing House, Delhi, 1995.

Human Relations in Banking: How to get along better with people? Santha Publishing House, Cochin, 1988.

Human Rights: A Fair Trial of United Nations (Vol. I) (*ISBN: 978-93-8662-13-0*) Concept Publishing Company (Pvt.) Ltd., New Delhi, (Under Publication).

Human Rights: A Fair Trial of United Nations (Vol. II) (*ISBN: 978-93-86682-14-7*) Concept Publishing Company (Pvt.) Ltd., New Delhi, (Under Publication).

Human Rights and the Police in India, (*ISBN: 81-7024-722-5*), A.P.H. Publishing Corporation, Delhi, 1996.

Human Rights Friendly Police: A Myth or Reality?, (*ISBN: 81-7648-150-5*), A.P.H. Publishing Corporation, Delhi, 2000.

Human Values and Police Behaviour, Bureau of Police Research and Development, Ministry of Home Affairs, Government of India, 2000.

India's Supreme Court and Police: Consensus and Conflicts, (*ISBN: 81-7341-301-0*), Indian Publishers' Distributors, Delhi, 2003.

Indian Police 2001: What Went Wrong Here? (*ISBN: 81-7024-967-8*), A.P.H. Publishing Corporation, Delhi, 1998.

Indian Police and Equal Justice Under Law, (*ISBN: 81-7648-066-5*), A.P.H. Publishing Corporation, Delhi, 1999.

Indian Police and Miscarriage of Justice, (*ISBN: 81-7024-792-6*), A.P.H. Publishing Corporation, Delhi, 1997.

Indian Police and Nexus Crime, (*ISBN: 81-7835-037-8*), Kalpaz Publications, Delhi, 2002.

Judiciary and Juvinile Justice, (*ISBN: 81-7341-389-4*), Indian Publishers' Distributors, Delhi, 2005.

Juvenile Delinquency (Malayalam), State Literacy Mission, Thiruvananthapuram, 2000.

Kolayalikalude Pinnampuram, (Malayalam) (*ISBN: 81-7705-321-0*) Prabhath Book House, Thiruvananthapuram, 2015.

Kuttakrithyangalile Kazhukanmar, (Malayalam) (*ISBN: 978-81-300-1598-9*), Poorna Publications, Kozhikode, 2014.

Kuttakrithyangalude Baliyadukal, (Malayalam) (*ISBN:......*) Poorna Publications, Kozhikode [To be released soon].

Management Thoughts for Justice Administration, (*ISBN: 13-978-81-7268-233-0 (HB)*), Logos Press, New Delhi, 2013.

Management Thoughts on Police Administration, (*ISBN: 81-7024-914-7*), A.P.H. Publishing Corporation, Delhi, 1998.

Misguiding Philosophies and Millennium Police, (*ISBN: 81-7341-278-2*), Indian Publishers' Distributors, Delhi, 2003.

National Police Commission: Issues for Rethinking, (*ISBN: 81-7024-826-4*), A.P.H. Publishing Corporation, Delhi, 1998.

Police and the Society, Kairali Books International, Trivandrum, 1985.

Police and Human Rights,(ed.), Kerala Police Officers' Association, Thiruvananthapuram, 1994.

Police and the People (Translation of the title: Public Relations at the Cutting Edge Level: Case-study materials by Prof. C.K. Muhammed

Ummer), The State Institute of Language, Kerala, Thiruvananthapuram, 2000.

Police Criminology and Crimes, (*ISBN: 81-7835-094-7*) Kalpaz Publications, Delhi, 2002.

Police Enforcement Crimes and Injustice, (*ISBN: 81-212-0471-5*), Gyan Publishing House, Delhi, 2001.

Police Interrogation: DOs which the police do not DO, (*ISBN: 81-7024-974-0*), A.P.H. Publishing Corporation, Delhi, 1998.

Police Leadership: The Inside Story, (*ISBN: 81-7648-120-3*), A.P.H. Publishing Corporation, Delhi, 1999.

Police Morality, (*ISBN: 81-7835-038-6*), Kalpaz Publications, Delhi, 2001.

Police, Victim and Victim Justice, (*ISBN: 81-7479-043-8*), Kaveri Books. Delhi, 2001.

Police, Women and Gender Justice, (*ISBN: 81-7648-137-8*), A.P.H. Publishing Corporation, Delhi, 2000.

Policing the Largest Democracy: 50 Years and After, (*ISBN: 81-7024-979-1*), A.P.H. Publishing Corporation, Delhi, 1998.

Policing the Police: A Nation's Cry, (*ISBN:81-7479-060-81*), Kaveri Books, Delhi, 2003.

Professional Police Witness Interviewing, (*ISBN: 81-7648-061-4*), A.P.H. Publishing Corporation, Delhi, 1999.

Public Relations at the Cutting Edge Level: Case-study materials, National, Delhi, 1985.

Road Users' Guide (Malayalam), Assistant Motor Vehicle Inspectors'Association, Ernakulam, 1997.

Singapooril Ninnoru Kuttapathram, (Malayalam) (*ISBN:.........*) Prabhath Book House, Thiruvananthapuram, [To be released soon].

Society, Police and Crimes: Tasks and Challenges, (*ISBN: 81-7341-266-0*), Indian Publishers' Distributors, Delhi, 2002.

Sociology of Policing India: 2000 and Beyond, (*ISBN: 81-7341-279-0*), Indian Publishers' Distributors, Delhi, 2003.

The Complete Refrence Methodology of Research in Criminology Law Justice and Correction (Vol.I), (*ISBN: 81-7341-414-8*), Indian Publishers' Distributors, Delhi, 2007.

The Complete Refrence Methodology of Research in Criminology Law Justice and Correction (Vol.II), (*ISBN: 81-7341-448-0*), Indian Publishers' Distributors, Delhi, 2010.

The Complete Refrence Methodology of Research in Criminology Law Justice and Correction (Vol.III), (*ISBN: 81-7341-449-7*), Indian Publishers' Distributors, Delhi, 2010.

The Justice Less Administered, (*ISBN: 81-7341-380-0*), Indian Publishers' Distributors, Delhi, 2005.

The Police and Delinquency in India, (*ISBN: 81-7024-725-X*), A.P.H. Publishing Corporation, Delhi, 1996.

The Police, The Accused and Criminal Injustice, (*ISBN: 91-7024-80 -X*), A.P.H. Publishing Corporation, Delhi, 1997.

The Police, the Court and Injustice, (*ISBN: 81-7024-806-X*), A.P.H. Publishing Corporation, Delhi, 1997.

The Police, The People and Criminal Justice, (*ISBN: 81-7024-862-9*), A.P.H. Publishing Corporation, Delhi, 1999.

The Unseen Phases of Crimes, (Malayalam), (*ISBN: 81-909360-1-8*), H&C Publishing House, Trissur, 2009.

Third Millennium Police: Take off Trends in India, (*ISBN: 81-7648-062-2*), A.P.H. Publishing Corporation, Delhi, 1999.

U.N. Universal Declaration of Human Rights and Criminal Justice: The Total Rivision (*ISBN: 13-978-81-8069-912-2*) Concept Publishing Company (Pvt.) Ltd., New Delhi, 2012.

United Nations and Indian Mysticism: Parallels on Human Rights and Police, (*ISBN: 81-7022-664-2*), Concept Publishing Company, Delhi, 2002.

United Nations and Prison Justice: The Complete Revision of the Standard Minimum Rules for the Treatment of Prisoners, (*ISBN: 978-818-069-9610*), Concept Publishing Company (Pvt.) Ltd., New Delhi, 2014.

Values and God's Commandments, (Malayalam) Catechetical Centre, Thalassery, 1995.

Why I am not a policeman, (*ISBN: 81-7479-042-X*), Kaveri Books, Delhi, 2001.

Wounded Justice and the Story of Indian Police, (*ISBN: 81-7479-045-4*), Kaveri Books, Delhi, 2001.

Index

'...isms, ologies and sophies, 94, 124, 145

A priori based analysis, 158
A.Q. (Animality Quotient), 38, 39
Abnormal behaviour, 176, 178
Accountability, 64
Acquisitive crowd, 36
Acquisitiveness, 30-31, 36, 112, 168, 197-98
Acquisitorial system, 158, 159
Act centered, 127
Actual conscience, 107-8
Ad hoc justice, 98
Ad hominem justice, 98
Addiction to prayer, 144
Administrative justice, 61
Adulterated justice, 97, 98
Adultery, 40, 106
Adversary system, 159
Affluence based analysis, 153
After care services, 182
Aggressive crowd, 36
Agrarian justice, 74, 75
Agrarian unrest, 75
Ahimsa, 139
Amputation of limb, 18
Anal stage, 23, 43
Animal ancestry, 24
Animal dung, 117
Animal instincts
  accompanying, 41
  baby-infant's, 41
  control of, 43, 128, 131, 134
  intelligence control, 135
Animal waste, 137
Animalism, 42
Animality, 6, 23-24, 32, 37, 41, 89, 112, 125-26, 129-32, 136, 138, 155, 162-63, 182, 194-96
  ego state, 195
  quotient, 38-39
Animal-kingdoms, 29
Animals instincts, 108
Anthropology, 1
Anti-social activities, 84-85, 173
Apartheid, 57
Aristotle, 25, 91, 115
Atavism, 27, 134
Atrocities, 80, 87, 90, 93, 96
Auburn system, 180-81
Australopithecines, 25
Authoritarian morality, 111

Ballot papers, 103
Bar Council of India, 73
Benefit of doubt, 88
Bipes, 25
Biting Stage, 23, 42, 111
Blocked spirituality, 165

Blocking of Intelligence, 166
Blocking of morality/Ethics, 164, 165, 166
Blue collar employees, 132
Blue sex, 144
Bogus certificates, 82
Borstals, 182
Bowel control, 42
British Prison System, 181-82
Bureaucracy, 59-60, 152
Bureaucratic crime, 90, 174
Bureaucratic justice, 59, 60
Bureaucrats, 62, 77-78, 104, 152
Business crimes, 88, 172

Canadian Prisons, 182
Cancer patients, 57, 197
Capitation fees, 82
Caste discrimination, 147
Caste system, 147
Catholics, 9, 115, 119, 184
Cat-o-nine lashes, 17
Centre for Personality Development, 180
Charities with a hook, 71
Charity crimes, 170
Charity *Mafia*, 57
Child Ego, 15, 20
Chromosomes based analysis, 147, 148
Class struggles, 72
Classical school, 4, 18, 20, 126
Classical school of criminology, 125, 142, 168
Classification of prisoners, 182
Clinical Scale, 40
Cognate crimes, 170
Cognizable crimes, 3
Coleman, James C., 36, 146, 183-84, 202
Commercial bribery, 171
Commission of crimes, 4, 13, 17, 24, 41, 54, 88, 100, 114, 130, 132, 146, 150, 152-53, 162
Communal conflicts, 65, 147, 165
Communal fanaticism, 66
Communal insanity, 86
Communal justice, 65
Communal leaders, 65, 89
Communal morons, 88
Communal riot, 36
Communalism, 57, 65
Compensation, 190
Complementary sex, 44
Complex or connected political crimes, 61, 62
Con games, 88, 93
Conceptual Intelligence, 162
Concocting evidence, 87
Confessional, 190
Conscience
  ethical, 108
  good, 140-41
  habitual, 107-8
  human, 8-9, 15, 99, 106-7
  mature, 108, 112
  moral, 15, 57, 60, 108, 112
Consensus justice, 89, 90
Containment theory, 188
Contaminated Intelligence, 164, 166
Contamination, 163, 165
Continuous social control, 100
Conventional Crimes, 169
Corporal punishments, 8, 17, 127
Corporate crimes, 90
Correction based analysis, 141, 142
Correctional justice, 64, 65
Correctional science, 64, 65
Cosmic truth, 48
Crimes
  accidental, 126
  affluent, 151
  banking, 90
  bureaucratic, 90, 152, 169, 174
  causation, 4, 18, 21, 146, 173, 176, 178, 181, 202
  centric life, 175
  chains, 94

charity, 170
circumstantial, 126
consensus, 90
control, 63, 131-32, 141, 160, 178, 198
controlling, 116
corporate, 90, 153, 170
cruelest, 97
cyber, 90, 94-95, 149, 170
doers, 13, 16-17, 51, 67, 84, 115, 125, 134, 141-43, 148, 151, 157, 160-62, 169, 178
domestic, 170, 172
economic, 90-91, 108, 144, 170
environmental, 83
gang, 152
heinous, 4
hospital, 69
internet, 144, 170
interpreted, 149
investigation, 11, 175
investment, 94
meat eater, 77
noble, 71
non-cognizable, 3
preventing, 18
sexual, 33
syndicates, 90, 150
thrillers, 175
trials, 175
Criminal heroism, 47
Criminal intelligence, 161
Criminal liability, 10, 99, 143
Criminal morphing, 144
Criminal motives, 79
Criminal personality, 54, 176
Criminal police justice, 99, 100
Criminal politics, 170
Criminal sociology, 98
Criminal *Theosophism*, 95
Criminality, 81-82, 113-18, 126, 130-31, 133-34, 138, 140-42, 144-47, 149-50, 160-62, 169-73, 175, 178-82, 193-94, 198-202
organized, 125, 153
white collar, 162
Criminalization of police, 99
Criminals, 12, 22, 28, 47, 54, 72, 78-79, 84, 90-93, 99, 125-27, 134, 161-62, 166-67, 175-76
bureaucratic, 152
chaining, 17
cyber, 95
grass-eater, 91
hard-core, 83
hardened, 125, 191
political, 61, 125
potential, 125
Criminology, 1, 12-13, 27, 31, 37, 51, 54-55, 88, 94, 103, 116, 125-26, 137, 140, 168
Critical analysis, 131, 135
Critical criminology, 72
Cro Magnon Man, 27
Cross border terrorism, 66, 67
Cruel punishments, 18, 111
Cultural conflict theory, 137
Cultural justice, 79, 80
Cultural lag theory, 137
Cultural scale analysis, 137
Cultural tolerance, 137
Custodial torture, 36
Custom based analysis, 138, 139
Cyber crimes, 90
Cyber crime syndicates, 94
Cyber justice, 94, 95
Cyber world, 94

Daya (charity), 140
'*De facto*' power/authority, 61, 62
'*De jure*' power/authority, 61, 62
Death penalty, 14
Decalogue, 17
Defective personality, 39, 44
Defence lawyer's justice, 97
Definance Crimes, 170
Delinquency, 47, 50, 126, 143, 172
Democracy crimes, 170

Democratic justice, 62
Demonical possession, 146
Demonism, 148
Demonological analysis, 143
Demonology, 4, 52, 53, 116, 179, 180
Detention cum punishment centers, 180
Deterrent theory of punishment, 124
Dharma, 139
Diagnostic Scale, 39-40
Differential participation, 1183
Disciplinary inquiries, 71
Disciplinary justice, 70, 71
Disciplining, 51
Discrimination, 58, 80, 156
  cultural, 80
  racial, 169
Distributive justice, 67, 157
Divine influence, 114
Divine justice, 71
Domestic animals, 28, 41
Domestic crimes, 170, 171
Domestic justice, 60
Dominant culture, 48
Drug Trafficking & Flesh trade, 100
Ducking stool, 17
Durkheim, 168-69

Economic crimes, 90, 144, 170
Economic determinism, 91
Economic justice, 91
Educational institutions, 32, 82, 160, 172, 200
Ego, 2-3, 5, 21, 45-47, 129, 131-32, 167, 173-74, 188-96, 199
Election morality, 104
Electra complex, 44, 174
Elmira reformatory, 181
Emotion quotient, 38
Emotional behaviour, 41, 136
Emotional control, 38, 48, 138-39
Emotional self control, 41, 47-48
Empiricism based analysis, 141
Empiricism, 95, 124, 141, 143
Encyclopaedia Britanica, 33
Endocrinology based analysis, 147, 148
Enforcement crimes, 83, 88, 99, 155, 171
Enforcement justice, 82, 83, 87, 88
Environmentalists, 82-83
Epicurianism based analysis, 142
Equal justice based analysis, 157
Equal justice, 67
Escape crowd, 36
Essence and Existence, 32
Ethical
  ability, 108
  behaviour, 110, 140
  consciousness, 60
  decision, 106
  Ego, 131
  guidance, 107
  justifications, 107
  norms, 107
  qualities, 48
Ethics based analysis, 140
Ethics conflicts, 167
Ethics ego state, 195
Ethics principles, 167
Etiology of sin, 3
Euphoria, 96
Euthanasia, 165
Exodus, 118
Exorcism, 52, 81, 116-17, 179-80
Extremist justice, 66

Family based analysis, 149
Fanaticism, 57, 66, 95, 124, 166
Fatalism, 127
Fear morality, 111
Felony, 3, 4, 115
Felt concepts, 20
Flesh trade, 100, 156
Forgiveness, 140
Free moral animals, 126

Fundamentalism, 57, 66, 95, 124, 145-46, 166

Gang culture, 171
Gender and Sex Crimes, 170
Gender and sex-based analysis, 156
Gender discrimination, 58
Gender injustice, 156
Gender justice, 58, 139
Generation gap, 138
Generation scale analysis, 138
Genetic endowment, 176, 185
Genocide, 33, 39, 58, 86, 111, 137, 145, 166
Gentle punishment, 52
Geography based analysis, 149
Gherao, 82, 89, 172
Gladstone Committee, 181
Grandma-stories, 52
Grass-eater crimes, 170
Grass-eater criminal, 91, 92
Group ego, 199-200
Group intelligence, 137
Gun powder politics, 172

Habitual Conscience, 107, 108
Hammurabi, 17, 126, 179
Hartals and bandhs, 74, 83-84, 93
Hedonism, 4, 5, 6, 7, 17, 142, 168
Hedonism, 4, 7, 17, 142, 168
Hedonistic calculus, 125, 142
Hereditary potentialities, 185
Heredity, 146, 162, 176-77, 180, 183, 185
Hermaphrodites, 58-59, 139, 156, 183, 187
Hippocrites, 180
Hire and fire policy, 92
Holy crimes, 169
Holy nexus, 154
Homecentric period, 109, 110
Home-school centric, 109, 110
Home-School-Others Centric, 109, 110
Home-School-Others-Community-Society Centric, 110
Hominem justice delivery, 98
Hominem justice principles, 98
Homo Erectus, 25-27
Homo Neanderthalensis, 27
Homo Sapiens, 26-27
Homo Transvaalemsis, 25, 26
Homosexual stage, 45-46
Homosexuality, 46, 70, 102, 147
Hopes and Expectations, 124
Horizontal mobility, 100
Horse Trade, 104-5
Hospital crimes, 69
Hostel system, 182
HR.Q, 38
Human personality, 10, 14
Human relations quotient, 38
Human rights based analysis, 157
Human Rights Commission, 157
Human rights, 14, 59, 80, 140, 155, 157, 182
Human rights violations, 57, 80, 157, 170
Human sacrifice, 131, 145, 165, 169
Humanity, 32, 89
Humanization, 42, 43, 44
Hyper markets, 86-87

I am O.K, 20
I.Q., Intelligence Quotient, 161
I'm not O.K, 19, 20
id, 2, 4, 6-8, 10, 18, 20-21, 33
Idealism, 124
Immoralities, 15, 32, 173-74
Imprisonment, 4, 7, 52, 84, 125, 127, 191
Incantation, 117
Individualistic interpretation, 163-64
Individualistic Scale, 39
Indriyanigraha (self control), 140
Injustice
administrative, 61

domestic, 60
inhuman, 67
investment, 93
social, 159
Inner buffer, 188
Inner containment, 188
Inquiry officers, 70
Inquisitorial system, 158
Inquisitorial, 159
Instinct-control mechanisms, 128
Instinctological treatment, 180
Instinctology, 180
Instincts
aggressive, 43
controlling, 40
intense, 125
maternal, 35, 143
parental, 46
survival, 36
very powerful, 36
Instinctual
crimes, 36
energy, 6, 180-81
expression, 40
factors, 37
level, 39
Institutional crimes, 170
Institutions, 32, 40, 70-71, 73, 82-84, 155, 161, 176
Intellectual analysis, 136-37, 141, 144, 147, 162
Intellectual forces, 42
Intellectual infiltration, 49
Intelligence
blocked, 166
conceptual, 162
criminal, 161-62
function of, 26, 31, 135
mechanical, 162
moral, 136, 162
oriented, 142
pervert, 131
quotient, 38
religious, 162
social, 137, 162
tests, 160-61
upright, 149
Intelligent
analysis, 135, 139, 142
animals, 25, 31
Interest based analysis, 144
Interest-free loans, 82
Interiorization, 110, 111
International cyber crimes-syndicates, 94
Internet
addiction, 54
crimes, 170
Investment justice, 93

Jail bird, 19
Japanese prisons, 182
JEL crimes, 104, 155
Jnana (wisdom), 140
Journalist justice, 78, 79
Journalistic
ethics, 101
justice, 101
prostitution, 101
Judicial crimes, 170
Judicial justice, 63, 64, 72, 73, 74
Judicial Officer's justice, 97
Judiciary based analysis, 155
Just justice, 63, 159
Justice
adulterate, 97-98
adulterated, 97-98
clear, 63
correctional, 64
criminal, 58, 67, 84, 99-100, 157
delivery system, 14
disciplinary, 70-71
distributive, 67
enforcement, 87
goddess of, 87-88
hominem, 98
journalistic, 78, 101
judicial, 63-64, 73-74

miscarriage of, 57, 68, 71, 79-81, 85, 156, 158-59
nebulous, 63
principles of, 98, 141
retributive, 126-27, 179
rule of, 73
social, 58, 158-59
to the insane, 85, 86
to the mentally challenged, 89
victimological, 58
wholistic, 67-68
Juvenile Justice Act, 110
Juveniles Justice, 101

Kamala and Amala, 24, 29
Knead, 188, 189, 191, 192, 193, 196
Ksama (Forbearance), 140

Labeling theory, 175
Latency stage, 44, 45
Law and order justice, 92, 93
Law Commission of India, 90
Law Enforcement based analysis, 155
Laws
agrarian, 74
ancient Roman, 158
anti-sati, 138
bad, 104
comprehensive, 140
cosmic, 115, 124
criminal, 86
cultural, 106-7, 147
custom-made, 14
divine, 71, 123, 126
effective, 14
ethical, 14, 84
human rights, 157
institutional, 9
penal, 72, 106, 165, 174, 198
religious, 13, 50, 161, 169, 197-98
rule of, 73
spiritual, 46, 186
state, 40
traffic, 194
Legal
justice, 85
morons, 89
sanctity, 72
Less justice, 57, 68, 156, 159
Lex Talionis, 17, 126, 142, 179
Libido, 55
Lier justice, 102, 103
Life
experience, 135-36
imprisonment, 4, 7, 19, 163, 179
introspect, 167
retrospect, 129-31, 133, 135-36, 167
script analysis, 135, 136, 167
'Living Together', 60
Low intelligence, 134

M.Q. (Morality Quotient), 38, 39
M/E.Q. (Morality/Ethics Quotient), 38, 39
Mafia, 47, 83, 150
crimes, 90, 125, 144, 152,
justice, 77, 78
and syndicates, 169
Majority scale, 39, 40, 137
Male prostitutes, 70
Man centered, 127
Management justice, 92
Manias and Phobias, 143
Maoism, 39, 124, 145
Maoist ethics, 131
Market justice, 86
Marxist criminology, 72
Marxist justice, 72
Mass media, 150
Mature conscience, 108, 112
Meat-eater crimes, 77, 169-70
Meat-eater criminals, 91
Mechanical intelligence, 162
Media crimes, 77, 170
Mental age, 38
Mental conflicts, 45-46, 151

Mental disorders, 15, 116, 127, 143, 179, 181
Mental peace, 13, 168
Mental retardation, 166, 178-79
Mercy killing, 165
Mic justice, 95, 96
Migrant justice, 76
Mind justice, 97
Misdemeanor, 3, 4, 15
Mob behaviour, 36, 137, 200
Mob justice, 98, 99
Mob violence, 98-99
Mobility justice, 100
Modern criminology, 27
Money chain and multi-marketing, 77, 93
Money justice, 97
Money order swindles, 93
Moral conscience, 112
Moral intelligence, 162
Moral justifications, 58
Moral laws, 9, 14, 26, 85, 106-8, 139, 198
Moral morons, 62
Moral personality, 110-11
Moral principles, 36, 56, 58, 61, 63, 65-67, 73, 81, 89, 96, 99, 105-7, 112, 126, 130
Moral sanctity, 72
Moral thinking, 110, 112
Moral training, 111-12
Morality, 26-29, 31-43, 48, 56-59, 63-69, 71-75, 80-81, 93-94, 96-99, 103-13, 128-33, 139-40, 152-57, 159-70, 194-97
  authoritarian, 111
  based analysis, 139
  cyber, 95
  disfavouring, 167
  election, 104
  fear, 111
  honour, 65
  individualistic, 107, 163
  international, 15
  justice, 100, 101
  overpower, 130
  political, 62, 76
  right, 111
  sentimental, 111
  sexual, 33
  spirituality, 162
  subjective, 58
Moralizing agents, 108
Moron
  administration, 89
  judgements, 89
Mortal sins, 3-4, 8, 115
Murder politics, 75-76
Murder-suicide, 174
Muscle justice, 97
Mutuality, 149-50

Naked animals, 29
National Police Commission, 74-76
Naxalism, 124
Naxalite ethics, 131
Neanderthalaman, 27
Negative emotions, 49-51, 137, 142
Neta-Babu-Dalal-Dada, 77
[illegible]xus crimes, 40, 83, 90, 104
[illegible]xus justice justice, 76, 77
'Noble Crimes', 71
Nokkukooli, 74
Non-criminal environments, 162
Noquisitorial system, 158-59, 170
Norma Normans, 105, 106
Norma Normata, 105, 106
Normative principles, 136
Normative scale, 39, 136

Occasional property crimes, 169
Occupational crimes, 169
Oedipus complex, 44, 174
Old Testament, 16, 117-18, 131, 173, 179
Opposite sex, 44
Oral stage, 23, 42, 111
Organized racketeering, 85

Othello, 174
Oyster Bay definition, 153

Papal prison, 127
Paper society or NGO, 82
Parent Ego, 15, 18, 20
Parental control, 45
Parole, 182
Patriarchal system, 139
Pedophilia, 102
Penance and penalty, 50, 51
Penance and prayer, 50, 51
Penn's Charter of 1862, 180
Pennsylvania system, 180-81
Penological analysis, 141
Penologist, 18
Personal crimes, 88
Personality based analysis, 148
Personality development, 23, 42, 44, 126, 162, 176, 180, 184-85
Personality traits, 24, 146
Personalization, 110, 111
Personnel environment, 102
Persuasion, 51-52
Pervert personality, 44, 127, 132
Phallic stage, 44
Philadelphian prison, 180
Pleasure-pain, 109
Pleasure-pain theory, 18
POCSO Act, 44, 102
Police ethics, 131
Police justice, 72, 73, 97
Police patronage, 93
Political agitation, 36
Political crimes, 61-62, 75, 90, 154, 169-70, 174
Political economy of crime, 72
Political god fathering, 93
Political insanity, 86
Political justice, 61
Political morality, 62, 76
Political morons, 88
'Political' based analysis, 154
Politicization of crimes, 75, 76
Politicization of criminals, 92
Politicized bureaucracy, 59, 60
Pontius Pilot, 173
Pornography, 54
Poverty based analysis, 151
Pre-delinquency, 45
Primates, 25
Prison Act, 1898 (England), 181
Prison Commission, 1962 (Britain), 182
Prison justice, 64, 65, 97
Prison reforms, 181-82
Problem families, 19
Professional ethics, 81
Prosecutor's justice, 97
Protection of Human Rights Act, 157
Psychoanalysis, 2, 4, 10, 15, 18, 20
Psychological position, 19
Psychoneurosis, 178-79
Psychopath, 9, 116
Psychopathic, 116
Psychosis, 178
Psychotherapeutic analysis, 143
Psychotherapist, 5, 8, 192
Puberty, 46-47
Public order crimes, 169
Pull factors, 14, 19, 22, 34, 43-45, 47-49, 128-29, 131-33, 145-46, 162-63, 183, 185, 188-90, 192-93, 199-200
Punishments, 7-9, 11, 13-14, 17-18, 43, 50-52, 69-71, 84, 97, 109, 117, 119, 124-28, 141-43, 180-81
  capital, 7, 52, 156
  divine, 9, 71-72
  emotional, 141
  severity of, 13, 52
Pure political crimes, 61, 62
Purgatory, 3, 8, 115, 119
Push-Pull-Ego Factor Theory of Crimes Causation, 1, 23, 25-27, 31, 33, 37, 41-43, 53, 105, 114-15, 119, 121, 125, 133-35, 161-63

Quaker's Movement, 177, 180

Radical criminology, 72
Radicalism, 67
Ramapithecus, 25
Rationalism based analysis, 140
Rationalism, 95, 124, 140, 143
Rationality, 31, 57
Rationalization, 36
Recidivist, 19, 64, 65, 84, 127, 151, 180
Reformation based analysis, 142
Regression, 24
Reinforcement, 49, 192
Relics and religious *mafia*, 77
Religious
- belief, 66
- bigotry, 33, 65-66, 146-47, 150, 165
- emotions, 144
- faith, 118
- fundamentalism, 66
- groups, 60, 78, 86, 99, 147
- intelligence, 162
- justice, 65, 66
- mafia, 77
- morons, 88
- rites, 119
- values, 186

Remote ancestors, 134
Repression, 45
Responsible parenting, 53
Retribution, 126, 180
Retributive
- approach, 141
- justice, 126, 127
- theory, 17, 18

Reward-punishment, 109
Rhetoric capacity, 96
Rhetoric justice, 95, 96
Right personality, development of, 141
Rituals based religions, 66
Roman Catholics, 4, 9
Roman Jurisprudence, 158
Rule of justice, 72
Rule of law, 72
Russian Prison System, 182

S.Q. (Spirituality Quotient), 38, 39
Sadharanadharma, 139
Satan worship, 116
Sati, 138
Satya (Truth), 140
Saucal (purity), 140
Scholastic psychology, 2
Scold's bridle, 17
Self analysis, 198-99
Self assertion, 30, 45, 194-95, 199
Self concept, 188, 189
Self identity, 191
Self structure, 188, 189
Self-destruction Crimes, 170
Self-financing courses, 82
Sentimental morality, 111
Sex
- crimes, 59, 100, 156, 170
- equality, 139
- instinct, 45
- justice, 59, 156
- morality, 59
- trade, 57
- values, 186

Sexual
- activities, 102
- excitement, 102
- exploitation, 144
- gratification, 44

Shark crimes, 151, 169
Sivadharma, 139
Slave trade, 58
Slavery, 57
Slum crimes, 169
Slum culture, 172
Social Crimes, 170
Social fabric of life, 26
Social intelligence, 137, 161, 162
Social justice based analysis, 158

Social media, 47, 54, 78-79, 88, 94, 98, 144
crimes, 79, 90, 94, 170
justice, 79
peers, 54
Social scale analysis, 137
Socialization, 10, 24, 42, 44
Socio-cultural environments, 183, 185
Socio-cultural factors based analysis, 147
Socio-economic conditions, 149
Solitary confinement, 181
Special Marriage Act, 197
Special mobility, 100
Spiritual animals, 31, 202
Spiritual communication, 50
Spirituality principle, 164, 167, 195-96
St. Paul, 2
Standard Minimum Rules, 180
Stock and pillory, 17
Stone age cave men, 179
Stone Age Cave, 179
Stress and Frustration based analysis, 151
Sub-human people, 86
Subjective analysis, 136
Subjective interpretation, 164
Subjective morality, 58
Subjective scale analysis, 136
Sucking stage, 23, 42, 111
Suggestive effects, 47
Suicide squad, 125
Suite crimes, 77, 91
Super ego, 2- 6, 8-11, 14, 16, 18, 20, 143, 191, 186, 191
Supernatural, 114
Superstition, 26, 144-45
Superstition based analysis, 144, 145
Syndicate based analysis, 153
Syndicate-crimes, 77

Tabula Rasa, 119
Tactual pleasure, 43
Tapas (Penance), 140
'Temple care', centers, 60
Ten Commandments, 17
Terrorism, 57, 66-67, 95, 124, 145-46, 166, 172
Terrorist Crimes, 169
Theology based analysis, 144
Theomachy, 145
Theopathy, 144
Theophany, 144
Theory of *Karma*, 13, 124
Theory of mutation, 24
Theosophism, 103, 145, 169
Theosophy, 124, 145
Thermal theory, 149
Third degree justice, 96, 97
Third degree methods, 87
Thomist approach, 3-4
Thought concepts, 20
Topography, 149
Torture commission, 96
Trade union, 74
Tradition based analysis, 139
Traditional crimes, 170
Traffic rage, 34
Transactional analysis, 5
Transgender, 58-59, 70, 139, 156, 183, 187
Transgression, 126
Transportation of criminals, 127
Trephining, 116
Tribal culture, 137
Truancy, 45, 100

Unborn children, 60, 90-91
Uncontrollable children, 45
Uncontrollable forces, 152
Unemployment based crimes, 152
Unfavourable conditions, 183
Unholy nexus, 75, 80, 154
United Nations Organisation (UNO), 182
Universal principles, 130

Untouchability, 80, 147

Vagrancy, 45, 100
Value assumptions, 190
Value oriented education, 82
Value system, 186
Venial sins, 3-4, 8, 115
Verbal diarrhea, 96
Vertical mobility, 100, 101
Victim justice, 58
Victimization, 44
Victimological compensation, 67, 190
Victimological crimes, 170
Victimology based analysis, 148
Visual media, 73, 78, 101, 150
Voting machine justice, 103, 104
Vultures amidst criminals, 175

Warring functions, 2
Weak mindedness, 134
White collar, 88
  crimes, 88, 90, 93
  criminality, 162
  justice, 88, 89
  professionals, 132, 160
Wholistic justice, 67, 68
Witch mania, 146
Witchcrafts, 146
Women Liberation Movement, 139
World Wars, 33, 161
Wounded justice, 57, 68, 97, 156, 159

Xenephone, 91

XXY or Kline Filter Syndrome, 147, 148
XXYY males, 147
XYY chromosomal pattern, 147

Yellow journalism, 78
You're not O.K, 19, 20
You're O.K, 19, 20

Zooplasty, 153